Hiram Corson

An Introduction to the Prose and Poetical Works of John Milton

Hiram Corson

An Introduction to the Prose and Poetical Works of John Milton

ISBN/EAN: 9783337098520

Printed in Europe, USA, Canada, Australia, Japan

Cover: Foto ©Thomas Meinert / pixelio.de

More available books at **www.hansebooks.com**

AN INTRODUCTION

TO THE

PROSE AND POETICAL WORKS

OF

JOHN MILTON

Comprising all the Autobiographic Passages in his Works, the more Explicit Presentations of his Ideas of True Liberty

COMUS, LYCIDAS, and SAMSON AGONISTES

With Notes and Forewords

BY

HIRAM CORSON, LL.D.

Professor of English Literature in the Cornell University

New York
THE MACMILLAN COMPANY
LONDON: MACMILLAN & CO., LTD.
1899

All rights reserved

CONTENTS xi

PAGES

Comus: a Masque presented at Ludlow Castle, 1634, before the
Earl of Bridgewater, then President of Wales . . . 126–164
Lycidas 165–179
Samson Agonistes 181–244

NOTES 245–303

INTRODUCTION

MILTON's prose works are perhaps not read, at the present day, to the extent demanded by their great and varied merits, among which may be named their uncompromising advocacy of whatsoever things are true, honest, just, pure, lovely, and of good report; their eloquent assertion of the inalienable rights of men to a wholesome exercise of their intellectual faculties, the right to determine for themselves, with all the aids they can command, what is truth and what is error; the right freely to communicate their honest thoughts from one to another,— rights which constitute the only sure and lasting foundation of individual, civil, political, and religious liberty; the ever-conscious sentiment which they exhibit, on the part of the poet, of an entire dependence upon 'that Eternal Spirit, who can enrich with all utterance and knowledge, and sends out his Seraphim with the hallowed fire of his altar, to touch and purify the lips of whom he pleases'; the ever-present consciousness they exhibit of that stewardship which every man as a probationer of immortality must render an account, according to the full measure of the talents with which he has been intrusted — of the sacred obligation, incumbent upon every one, of acting throughout the details of life, private or public, trivial or momentous, 'as ever in his great Task-Master's eye.'

Some of his poetical works are extensively 'studied' in the schools, and a style study of some of his prose works is made in departments of rhetoric; but his prose works cannot be said to be much read in the best sense of the word,— that is, with all the faculties alert upon the subject-matter as of prime importance, with an openness of heart, and with an accompanying interest in the general loftiness of their diction; in short, as every one should train himself to read any great author, with the fullest loyalty to the author — by which is not meant that all his thoughts and opinions and beliefs are to be accepted, but that what they really are be adequately, or *ad modum recipientis*, apprehended; in other words, loyalty to an author means that the most favorable attitude possible for each and every reader be taken for the reception of his meaning and spirit.

Mark Pattison, in his life of Milton, in the 'English Men of Letters,' while fully recognizing the grand features of the prose works as monuments of the English language, notwithstanding what he calls their 'asyntactic disorder,' undervalues, or rather does not value at all, Milton's services to the cause of political and religious liberty as a polemic prose writer, and considers it a thing to be much regretted that he engaged at all in the great contest for political, religious, and other forms of liberty. This seems to be the one unacceptable feature of his very able life of the poet. 'But for the Restoration,' he says, 'and the overthrow of the Puritans, we should never have had the great Puritan epic.' Professor Goldwin Smith, in his article in the *New York Nation* on Pattison's 'Milton,' remarks: 'Looking upon the life of. Milton the politician merely as a sad and ignominious interlude in the life of Milton the poet, Mr. Pattison cannot be expected to entertain the idea that the poem is in any sense the work of the politician. Yet we cannot help thinking that the tension and elevation which Milton's nature had undergone in the mighty struggle, together with the heroic dedication of his faculties to the most serious objects, must have had not a little to do both with the final choice of his subject and with the tone of his poem. "The great Puritan epic" could hardly have been written by any one but a militant Puritan.'

Dr. Richard Garnett, in his 'Life of Milton,' pp. 68, 69, takes substantially the same view as does Professor Smith: 'To regret with Pattison that Milton should, at this crisis of the State, have turned aside from poetry to controversy, is to regret that "Paradise Lost" should exist. Such a work could not have proceeded from one indifferent to the public weal. . . . It is sheer literary fanaticism to speak with Pattison of "the prostitution of genius to political party." Milton is as much the idealist in his prose as in his verse; and although in his pamphlets he sides entirely with one of the two great parties in the State, it is not as its instrument, but as its prophet and monitor.'

Milton was writing prose when, Mr. Pattison thinks, he should have been writing poetry, 'and that most ephemeral and valueless kind of prose, pamphlets, extempore articles on the topics of the day. He poured out reams of them, *in simple unconsciousness that they had no influence whatever on the current of events.*'

But they certainly had an influence, and a very great influence, on the current of events not many years after. The restoration of Charles II. did not mean that the work of Puritanism was undone, and that Milton's pamphlets were to be of no effect. It was in a large measure due to that work and to those pamphlets that in a few years — fourteen only after Milton's death — the constitutional basis of the monarchy underwent a quite radical change for the better, — a change which would have been a solace to Milton, if he could have lived to see it; and he could then have justly felt that he had contributed to the change. He would have been but eighty years old, if he had lived till the revolution of 1688.

A man constituted as Milton was could not have kept himself apart from the great conflicts of his time. He was a patriot in every fibre of his being. He realized in the cultivation of himself his definition of education, given in his tractate 'Of Education. To Master S. Hartlib': 'I call a complete and generous education that which fits a man to perform justly, skilfully, and magnanimously all the offices, both private and public, of peace and war.' Of course he did not mean that that was all of education. And in his 'Areopagitica,' he says, after defining 'the true warfaring Christian,' 'I cannot praise a fugitive and cloistered virtue, unexercised and unbreathed, that never sallies out and sees her adversary, but slinks out of the race, where that immortal garland is to be run for, not without dust and heat.'

Although the direct subjects of his polemic prose works may not have an interest for the general reader at the present day, they are all, independently of their direct subjects, charged with 'truths that perish never,' most vitally expressed. And this is as true of the 'Treatises on Divorce' as it is of any of the other prose works. They are full of bright gems of enduring truth.

Lord Macaulay's article on Milton, first published in the *Edinburgh Review* for August, 1825, is a brilliant and, in many respects, a valuable production, but he certainly says some things on the favorableness of an uncivilized age, and the unfavorableness of a civilized and learned age, to poetical creativeness, which are quite remote from the truth, and which Milton would certainly have regarded as abundantly absurd. So, too, he would have regarded what is said of the necessary struggle which a great poet must make against the spirit of his age. All these views are as completely at variance with Milton's own as are those of Mark Pattison in regard to Milton the politician.

Lord Macaulay's article was occasioned by the publication

of an English version, by Rev. Charles Richard Sumner, afterwards Bishop of Winchester, of Milton's 'Treatise on Christian Doctrine,' the existence of which was unknown up to the year 1823, when the original manuscript in Latin was found in a press of the old State Paper office, in Whitehall.

In this essay the author sets forth an opinion, still widely entertained, it may be, by a large number of cultivated people, namely, that as learning and general civilization, and science, with its applications to the physical needs and comforts of life, advance, Poetry recedes, and 'hides her diminished head,' and men become more and more subject to facts as facts, losing sight more and more of the poetical, that is, spiritual, relations of facts.

'Milton knew,' Macaulay tells us, 'that his poetical genius derived no advantage from the civilization which surrounded him, or from the learning which he had acquired; and he looked back with something of regret to the ruder age of simple words and vivid impressions.'

But it appears from Milton's own authority that he did not know this; that, on the contrary, he thought the poet should be master of all human learning, ancient and modern, should know many languages and many literatures; that 'by labour and *intense study*, which,' he adds, 'I take to be my portion in this life, joined with the strong propensity of nature, I might perhaps leave something so written to after-times, as they should not willingly let it die.' Some of the autobiographic passages contained in this book will be found a sufficient refutation of what has been quoted from Macaulay.

The view which Milton took of learning, and acted upon, is one which should be kept before the minds of students at the present day, when the tendency is so strong toward learning for its own sake. As well talk of beefsteak for its own sake. Learning was with Milton a means of enlarging his capacity — a means toward *being* and *doing*. Mark Pattison well says, 'He cultivated, not letters, but himself, and sought to enter into possession of his own mental kingdom, not that he might reign there, but that he might royally use its resources in building up a work which should bring honour to his country, and his native tongue.'

"Though we admire,' Lord Macaulay continues, 'those great works of imagination which have appeared in dark ages, we do not admire them the more because they have appeared in dark ages. On the contrary, we hold that the most wonderful and splendid proof of genius is a great poem produced in a civilized age. We cannot understand why those who believe in that most orthodox article of literary faith, that the earliest poets are generally the best, should wonder at the rule as if it were the exception. Surely the uniformity of the phenomenon indicates a corresponding uniformity in the cause.'

Further on he says: 'He who, in an enlightened and literary society, aspires to be a great poet, must first become a little child.' The most highly learned and cultured (eternalized), the most fully developed in every direction, are the most *childlike*, the least knowledge-proud, and the more spiritual vitality they have, the greater will be their humility and simplicity — the gates to true wisdom. 'He [the poet] must take to pieces,' says Macaulay, 'the whole web of his mind.' Rather a difficult piece of unravelling to impose upon the poor fellow! 'He must unlearn much of that knowledge which has perhaps constituted hitherto his chief title of superiority.' Oh, who would be a poet in a civilized age! 'His very talents will be a hindrance to him.' What an irredeemable numskull he would have a poet to be! According to this doctrine, our institutions for feeble-minded children are likely to send forth the best poets into the world. 'His difficulties will be proportioned to his proficiency in the pursuits which are fashionable among his contemporaries, and that proficiency will in general be proportioned to the vigor and activity of his mind. . . . We have seen in our own time, great talents, intense labor, and long meditation, employed in this struggle against the spirit of the age, and employed, we will not say absolutely in vain, but with dubious success and feeble applause.'

Of all the flimsy theories in regard to the conditions of poetic creativeness that the mind of man could devise, this is certainly the flimsiest. It is only necessary to give a hasty glance at the works of those poets who are regarded as Masters of Song in the various literatures of the ancient and the modern world, to learn the secret of their vitality and power — that secret being, first, that they all possessed the best knowledge and learning of their times and places; and, secondly, that they all held the widest and most intimate relations with their several ages and countries, and drank deepest of, and most intensely reflected, the spirit of those ages and countries. If Shakespeare was not a learned man, he was the best educated man that ever lived. He had a fulness of life, intellectual and spiritual, and an easy command of all his faculties, to which but few of the sons of men have ever attained; and he lived in an age the most favorable in human history for the exercise of dramatic genius, and an age, on the whole, more civilized than any that had ever preceded it.

No true poet could live in any age without imbibing and reflecting its spirit, and that to a much greater degree than other men. For the poetic nature is distinguished from ordinary natures by its greater impressibility and its keener, more penetrating insight, and to suppose that a poet can keep apart from the spirit of his age and the state of society around him is to lose sight of the very *differentia* of the poetic nature, and implicitly to admit its feebleness. In one respect he may be said to keep apart from his age, in the sense of rejecting, in having no affinities for, what in it is ephemeral, while appropriating what of vital and eternal is in it. His affinities, by virtue of his poetic nature, are for what is enduring in the transient. And every age must have the vital and eternal in it, as the vital and eternal are omnipresent at all times and in all places.

The great poet is great because he is intensely *individual*, and there can be no intense individuality, paradoxical as it may appear, that is not subject, in a more than ordinary degree, to impressions of time and place. An individual in the fullest sense of the word, one who legitimates, as it were, in the eyes of his country or his age, his decisive influence over its destiny, is generally characterized, not so much by his rejecting power, though he will always, and necessarily, have this in a high degree, as by his appropriating power. He brings to the special unity of his nature all that that nature, in its healthiest activity, can assimilate, and throws off only the to him non-assimilable dross of things. The more complete his life becomes, the more it is bound up with what surrounds it, and he is susceptible of impressions the more numerous and the more profound.

The greater impressibility (spiritual sensitiveness) and its resultant, the keener, more penetrating insight ('the vision and the faculty divine'), which preëminently distinguish poetic genius from ordinary natures, render great poets the truest historians of their times and the truest prophets. The poetic and dramatic literature of a people is a mirror in which is most clearly reflected their real and essential life. History gives rather their phenomenal life. It is the essential spirit only of an age, the permanent, the absolute, in it, as assimilated and 'married to immortal verse' by a great poet, that can retain a hold upon the interests and sympathies of future generations.

Milton was most emphatically a man of his age, and its clearest reflector, sustaining to it the most intimate and sympathetic and intensely active relationship; and, of all that was enduring in it, his works, both prose and poetical, are the best existing exponent. His intimate relationship with his age has been set forth in Dr. Masson's exhaustive and grandly monumental work, in six large octavo volumes, 'The Life of John Milton: narrated in connexion with the political, ecclesiastical, and literary history of his time.' No other poet in universal literature, unless Dante be an exception, ever sustained such a relationship to the great movements of his time and country that an exhaustive biography of him would need to be, to the same extent, 'narrated in connexion with the political, ecclesiastical, and literary history of his time.'

Milton might justly and proudly have said of himself, with reference to the fierce political and ecclesiastical conflicts of his time, '*quorum pars magna fui.*' And who can doubt that by these conflicts, and even, also, by his loss of sight therein, he was *tempered* to write the 'Paradise Lost,' the 'Paradise Regained,' and the 'Samson Agonistes'? He might have written some other great work, if he had kept himself apart from these conflicts, as Pattison thinks he ought to have done, but he certainly could not have written the 'Paradise Lost.' Of the principles involved in the great contest for civil and religious liberty his prose works are the fullest exponent. In the 'Paradise Lost' can be seen the influence of his classical and Italian studies. Homer and Virgil and Dante are in it, but its essential, vitalizing, controlling spirit is that of a refined exalted Puritanism, freed from all that was in it of the contingent and the accidental; and thus that spirit will be preserved for ever in the pure amber of the poem.

It was not within the scope of this little book, as a primary introduction to the study of Milton, to include any extended presentation of the 'Paradise Lost.' But two grand features may be alluded to here. It is, in some respects, one of the most *educating* of English poems. The grand feature of the poem, that feature which distinguishes it from all other works of genius, both ancient and modern, is its essential, constitutional sublimity. So universally has this feature been recognized as peculiar to the poem, that the word Miltonic has become synonymous with the sublime. The loftiness of the diction, which is without all touch of bombast, every sympathetic reader must feel to be an emanation from the august personality of the poet. There is no perceptible strain anywhere, as there is no perceptible lapse of power, on the part of the poet. He keeps ever up to the height of his great argument. To come into the fullest possible sympathetic relationship with the poem's constitutional sublimity, to be impressed by its loftiness of diction, by the contriving spirit of its eloquence, are educating experiences of the highest order — experiences which imply an exercise, most vitalizing and uplifting, of the reader's higher organs of apprehension and discernment. The theology of the poem need not obstruct for any one these educating influences. They are quite independent of the theology, as are the educating influences of the 'Divina Commedia' independent of its mediæval Catholicism. The absolute man was in the ascendent in both Dante and Milton; and by virtue of that ascendency, they are, and ever will continue to be, great educating personalities, whatever false science and false opinions on various subjects are embodied in their works, and however much the world's faith in things which they most vitally believed may decline and entirely cease to be. Their personalities and their works are consubstantial. This fact — an immortal fact — was, perhaps, not taken sufficient account of by Mark Pattison when he wrote in his 'Life of Milton' that 'the demonology of the poem has already, with educated readers, passed from the region of fact into that of fiction. Not so universally, but with a large number of readers, the angelology can be no more than what the critics call machinery. And it requires a violent effort from any of our day to accommodate our conceptions to the anthropomorphic theology of "Paradise Lost." Were the sapping process to continue at the same rate for two more centuries, the possibility of epic illusion would be lost to the whole scheme and economy of the poem.' But there is a power in 'Paradise Lost' which is, and ever will be, independent of all manner of obsolete beliefs.

Both the 'Paradise Lost' and the 'Divina Commedia' belong, in a supereminent degree, to what Thomas De Quincey calls, in his 'Essay on Pope,' the literature of *power*, as distinguished from the literature of *knowledge;* and, as a consequence, the statement of Mark Pattison that 'there is an element of decay and death in poems which we vainly style immortal,' is not applicable to them. By the literature of power is meant that which is, in whatever form, an adequate embodiment of eternal verities — verities of the human soul and of the divine constitution of things, and their mutual adaptation, however much the former may be estranged from the latter. Such embodiment will maintain its individual existence.

'In that great social order, which collectively we call literature,' says De Quincey, 'there may be distinguished two separate offices that may blend and often *do* so, but capable severally of a severe insulation, and naturally fitted for reciprocal repulsion. There is, first, the literature of knowledge, and, secondly, the literature of *power*. The function of the first is to *teach;* the function of the second is to *move*. . . . The first speaks to the *mere* discursive understanding; the second speaks ultimately, it may happen, to the higher understanding or reason, but always *through* affections of pleasure and sympathy. . . . Whenever we talk in ordinary language of seeking information or gaining knowledge, we understand the words as connected with something of absolute novelty. But it is the grandeur of all truth which can occupy a very high place in human interests, that it is never absolutely novel to the meanest of minds: it exists eternally by way of germ or latent principle in the lowest as in the highest, needing to be developed, but never to be planted. To be capable of transplantation is the immediate criterion of a truth that ranges on a lower scale. Besides which, there is a rarer thing than truth, namely, *power* or deep sympathy with truth.'

By the truth which 'is never absolutely novel to the meanest of minds,' De Quincey means absolute, eternal truth, inherent in the human soul, as distinguished from relative, temporal truth, the former being more or less 'cabined, cribbed, confined' in all men. As Paracelsus is made to express it, in Browning's poem 'Paracelsus,' 'There is an inmost centre in us all, where truth abides in fulness; . . . and "to know" rather consists in opening out a way whence the imprisoned splendor may escape, than in effecting entry for a light supposed to be without.'

To continue with De Quincey: 'What you owe to Milton [and he has the 'Paradise Lost' specially in his mind] is not any knowledge, of which a million separate items are still but a million of advancing steps on the same earthly level; what you owe is *power*, that is, exercise and expansion to your own latent capacity of sympathy with the infinite, where every pulse and each separate influx is a step upwards — a step ascending as upon a Jacob's ladder from earth to mysterious altitudes above the earth. *All* the steps of knowledge, from first to last, carry you further on the same plane, but could never raise you one foot above your ancient level of earth; whereas the very *first* step in power is a flight — is an ascending into another element where earth is forgotten. . . . The very highest work that has ever existed in the literature of knowledge is but a *provisional* work: a book upon trial and sufferance, and *quamdiu bene se gesserit.* Let its teaching be even partially revised, let it be but expanded, nay, even let its teaching be but placed in a better order, and instantly it is superseded. Whereas the feeblest works in the literature of power, surviving at all, survive as finished and unalterable amongst men. For instance, the "Principia" of Sir Isaac Newton was a book *militant* on earth from the first. In all stages of its progress it would have to fight for its existence; first, as regards absolute truth; secondly, when that combat is over, as regards its form or mode of presenting the truth. And as soon as a La Place, or anybody else, builds higher upon the foundations laid by this book, effectually he throws it out of the sunshine into decay and darkness; by weapons won from this book he superannuates and destroys this book, so that soon the name of Newton remains as a mere *nominis umbra*, but his book, as a living power, has transmigrated into other forms. Now, on the contrary, the "Iliad," the "Prometheus" of Æschylus, — the "Othello" or "King Lear," — the "Hamlet" or "Macbeth," — and the "Paradise Lost," are not militant, but triumphant forever as long as the languages exist in which they speak or can be taught to speak. They never *can* transmigrate into new incarnations. . . . All the literature of knowledge builds only ground-nests, that are swept away by floods, or confounded by the plough; but the literature of power builds nests in aërial altitudes of temples, sacred from violation, or of forests inaccessible to fraud.'

I would not give these extended quotations from De Quincey were it not that there may be many students who will read this book, and who will not have access to the works of De

Quincey. Those who have, should read all that he says on the subject. The distinction which he makes between the literature of knowledge and the literature of power was never before so clearly and eloquently made, and it is a distinction which needs to be especially emphasized in these days of excessive knowledge-mongery, apart from education. Literature is largely made in the schools a knowledge subject. The great function of literature, namely, to bring into play the spiritual faculties, is very inadequately recognized, and the study of English Literature is made too much an objective job — the fault of teachers, not students. When the literature is studied as a life-giving power, students are always more interested than when everything else except the one thing needful receives attention, — the sources of works of genius, the influences under which they were produced, their relations to history and to time and place, and whatever else may be made to engage the minds of students in the absence of the teacher's ability to bring them into a sympathetic relationship with the informing life of the works 'studied' — with that which constitutes their absolute power.

Another important feature of the 'Paradise Lost' to which I would call attention, and of which much should be made in the study of the poem, as a condition of assimilating its educating power, is the verse, which more fully realizes Wordsworth's definition and notion of harmonious verse, given by Coleridge in the third of his 'Satyrane's Letters,' than any other blank verse in the language. The definition, it is evident, was meant to apply more particularly to non-dramatic blank verse. Wordsworth's definition is, as given by Coleridge, that 'harmonious verse consists (the English iambic blank verse above all) in the apt arrangement of pauses and cadences and the sweep of whole paragraphs,

> "with many a winding bout
> Of linkèd sweetness long drawn out,"

and not in the even flow, much less in the prominence or antithetic vigor of single lines, which are indeed injurious to the total effect, except where they are introduced for some specific purpose.'

In my 'Primer of English Verse' (Ginn & Co., Boston), I have presented the two grand features of Milton's blank verse, namely: (1) The melodious variety of his cadences closing within verses, this being one of the essentials of 'true musical delight' which Milton mentions, in his remarks on 'The Verse,' 'the sense variously drawn out from one verse into another'; and (2) the melodious and harmonious grouping of verses into what may, with entire propriety, be called stanzas — stanzas which are more organic than the uniformly constructed stanzas of rhymed verse. The latter must be more or less artificial, by reason of the uniformity which is maintained. But the stanzas of Milton's blank verse are waves of melody and harmony which are larger or smaller, and with ever varied cadences, according to the propulsion of the thought and feeling which produces them, which propulsion may be sustained through a dozen verses or more, or may expend itself in two or three. No other blank verse in the language exhibits such a masterly skill in the variation of its pauses — pauses, I mean, where periodic groups, or logical sections of groups, terminate after, or within, it may be, the first, second, third, or fourth foot of a verse. There are five cases where the termination is within the fifth foot.

Stanza is quite exclusively applied to uniform groups of rhymed verses, but it can be with equal propriety applied to the *varied* groups of blank verses, especially those of the 'Paradise Lost.' For the proper appreciation of the individual verses in Milton's blank verse, they must be read in groups, — a group sometimes, perhaps generally, beginning within a verse and ending within a verse. These groups are due to the unifying action of feeling, just as much as rhymed stanzas are, and, indeed, often, if not generally, more so.

The autobiographical passages which have been brought together from the prose and poetical works, occupying 103 pages of the book, exhibit the man, Milton, better than could any regular biography of the same extent. The latter could give more of the details of his outward life and experiences, but could not so reflect his personality, his inmost being. He was most emphatically a *person*. He realized in himself what is expressed in the following verses from Tennyson's 'Œnone':

> 'Self-reverence, self-knowledge, self-control,
> These three alone lead life to sovereign power.
> Yet not for power (power of herself
> Would come uncalled for), but to live by law,
> Acting the law we live by without fear;
> And, because right is right, to follow right
> Were wisdom in the scorn of consequence.'

He also realized in himself what he says in his 'Areopagitica': 'He that can apprehend and consider vice with all her baits and seeming pleasures, and yet abstain, and yet distinguish, and yet prefer that which is truly better, he is the true warfaring Christian.'

What he says of himself in reply to the base and scurrilous and utterly unfounded charges against his private character is more than what Mark Pattison truly characterizes as 'a superb and ingenuous egotism'; is more than an *apologia pro vita sua*; it was also prompted by the consideration that what he was agonizingly contending for in the cause of civil, political, and religious liberty might suffer, if his private character were not freed from the charges made against it. In the extended autobiographical passage in the 'Second Defence of the People of England,' he assigns two other reasons for acquitting himself of the charges made against his private character, namely, 'that those illustrious worthies, who are the objects of my praise, may know that nothing could afflict me with more shame than to have any vices of mine diminish the force or lessen the value of my pangeyric upon them; and that the people of England, whom fate or duty, or their own virtues, have incited me to defend, may be convinced from the purity and integrity of my life, that my defence, if it do not redound to their honour, can never be considered as their disgrace.'

A noble motive nobly presented!

There are no authors in the literature more distinctly revealed in their writings than is John Milton. His personality is felt in his every production, poetical and prose, and felt almost as much in the earliest as in the latest period of his authorship. And there is no epithet more applicable to his personality than the epithet august. He is therefore one of the most educating of authors, in the highest sense of the word, that is, educating in the direction of sanctified character.

> ' 'Tis human fortune's happiest height to be
> A spirit melodious, lucid, poised, and whole:
> Second in order of felicity
> I hold it, to have walked with such a soul.'

The prime value attaching to the prose works of Milton at the present day is their fervent exposition of true freedom, — a freedom which involves a deep sympathy with truth; a freedom which is induced by a willing and, in its final result, a spontaneous obedience to one's higher nature. Without such obedience no one can be truly free. Outward freedom, so called, may only afford an opportunity to one with evil inward tendencies to become, morally, an invertebrate. Lord Byron speaks of his Lara as

> 'Left by his sire, too young such loss to know,
> *Lord of himself; that heritage of woe*,
> That fearful empire which the human breast
> But holds to rob the heart within of rest! —
> With none to check, and few to point in time
> The thousand paths that slope the way to crime.'

There is more outward freedom at the present time than there was ever before, perhaps, in the world's history, and the temptations which it involves can be adequately resisted only by the subjective freedom which Milton so strenuously advocated. His ideas of all kinds of true freedom (explicit expressions of which have been brought together in the second section of this book) need to be instilled into all young minds, first, for their own intrinsic value, and, secondly, as a means — the sole means — of checking the present and ever increasing tendency toward unrestrained desires, toward what many mistake for true freedom, namely, *license*. Of such, Milton says, in one of his sonnets,

> 'License they mean when they cry liberty;
> For who loves that must first be wise and good.'

The passage on Discipline (pp. 108-111) from 'The Reason of Church Government urged against Prelaty,' should be learned *by heart* (in the vital sense of the phrase, not in the sense of merely memorizing) by all young people in our schools. Everything should be done to induce a sympathetic assimilation on their part of the lofty utterances in this passage on Discipline, ' whose golden surveying rod,' says Milton, 'marks out and measures every quarter and circuit of New Jerusalem.'

The translations (not acknowledged in the text) of the two Latin poems addressed to the poet's Anglo Italian friend, Charles Diodati ('*Elegia Prima. Ad Carolum Diodatum*,' p. 28, and '*Elegia Sexta. Ad Carolum Diodatum, ruri com-*

morantem,' p. 31), and of the Familiar Letters ('*Epistolæ Familiares*'), Nos. III.-X., XII., XIV., XXI., XXIX., and XXXI. are by Dr. Masson. His translations of the latter are much closer to the meaning and tone of the original than those by Robert Fellowes, given in the Bohn edition of the prose works, which hardly warrant the characterization of them by the editor, J. A. St. John, as 'the very elegant translation of Mr. Fellowes, of Oxford, who, in most instances, has happily and with much feeling entered into and expressed the views of Milton.' The translation of No. XV. of the Familiar Letters, 'To Leonard Philaras, Athenian,' is by my colleague, Professor Charles E. Bennett.

Students who are sufficiently good Latin scholars should read Milton's Latin poems in the original, especially the '*In Quintum Novembris : anno ætatis* 17,' the '*Ad Patrem,*' and the '*Epitaphium Damonis.*' The '*In Quintum Novembris*' (On the fifth of November, that is, the anniversary of the discovery of the Gunpowder Plot) is described by Masson as 'one of the very cleverest and most poetical of all Milton's youthful productions, and certainly one of the most characteristic.' The '*Epitaphium Damonis*' has been admirably edited with notes by C. S. Jerram, M.A. Trin. Coll. Oxon., along with 'Lycidas.'

The student should first read carefully all the selections, prose and poetical, without referring to the notes. Notes are a necessary evil, and should not be read until after a requisite general impression has been received from an independent reading; often two or more independent readings should precede any attention to explanatory notes. Even such a poem as Browning's 'The Ring and the Book,' abounding as it does in out of the way allusions, difficult syntactical constructions, etc., requiring explanation, should be so read. The student would thus get a better impression of the poem as a whole, and would derive from it a greater pleasure (the pleasure resulting from the less interrupted exercise of his higher faculties) than if he should read it at first with the aid of abundant notes explanatory of details. A special attention to the details should be given only after the reader has, in a general way, taken in the articulating thought and the informing life of the poem.

There are thousands of allusions in the 'Paradise Lost' which a reader might not know, and yet be able to read the whole poem for the first time and enjoy it, and, what is all-important, be uplifted by it, without a single explanatory note.

The portrait of Milton is from that first drawn in crayons by William Faithorne, and afterward engraved by him for the poet's 'History of Britain,' published in 1670. Underneath the original engraving is the inscription, '*Joannis Miltoni Effigies Ætat*: 62. 1670. *Gul. Faithorne ad Vivum Delin. et Sculpsit*' (John Milton's effigy at the age of 62. 1670. Drawn from life and engraved by William Faithorne).

Faithorne was the most distinguished portrait artist and engraver of the time. He appears to have especially excelled in crayon-drawing rather than in painting. His numerous engravings are both from his own studies and from those of other artists, especially of Vandyke. 'No one,' says Masson, 'can desire a more impressive and authentic portrait of Milton in his later life. The face is such as has been given to no other human being; it was and is uniquely Milton's. Underneath the broad forehead and arched temples there are the great rings of eye-socket, with the blind unblemished eyes in them, drawn straight upon you by your voice, and speculating who and what you are; there is a severe composure in the beautiful oval of the whole countenance, disturbed only by the singular pouting round the rich mouth; and the entire expression is that of English intrepidity mixed with unutterable sorrow.' H. C.

CASCADILLA COTTAGE, July, 1899.

MILTON'S AUTOBIOGRAPHY

*made up of all the more important autobiographical passages
contained in his prose and poetical works*

It was found quite impossible to avoid somewhat of a jumble in bringing together the many autobiographic passages scattered throughout Milton's prose and poetical works. The passage in the 'Second Defence of the People of England,' in reply to the scurrilous abuse and utterly unfounded charges against his private character contained in the *Regii Sanguinis Clamor ad Cœlum, adversus Parricidas Anglicanos*, 1652, which occasioned the 'Second Defence,' covers a larger period of Milton's life than any other, extending, as it does, from his birth to the time of his writing the 'Second Defence,' published in 1654, Milton being then in his forty-sixth year; and as there is an autobiographic passage of some importance in the preface to the 'First Defence' (published in 1651), this passage and that in the 'Second Defence' are kept together and given first. In the former he expresses his sense of the honor done him in his having been engaged to reply to the *Defensio Regia pro Carolo I.*, by Salmasius; and he evidently felt, and justly, too, that no abler man could have been engaged for that important function. The extract from 'A Defence of the People of England' is from the translation ascribed by Milton's biographer, John Toland, to Mr. Washington, a gentleman of the Temple, and that from the 'Second Defence,' from the translation by Robert

Fellowes, A.M., Oxon. These are very free translations, and sometimes far from being adequate representations of Milton's thought. It is much to be regretted that Milton did not himself make an English translation, for the general English reader, of these two noble Defences.

The other autobiographic passages are given, as far as may be, in their chronological order, — that is, not always according to the dates of their composition, but according to their order in Milton's life.

From the Preface to 'A Defence of the English People'

Although I fear, lest, if in defending the people of England, I should be as copious in words, and empty of matter, as most men think Salmasius has been in his defence of the king, I might seem to deserve justly to be accounted a verbose and silly defender; yet since no man thinks himself obliged to make so much haste, though in the handling but of any ordinary subject, as not to premise some introduction at least, according as the weight of the subject requires; if I take the same course in handling almost the greatest subject that ever was (without being too tedious in it) I am in hopes of attaining two things, which indeed I earnestly desire : the one, not to be at all wanting, as far as in me lies, to this most noble cause and most worthy to be recorded to all future ages : the other, that I may appear to have myself avoided that frivolousness of matter, and redundancy of words, which I blame in my antagonist. For I am about to discourse of matters neither inconsiderable nor common, but how a most potent king, after he had trampled upon the laws of the nation, and given a shock to its religion, and begun to rule at his own will and pleasure, was at last subdued in the field by his own subjects, who had undergone a long slavery under him; how afterwards he was cast into prison, and when he gave no ground, either by words or actions, to hope better things of him, was finally by the supreme council of the kingdom condemned to die, and beheaded before the very gates of the royal palace. I shall likewise relate (which will much conduce to the easing men's minds of a great superstition) by what right, especially according to our law, this judgment was given, and all these matters transacted; and shall easily defend my valiant and worthy countrymen (who have extremely well deserved of all subjects and nations in the world) from the most wicked calumnies, both of domestic and foreign railers, and especially from the reproaches of this most vain and empty sophist, who sets up for a captain and ringleader to all the rest. For what king's majesty sitting upon an exalted throne, ever shone so brightly, as that of the people of England then did, when, shaking off that old superstition, which had prevailed a long time, they gave judgment upon the king himself, or rather upon an enemy who had been their king, caught as it were in a net by his own laws, (who alone of all mortals challenged to himself impunity by a divine right,) and scrupled not to inflict the same punishment upon him, being guilty, which he would have inflicted upon any other? But why do I mention these things as performed by the people, which almost open their voice themselves, and testify the presence of God throughout? who, as often as it seems good to his infinite wisdom, uses to throw down proud and unruly kings, exalting themselves above the condition of human nature, and utterly to extirpate them and all their family. By his manifest impulse being set at work to recover our almost lost liberty, following him as our guide, and adoring the impresses of his divine power manifested upon all occasions, we went on in no obscure, but an illustrious passage, pointed out and made plain to us by God himself. Which things, if I should so much as hope by any diligence or ability of mine, such as it is, to discourse of as I ought to do, and to commit them so to writing, as that perhaps all nations and all ages may read them, it would be a very vain thing in me. For what style can be august and magnificent enough, what man has ability sufficient to undertake so great a task? Since we find by experience, that in so many ages as are gone over the world, there has been but here and there a man found, who has been able worthily to recount the actions of great heroes, and potent states; can any man have so good an opinion of his own talents, as to think himself capable of reaching these glorious and wonderful works of Almighty God, by any language, by any style of his? Which enterprise, though some of the most eminent persons in our commonwealth have prevailed upon me by their authority to undertake, and would have it be my business to vindicate with my pen against envy and calumny (which are proof against arms) those glorious performances of theirs, (whose opinion of me I take as a very great honour, that they should pitch upon me before others to be serviceable in this kind of those most valiant deliverers of my native country; and true it is, that from my very youth, I have been bent extremely upon such sort of studies, as inclined me, if not to do great things myself, at least to celebrate those that did,) yet as having no confidence in any such advantages, I have recourse to the divine assistance; and invoke the great and holy God, the giver of all good gifts, that I may as substantially, and as truly, discourse and refute the sauciness and lies of this foreign declaimer, as our noble generals piously and successfully by force of arms broke the king's pride, and his unruly domineering, and afterwards put an end to both by inflicting a memorable punishment upon himself, and as thoroughly as a single person did with ease but of late confute and confound the king himself, rising as it were from the grave, and recommending himself to the people in a book published after his death, with new artifices and allurements of words and expressions. Which antagonist of mine, though he be a foreigner, and, though he deny it a thousand times over, but a poor grammarian; yet not contented with a salary due to him in that capacity, chose to turn a pragmatical coxcomb, and not only to intrude in state-affairs, but into the affairs of a foreign state: though he brings along with him neither modesty, nor understanding, nor any other qualification requisite in so great an arbitrator, but sauciness, and a little grammar only. Indeed if he had published here, and in English, the same things as he has now written in Latin, such as it is, I think no man would have thought it worth while to return an answer to them, but would partly despise them as common, and exploded over and over already, and partly abhor them as sordid and tyrannical maxims, not to be endured even by the most abject of slaves: nay, men that have sided with the king, would have had these thoughts of his book. But since he has swoln it to a considerable bulk, and dispersed it amongst foreigners, who are altogether ignorant of our affairs and constitution, it is fit that they who mistake them should be better informed; and that he, who is so very forward to speak ill of others, should be treated in his own kind. If it be asked, why we did not then attack him sooner? why we suffered him to triumph so long, and pride himself in our silence? For others I am not to answer; for myself I can boldly say, that I had neither words nor arguments long to seek for the defence of so good a cause, if I had enjoyed such a measure of health, as would have endured the fatigue of writing. And being but weak in body, I am forced to write by piecemeal, and break off almost every hour, though the subject be such as requires an uninterrupted study and intenseness of mind. But though this bodily indisposition may be a hindrance to me in setting forth the just praises of my most worthy countrymen, who have been the saviours of their native country, and whose exploits, worthy of immortality, are already famous all the world over; yet I hope it will be no difficult matter for me to defend them from the insolence of this silly little scholar, and from that saucy tongue of his, at least. Nature and laws would be in an ill case, if slavery should find what to say for itself, and liberty be mute; and if tyrants should find men to plead for them, and they that can master and vanquish tyrants, should not be able to find advocates. And it were a deplorable thing indeed, if the reason mankind is endued withal, and which is the gift of God, should not furnish more arguments for men's preservation, for their deliverance, and, as much as the nature of the thing will bear, for making them equal to one another, than for their oppression, and for their utter ruin under the domineering power of one single person. Let me therefore enter upon this noble cause with a cheerfulness grounded upon this assurance, that my adversary's cause is maintained by nothing but fraud, fallacy, ignorance, and barbarity; whereas mine has light, truth, reason, the practice and the learning of the best ages of the world, on its side.

From the 'Second Defence of the People of England in Reply to an Anonymous Libel, entitled "The Cry of the Royal Blood to Heaven against the English Parricides"'

A grateful recollection of the divine goodness is the first of human obligations; and extraordinary favours demand more solemn and devout acknowledgments: with such acknowledgments I feel it my duty to begin this work. First, because I was born at a time when the virtue of my fellow-citizens, far exceeding that of their progenitors in greatness of soul and vigour of enterprise, having invoked Heaven to witness the justice of their cause, and been clearly governed by its directions, has succeeded in delivering the commonwealth from the most grievous tyranny, and religion from the most ignominious degradation. And next, because when there suddenly arose many who, as is usual with the vulgar, basely calumniated the most illustrious achievements, and when one eminent above the rest, inflated with literary pride, and the zealous applauses of his partisans, had in a scandalous publication, which was particularly levelled against me, nefariously undertaken to plead the cause of despotism, I, who was neither deemed unequal to so renowned an adversary, nor to so great a subject, was particularly selected by the deliverers of our country, and by the general suffrage of the public, openly to vindicate the rights of the English nation, and consequently of liberty itself. Lastly, because in a matter of so much moment, and which excited such ardent expectations, I did not disappoint the hopes nor the opinions of my fellow-citizens; while men of learning and eminence abroad honoured me with unmingled approbation; while I obtained such a victory over my opponent that, notwithstanding his unparalleled assurance, he was obliged to quit the field with his courage broken and his reputation lost; and for the three years which he lived afterwards, much as he menaced and furiously as he raved, he gave me no further trouble, except that he procured the paltry aid of some despicable hirelings, and suborned some of his silly and extravagant admirers to support him under the weight of the unexpected and recent disgrace which he had experienced. This will immediately appear. Such are the signal favours which I ascribe to the divine beneficence, and which I thought it right devoutly to commemorate, not only that I might discharge a debt of gratitude, but particularly because they seem auspicious to the success of my present undertaking. For who is there, who does not identify the honour of his country with his own? And what can conduce more to the beauty or glory of one's country than the recovery not only of its civil but its religious liberty?

* * * * * * * * *

... I can easily repel any charge which may be adduced against me, either of want of courage, or want of zeal. For though I did not participate in the toils or dangers of the war, yet I was at the same time engaged in a service not less hazardous to myself and more beneficial to my fellow-citizens; nor, in the adverse turns of our affairs, did I ever betray any symptoms of pusillanimity and dejection: or show myself more afraid than became me of malice or of death: For since from my youth I was devoted to the pursuits of literature, and my mind had always been stronger than my body, I did not court the labours of a camp, in which any common person would have been of more service than myself, but resorted to that employment in which my exertions were likely to be of most avail. Thus, with the better part of my frame I contributed as much as possible to the good of my country, and to the success of the glorious cause in which we were engaged; and I thought that if God willed the success of such glorious achievements, it was equally agreeable to his will that there should be others by whom those achievements should be recorded with dignity and elegance; and that the truth, which had been defended by arms, should also be defended by reason; which is the best and only legitimate means of defending it. Hence, while I applaud those who were victorious in the field, I will not complain of the province which was assigned me; but rather congratulate myself upon it, and thank the Author of all good for having placed me in a station, which may be an object of envy to others rather than of regret to myself. I am far from wishing to make any vain or arrogant comparisons, or to speak ostentatiously of myself; but, in a cause so great and glorious, and particularly on an occasion when I am called by the general suffrage to defend the very defenders of that cause, I can hardly refrain from assuming a more lofty and swelling tone than the simplicity of an exordium may seem to justify: and much as I may be surpassed in the powers of eloquence and copiousness of diction by the illustrious orators of antiquity, yet the subject of which I treat was never surpassed, in any age, in dignity or in interest. It has excited such general and such ardent expectation, that I imagine myself, not in the forum or on the rostra, surrounded only by the people of Athens or of Rome, but about to address in this, as I did in my former Defence, the whole collective body of people, cities, states, and councils of the wise and eminent, through the wide expanse of anxious and listening Europe. I seem to survey, as from a towering height, the far extended tracts of sea and land, and innumerable crowds of spectators, betraying in their looks the liveliest interest, and sensations the most congenial with my own. Here I behold the stout and manly prowess of the Germans disdaining servitude; there the generous and lively impetuosity of the French; on this side, the calm and stately valour of the Spaniard; on that, the composed and wary magnanimity of the Italian. Of all the lovers of liberty and virtue, the magnanimous and the wise, in whatever quarter they may be found, some secretly favour, others openly approve; some greet me with congratulations and applause; others, who had long been proof against conviction, at last yield themselves captive to the force of truth. Surrounded by congregated multitudes, I now imagine that, from the columns of Hercules to the Indian Ocean, I behold the nations of the earth recovering that liberty which they so long had lost; and that the people of this island are transporting to other countries a plant of

more beneficial qualities, and more noble growth, than that
which Triptolemus is reported to have carried from region to
region; that they are disseminating the blessings of civilization
and freedom among cities, kingdoms, and nations. Nor shall
I approach unknown, nor perhaps unloved, if it be told that I
am the same person who engaged in single combat that fierce
advocate of despotism; till then reputed invincible in the opin-
ion of many, and in his own conceit; who insolently challenged
us and our armies to the combat; but whom, while I repelled
his virulence, I silenced with his own weapons; and over
whom, if I may trust to the opinions of impartial judges, I
gained a complete and glorious victory. That this is the plain
unvarnished fact appears from this: that, after the most noble
queen of Sweden, than whom there neither is nor ever was a
personage more attached to literature and to learned men, had
invited Salmasius or Salmatia (for to which sex he belonged is
a matter of uncertainty) to her court, where he was received
with great distinction, my Defence suddenly surprised him in
the midst of his security. It was generally read, and by the
queen among the rest, who, attentive to the dignity of her sta-
tion, let the stranger experience no diminution of her former
kindness and munificence. But, with respect to the rest, if I
may assert what has been often told, and was matter of public
notoriety, such a change was instantly effected in the public
sentiment, that he, who but yesterday flourished in the highest
degree of favour, seemed to-day to wither in neglect; and soon
after receiving permission to depart, he left it doubtful among
many whether he were more honoured when he came, or more
disgraced when he went away; and even in other places it is
clear, that it occasioned no small loss to his reputation; and
all this I have mentioned, not from any futile motives of vanity
or ostentation, but that I might clearly show, as I proposed in
the beginning, what momentous reasons I had for commencing

this work with an effusion of gratitude to the Father of the universe. Such a preface was most honourable and appropriate, in which I might prove, by an enumeration of particulars, that I had not been without my share of human misery; but that I had, at the same time, experienced singular marks of the divine regard; that in topics of the highest concern, the most connected with the exigencies of my country, and the most beneficial to civil and religious liberty; the supreme wisdom and beneficence had invigorated and enlarged my faculties, to defend the dearest interests, not merely of one people, but of the whole human race, against the enemies of human liberty; as it were in a full concourse of all the nations on the earth: and I again invoke the same Almighty Being, that I may still be able, with the same integrity, the same diligence, and the same success, to defend those actions which have been so gloriously achieved; while I vindicate the authors as well as myself, whose name has been associated with theirs, not so much for the sake of honour as disgrace, from unmerited ignominy and reproach.

* * * * * * * * *

But the conflict between me and Salmasius is now finally terminated by his death; and I will not write against the dead; nor will I reproach him with the loss of life as he did me with the loss of sight; though there are some who impute his death to the penetrating severity of my strictures, which he rendered only the more sharp by his endeavours to resist. When he saw the work which he had in hand proceed slowly on, the time of reply elapsed, the public curiosity subsided, his fame marred, and his reputation lost; the favour of the princes, whose cause he had so ill defended, alienated, he was destroyed, after three years of grief, rather by the force of depression than disease.

* * * * * * * * *

If I inveigh against tyrants, what is this to kings? whom I am far from associating with tyrants. As much as an honest man differs from a rogue, so much I contend that a king differs from a tyrant. Whence it is clear, that a tyrant is so far from being a king, that he is always in direct opposition to a king. And he who peruses the records of history, will find that more kings have been subverted by tyrants than by their subjects. He, therefore, who would authorize the destruction of tyrants, does not authorize the destruction of kings, but of the most inveterate enemies to kings.

* * * * * * * * *

Let us now come to the charges which were brought against myself. Is there anything reprehensible in my manners or my conduct? Surely nothing. What no one, not totally divested of all generous sensibility, would have done, he reproaches me with want of beauty and loss of sight.

'Monstrum horrendum, informe, ingens, cui lumen ademptum.'

I certainly never supposed that I should have been obliged to enter into a competition for beauty with the Cyclops; but he immediately corrects himself, and says, 'though not indeed huge, for there cannot be a more spare, shrivelled, and bloodless form.' It is of no moment to say anything of personal appearance, yet lest (as the Spanish vulgar, implicitly confiding in the relations of their priests, believe of heretics) any one, from the representations of my enemies, should be led to imagine that I have either the head of a dog, or the horn of a rhinoceros, I will say something on the subject, that I may have an opportunity of paying my grateful acknowledgments to the Deity, and of refuting the most shameless lies. I do not believe that I was ever once noted for deformity, by any one who ever saw me; but the praise of beauty I am not anxious to obtain. My stature certainly is not tall; but it rather approaches the middle than the diminutive. Yet what if it were diminutive, when so many men, illustrious both in peace and war, have been the same? And how can that be called diminutive, which is great enough for every virtuous achievement? Nor, though very thin, was I ever deficient in courage or in strength; and I was wont constantly to exercise myself in the use of the broadsword, as long as it comported with my habit and my years. Armed with this weapon, as I usually was, I should have thought myself quite a match for any one, though much stronger than myself; and I felt perfectly secure against the assault of any open enemy. At this moment I have the same courage, the same strength, though not the same eyes; yet so little do they betray any external appearance of injury, that they are as unclouded and bright as the eyes of those who most distinctly see. In this instance alone I am a dissembler against my will. My face, which is said to indicate a total privation of blood, is of a complexion entirely opposite to the pale and the cadaverous; so that, though I am more than forty years old, there is scarcely any one to whom I do not appear ten years younger than I am; and the smoothness of my skin is not, in the least, affected by the wrinkles of age. If there be one particle of falsehood in this relation, I should deservedly incur the ridicule of many thousands of my countrymen, and even many foreigners to whom I am personally known. But if he, in a matter so foreign to his purpose, shall be found to have asserted so many shameless and gratuitous falsehoods, you may the more readily estimate the quantity of his veracity on other topics. Thus much necessity compelled me to assert concerning my personal appearance. Respecting yours, though I have been informed that it is most insignificant and contemptible, a perfect mirror of the worthlessness of your character and the malevolence of your heart, I say nothing, and no one will be anxious that anything should be said. I wish that I could with equal facility refute what this barbarous opponent has said of my blindness; but I cannot do it; and I must submit to the affliction. It is not so wretched to be blind, as it is not to be capable of enduring blindness. But why should I not endure a misfortune which it behooves everyone to be prepared to endure if it should happen; which may, in the common course of things, happen to any man; and which has been known to happen to the most distinguished and virtuous persons in history? Shall I mention those wise and ancient bards, whose misfortunes the gods are said to have compensated by superior endowments, and whom men so much revered, that they chose rather to impute their want of sight to the injustice of heaven than to their own want of innocence or virtue? What is reported of the Augur Tiresias is well known; of whom Apollonius sung thus in his Argonautica:

> 'To men he dared the will divine disclose,
> Nor feared what Jove might in his wrath impose.
> The gods assigned him age, without decay,
> But snatched the blessing of his sight away.'

But God himself is truth; in propagating which, as men display a greater integrity and zeal, they approach nearer to the similitude of God, and possess a greater portion of his love. We cannot suppose the deity envious of truth, or unwilling that it should be freely communicated to mankind. The loss of sight, therefore, which this inspired sage, who was so eager in promoting knowledge among men, sustained, cannot be considered as a judicial punishment. Or shall I mention those worthies who were as distinguished for wisdom in the cabinet as for valour in the field? And first, Timoleon of Corinth, who delivered his city and all Sicily from the yoke of slavery; than whom there never lived in any age a more virtuous man or a more incorrupt statesman : Next Appius Claudius, whose discreet counsels in the senate, though they could not restore sight to his own eyes, saved Italy from the formidable inroads of Pyrrhus : then Cæcilius Metellus the high-priest, who lost his sight, while he saved, not only the city, but the palladium, the protection of the city, and the most sacred relics, from the destruction of the flames. On other occasions Providence has indeed given conspicuous proofs of its regard for such singular exertions of patriotism and virtue ; what, therefore, happened to so great and so good a man, I can hardly place in the catalogue of misfortunes. Why should I mention others of later times, as Dandolo of Venice, the incomparable Doge ; or Zisca, the bravest leader of the Bohemians, and the champion of the cross ; or Jerome Zanchius, and some other theologians of the highest reputation? For it is evident that the patriarch Isaac, than whom no man ever enjoyed more of the divine regard, lived blind for many years ; and perhaps also his son Jacob, who was equally an object of the divine benevolence. And in short, did not our Saviour himself clearly declare that that poor man whom he restored to sight had not been born blind, either on account of his own sins or those of his progenitors? And with respect to myself, though I have accurately examined my conduct, and scrutinized my soul, I call thee, O God, the searcher of hearts, to witness, that I am not conscious, either in the more early or in the later periods of my life, of having committed any enormity which might deservedly have marked me out as a fit object for such a calamitous visitation. But since my enemies boast that this affliction is only a retribution for the transgressions of my pen, I again invoke the Almighty to witness, that I never, at any time, wrote anything which I did not think agreeable to truth, to justice, and to piety. This was my persuasion then, and I feel the same persuasion now. Nor was I ever prompted to such exertions by the influence of ambition, by the lust of lucre or of praise; it was only by the conviction of duty and the feeling of patriotism, a disinterested passion for the extension of civil and religious liberty. Thus, therefore, when I was publicly solicited to write a reply to the Defence of the royal cause, when I had to contend with the pressure of sickness, and with the apprehension of soon losing the sight of my remaining eye, and when my medical attendants clearly announced, that if I did engage in the work, it would be irreparably lost, their premonitions caused no hesitation and inspired no dismay. I would not have listened to the voice even of Æsculapius himself from the shrine of Epidaurus, in preference to the suggestions of the heavenly monitor within my breast; my resolution was unshaken, though the alternative was either the loss of my sight, or the desertion of my duty: and I called to mind those two destinies, which the oracle of Delphi announced to the son of Thetis:

> 'I by my Goddess-mother have been warned,
> The silver-footed Thetis, that o'er me
> A double chance of destiny impends:
> If here remaining, round the walls of Troy
> I wage the war, I ne'er shall see my home,
> But then undying glory shall be mine:
> If I return, and see my native land,
> My glory all is gone; but length of life
> Shall then be mine, and death be long deferred.'
>
> — *Iliad*, ix. 410-416.

I considered that many had purchased a less good by a greater evil, the meed of glory by the loss of life; but that I might procure great good by little suffering; that though I am blind, I might still discharge the most honourable duties, the performance of which, as it is something more durable than glory, ought to be an object of superior admiration and esteem; I resolved, therefore, to make the short interval of sight, which was left me to enjoy, as beneficial as possible to the public interest. Thus it is clear by what motives I was governed in the measures which I took, and the losses which I sustained. Let then the calumniators of the divine goodness cease to revile, or to make me the object of their superstitious imaginations. Let them consider, that my situation, such as it is, is neither an object of my shame nor my regret, that my resolutions are too firm to be shaken, that I am not depressed by any sense of the divine displeasure; that, on the other hand, in the most momentous periods, I have had full experience of the divine favour and protection; and that, in the solace and the strength which have been infused into me from above, I have been enabled to do the will of God; that I may oftener think on what he has bestowed, than on what he has withheld; that, in short, I am unwilling to exchange my consciousness of rectitude with that of any other person; and that I feel the recollection a treasured store of tranquillity and delight. But, if the choice were necessary, I would, sir, prefer my blindness to yours; yours is a cloud spread over the mind, which darkens both the light of reason and of conscience; mine keeps from my view only the coloured surfaces of things, while it leaves me at liberty to contemplate the beauty and stability of virtue and of truth. How many things are there besides which I would not willingly see; how many which I must see against my will; and how few which I feel any anxiety to see! There is, as the apostle has remarked, a way to strength through weakness. Let me then be the most feeble creature alive, as long as that feebleness serves to invigorate the energies of my rational and immortal spirit; as long as in that obscurity, in which I am enveloped, the light of the divine presence more clearly shines, then, in proportion as I am weak, I shall be invincibly strong; and in proportion as I am blind, I shall more clearly see. Oh, that I may thus be perfected by feebleness, and irradiated by obscurity! And, indeed, in my blindness, I enjoy in no inconsiderable degree the favour of the Deity, who regards me with more tenderness and compassion in proportion as I am able to behold nothing but himself. Alas! for him who insults me, who maligns and merits public execration! For the divine law not only shields me from injury, but almost renders me too sacred to attack; not indeed so much from the privation of my sight, as from the overshadowing of those heavenly wings which seem to have occasioned this obscurity; and which, when occasioned, he is wont to illuminate with an interior light, more precious and more pure. To this I ascribe the more tender assiduities of my friends, their soothing attentions, their kind visits, their reverential observances; . . . This extraordinary kindness which I experience, cannot be any fortuitous combination; and friends, such as mine, do not suppose that all the virtues of a man are contained in his eyes. Nor do the persons of principal distinction in the commonwealth suffer me to be bereaved of comfort, when they see me bereaved of sight, amid the exertions which I made, the zeal which I showed, and the dangers which I run for the liberty which I love. But, soberly reflecting on the casualties of human life, they show me favour and indulgence, as to a soldier who has served his time, and kindly concede to me an exemption from care and toil. They do not strip me of the badges of honour which I have once worn; they do not deprive me of the places of public trust to which I have been appointed; they do not abridge my salary or emoluments; which, though I may not do so much to deserve as I did formerly, they are too considerate and too kind to take away; and, in short, they honour me as much as the Athenians did those whom they determined to support at the public expense in the Prytaneum. Thus, while both God and man unite in solacing me under the weight of my affliction, let no one lament my loss of sight in so honourable a cause. And let me not indulge in unavailing grief, or want the courage either to despise the revilers of my blindness, or the forbearance easily to pardon the offence.

* * * * * * * * *

I must crave the indulgence of the reader if I have said already, or shall say hereafter, more of myself than I wish to say; that, if I cannot prevent the blindness of my eyes, the oblivion or the defamation of my name, I may at least rescue my life from that species of obscurity, which is the associate of unprincipled depravity. This it will be necessary for me to do on more accounts than one; first, that so many good and learned men among the neighbouring nations, who read my works, may not be induced by this fellow's calumnies to alter the favourable opinion which they have formed of me; but may be persuaded that I am not one who ever disgraced beauty of sentiment by deformity of conduct, or the maxims of a freeman by the actions of a slave; and that the whole tenor of my life has, by the grace of God, hitherto been unsullied by enormity or crime. Next, that those illustrious worthies, who are the objects of my praise, may know that nothing could afflict me with more shame than to have any vices of mine diminish the force or lessen the value of my panegyric upon them; and, lastly, that the people of England, whom fate, or duty, or their own virtues, have incited me to defend, may be convinced from the purity and integrity of my life, that my defence, if it do not redound to their honour, can never be considered as their disgrace. I will now mention who and whence I am. I was born in London, of an honest family; my father was distinguished by the undeviating integrity of his life; my mother, by the esteem in which she was held, and the alms which she bestowed. My father destined me from a child to the pursuits of literature; and my appetite for knowledge was so voracious, that, from twelve years of age, I hardly ever left my studies, or went to bed before midnight. This primarily led to my loss of sight. My eyes were naturally weak, and I was subject to frequent headaches; which, however, could not chill the ardour of my curiosity, or retard the progress of my improvement. My father had me daily instructed in the grammar-school, and by other masters at home. He then, after I had acquired a proficiency in various languages, and had made a considerable progress in philosophy, sent me to the University of Cambridge. Here I passed seven years in the usual course of instruction and study, with the approbation of the good, and without any stain upon my character, till I took the degree of Master of Arts. After this I did not, as this miscreant feigns, run away into Italy, but of my own accord retired to my father's house, whither I was accompanied by the regrets of most of the fellows of the college, who showed me no common marks of friendship and esteem. On my father's estate, where he had determined to pass the remainder of his days, I enjoyed an interval of uninterrupted leisure, which I entirely devoted to the perusal of the Greek and Latin classics; though I occasionally visited the metropolis, either for the sake of purchasing books, or of learning something new in mathematics or in music, in which I, at that time, found a source of pleasure and amusement. In this manner I spent five years till my mother's death. I then became anxious to visit foreign parts, and particularly Italy. My father gave me his permission, and I left home with one servant. On my departure, the celebrated Henry Wotton, who had long been king James's ambassador at Venice, gave me a signal proof of his regard, in an elegant letter which he wrote, breathing not only the warmest friendship, but containing some maxims of conduct which I found very useful in my travels. The noble Thomas Scudamore, king Charles's ambassador, to whom I carried letters of recommendation, received me most courteously at Paris. His lordship gave me a card of introduction to the learned Hugo Grotius, at that time ambassador from the queen of Sweden to the French court; whose acquaintance I anxiously desired, and to whose house I was accompanied by some of his lordship's friends. A few days after, when I set out for Italy, he gave me letters to the English merchants on my route, that they might show me any civilities in their power. Taking ship at Nice, I arrived at Genoa, and afterwards visited Leghorn, Pisa, and Florence. In the latter city, which I have always more particularly esteemed for the elegance of its dialect, its genius, and its taste, I stopped about two months; when I contracted an intimacy with many persons of rank and learning; and was a constant attendant at their literary parties; a practice which prevails there, and tends so much to the diffusion of knowledge, and the preservation of friendship. No time will ever abolish the agreeable recollections which I cherish of Jacopo Gaddi, Carlo Dati, Frescobaldi, Coltellini, Bonmattei, Chimentelli, Francini, and many others. From Florence I went to Siena, thence to Rome, where, after I had spent about two months in viewing the antiquities of that renowned city, where I experienced the most friendly attentions from Lucas Holstenius, and other learned and ingenious men, I continued my route to Naples. There I was introduced by a certain recluse, with whom I had travelled from Rome, to Giovanni Battista Manso, marquis of Villa, a nobleman of distinguished rank and authority, to whom Torquato Tasso, the illustrious poet, inscribed his book on friendship. During my stay, he gave me singular proofs of his regard: he himself conducted me around the city, and to the palace of the viceroy; and more than once paid me a visit at my lodgings. On my departure he gravely apologized for not having shown me more civility, which he said he had

been restrained from doing, because I had spoken with so little
reserve on matters of religion. When I was preparing to pass
over into Sicily and Greece, the melancholy intelligence which
I received of the civil commotions in England made me
alter my purpose; for I thought it base to be travelling for
amusement abroad, while my fellow-citizens were fighting for
liberty at home. While I was on my way back to Rome, some
merchants informed me that the English Jesuits had formed a
plot against me if I returned to Rome, because I had spoken
too freely on religion; for it was a rule which I laid down to
myself in those places, never to be the first to begin any con-
versation on religion; but if any questions were put to me
concerning my faith, to declare it without any reserve or fear.
I, nevertheless, returned to Rome. I took no steps to conceal
either my person or my character; and for about the space of
two months I again openly defended, as I had done before, the
reformed religion in the very metropolis of popery. By the
favour of God, I got safe back to Florence, where I was
received with as much affection as if I had returned to my
native country. There I stopped as many months as I had
done before, except that I made an excursion for a few days
to Lucca; and, crossing the Apennines, passed through Bologna
and Ferrara to Venice. After I had spent a month in survey-
ing the curiosities of this city, and had put on board a ship the
books which I had collected in Italy, I proceeded through
Verona and Milan, and along the Leman lake to Geneva. The
mention of this city brings to my recollection the slandering
More, and makes me again call the Deity to witness, that in all
those places in which vice meets with so little discouragement,
and is practised with so little shame, I never once deviated
from the paths of integrity and virtue, and perpetually reflected
that, though my conduct might escape the notice of men, it
could not elude the inspection of God. At Geneva I held

daily conferences with John Diodati, the learned professor of Theology. Then pursuing my former route through France, I returned to my native country, after an absence of one year and about three months; at the time when Charles, having broken the peace, was renewing what is called the episcopal war with the Scots, in which the royalists being routed in the first encounter, and the English being universally and justly disaffected, the necessity of his affairs at last obliged him to convene a parliament. As soon as I was able, I hired a spacious house in the city for myself and my books; where I again with rapture renewed my literary pursuits, and where I calmly awaited the issue of the contest, which I trusted to the wise conduct of Providence, and to the courage of the people. The vigour of the parliament had begun to humble the pride of the bishops. As long as the liberty of speech was no longer subject to control, all mouths began to be opened against the bishops; some complained of the vices of the individuals, others of those of the order. They said that it was unjust that they alone should differ from the model of other reformed churches; that the government of the church should be according to the pattern of other churches, and particularly the word of God. This awakened all my attention and my zeal. I saw that a way was opening for the establishment of real liberty; that the foundation was laying for the deliverance of man from the yoke of slavery and superstition; that the principles of religion, which were the first objects of our care, would exert a salutary influence on the manners and constitution of the republic; and as I had from my youth studied the distinctions between religious and civil rights, I perceived that if I ever wished to be of use, I ought at least not to be wanting to my country, to the church, and to so many of my fellow-Christians, in a crisis of so much danger; I therefore determined to relinquish the other pursuits in which I was engaged, and to transfer the whole force of my talents and my industry to this one important object. I accordingly wrote two books to a friend concerning the reformation of the church of England. Afterwards, when two bishops of superior distinction vindicated their privileges against some principal ministers, I thought that on those topics, to the consideration of which I was led solely by my love of truth, and my reverence for Christianity, I should not probably write worse than those who were contending only for their own emoluments and usurpations. I therefore answered the one in two books, of which the first is inscribed, Concerning Prelatical Episcopacy, and the other Concerning the Mode of Ecclesiastical Government; and I replied to the other in some Animadversions, and soon after in an Apology. On this occasion it was supposed that I brought a timely succour to the ministers, who were hardly a match for the eloquence of their opponents; and from that time I was actively employed in refuting any answers that appeared. When the bishops could no longer resist the multitude of their assailants, I had leisure to turn my thoughts to other subjects; to the promotion of real and substantial liberty; which is rather to be sought from within than from without; and whose existence depends, not so much on the terror of the sword, as on sobriety of conduct and integrity of life. When, therefore, I perceived that there were three species of liberty which are essential to the happiness of social life — religious, domestic, and civil; and as I had already written concerning the first, and the magistrates were strenuously active in obtaining the third, I determined to turn my attention to the second, or the domestic species. As this seemed to involve three material questions, the conditions of the conjugal tie, the education of the children, and the free publication of the thoughts, I made them objects of distinct consideration. I explained my sentiments, not only concerning the solemnization of the marriage, but the dissolution, if circumstances rendered it necessary; and I drew my arguments from the divine law, which Christ did not abolish, or publish another more grievous than that of Moses. I stated my own opinions, and those of others, concerning the exclusive exception of fornication, which our illustrious Selden has since, in his Hebrew Wife, more copiously discussed; for he in vain makes a vaunt of liberty in the senate or in the forum, who languishes under the vilest servitude, to an inferior at home. On this subject, therefore, I published some books which were more particularly necessary at that time, when man and wife were often the most inveterate foes, when the man often staid to take care of his children at home, while the mother of the family was seen in the camp of the enemy, threatening death and destruction to her husband. I then discussed the principles of education in a summary manner, but sufficiently copious for those who attend seriously to the subject; than which nothing can be more necessary to principle the minds of men in virtue, the only genuine source of political and individual liberty, the only true safeguard of states, the bulwark of their prosperity and renown. Lastly, I wrote my Areopagitica, in order to deliver the press from the restraints with which it was encumbered; that the power of determining what was true and what was false, what ought to be published and what to be suppressed, might no longer be entrusted to a few illiterate and illiberal individuals, who refused their sanction to any work which contained views or sentiments at all above the level of the vulgar superstition. On the last species of civil liberty, I said nothing, because I saw that sufficient attention was paid to it by the magistrates; nor did I write anything on the prerogative of the crown, till the king, voted an enemy by the parliament, and vanquished in the field, was summoned before the tribunal which condemned him to lose his head. But when, at length, some Presbyterian ministers, who had formerly been the most bitter enemies to Charles, became jealous of the growth of the Independents, and of their ascendency in the parliament, most tumultuously clamoured against the sentence, and did all in their power to prevent the execution, though they were not angry, so much on account of the act itself, as because it was not the act of their party; and when they dared to affirm, that the doctrine of the protestants, and of all the reformed churches, was abhorrent to such an atrocious proceeding against kings; I thought that it became me to oppose such a glaring falsehood; and accordingly, without any immediate or personal application to Charles, I showed, in an abstract consideration of the question, what might lawfully be done against tyrants; and in support of what I advanced, produced the opinions of the most celebrated divines; while I vehemently inveighed against the egregious ignorance or effrontery of men, who professed better things, and from whom better things might have been expected. That book did not make its appearance till after the death of Charles; and was written rather to reconcile the minds of the people to the event, than to discuss the legitimacy of that particular sentence which concerned the magistrates, and which was already executed. Such were the fruits of my private studies, which I gratuitously presented to the church and to the state; and for which I was recompensed by nothing but impunity; though the actions themselves procured me peace of conscience, and the approbation of the good; while I exercised that freedom of discussion which I loved. Others, without labour or desert, got possession of honours and emoluments; but no one ever knew me either soliciting anything myself or through the medium of my friends; ever beheld me in a supplicating posture at the doors of the senate, or the levees of the great. I usually kept myself secluded at home, where my own property, part of which had been withheld during the civil commotions, and part of which had been absorbed in the oppressive contributions which I had to sustain, afforded me a scanty subsistence. When I was released from these engagements, and thought that I was about to enjoy an interval of uninterrupted ease, I turned my thoughts to a continued history of my country, from the earliest times to the present period. I had already finished four books, when, after the subversion of the monarchy, and the establishment of a republic, I was surprised by an invitation from the council of state, who desired my services in the office for foreign affairs. A book appeared soon after, which was ascribed to the king, and contained the most invidious charges against the parliament. I was ordered to answer it; and opposed the Iconoclast to his Icon. I did not insult over fallen majesty, as is pretended; I only preferred queen Truth to king Charles. The charge of insult, which I saw that the malevolent would urge, I was at some pains to remove in the beginning of the work; and as often as possible in other places. Salmasius then appeared, to whom they were not, as More says, long in looking about for an opponent, but immediately appointed me, who happened at the time to be present in the council. I have thus, sir, given some account of myself, in order to stop your mouth, and to remove any prejudices which your falsehoods and misrepresentations might cause even good men to entertain against me. I tell thee then, thou mass of corruption, to hold thy peace; for the more you malign, the more you will compel me to confute; which will only serve to render your iniquity more glaring, and my integrity more manifest.

To Charles Diodati, Milton's schoolfellow at St. Paul's School, and his dearest friend

At length, dear friend, your letter has reached me, and the messenger-paper has brought me your words — brought me them from the western shore of Chester's Dee, where with prone stream it seeks the Vergivian wave. Much, believe me, it delights me that foreign lands have nurtured a heart so loving of ours, and a head so faithfully mine; and that a distant part of the country now owes me my sprightly companion, whence, however, it means soon, on being summoned, to send him back. Me at present that city contains which the Thames washes with its ebbing wave; and me, not unwilling, my father's house now possesses. At present it is not my care to revisit the reedy Cam; nor does the love of my forbidden rooms yet cause me grief (*nec dudum vetiti me laris angit amor*). Nor do naked fields please me, where soft shades are not to be had. How ill that place suits the votaries of Apollo! Nor am I in the humour still to bear the threats of a harsh master (*duri minas perferre magistri*), and other things not to be submitted to by my genius (*cæteraque ingenio non subeunda meo*). If this be exile (*si sit hoc exilium*), to have gone to my father's house, and, free from cares, to be pursuing agreeable relaxations, then certainly I refuse neither the name nor the lot of a fugitive (*non ego vel profugi nomen sortemque recuso*), and gladly I enjoy the condition of exile (*lætus et exilii conditione fruor*). Oh that that poet, the tearful exile in the Pontic territory had never endured worse things! Then had he nothing yielded to Ionian Homer, nor would the supreme reputation of having surpassed him be yours, O Maro! For it is in my power to give my leisure up to the placid Muses; and books, which are my life, have me all to themselves. When I am wearied, the pomp of the winding theatre takes me hence, and the garrulous stage calls me to its noisy applauses — whether it be the wary old gentleman that is heard, or the prodigal heir; whether the wooer, or the soldier with his helmet doffed, is on the boards, or the lawyer, prosperous with a ten years' lawsuit, is mouthing forth his gibberish to the unlearned forum. Often the wily servant is abetting the lover-son, and at every turn cheating the very nose of the stiff father; often there the maiden, wondering at her new sensations, knows not what love is, and, while she knows not, loves. Or, again, furious Tragedy shakes her bloody sceptre and rolls her eyes, with dishevelled locks, and it is a pain to look, and yet it is a pleasure to have looked and been pained; for sometimes there is a sweet bitterness in tears. Or the unhappy boy leaves his untasted joys, and falls off, a pitiful object, from his broken love; or the fierce avenger of crime recrosses the Styx from the shades, perturbing guilty souls with his funeral torch. Or the house of Pelops or that of noble Ilium is in grief, or the palace of Creon expiates its incestuous ancestry. But not always within doors, nor even in the city, do we mope; nor does the season of spring pass by unused by us. The grove also planted with thick elms, has our company, and the noble shade of a suburban neighborhood. Very often here, as stars breathing forth mild flames, you may see troops of maidens passing by. Ah! how often have I seen the wonders of a worthy form, which might even repair the old age of Jove! Ah! how often have I seen eyes surpassing all gems and whatever lights revolve round either pole; and necks twice whiter than the arms of living Pelops, and than the way which flows tinged with pure nectar; and the exquisite grace of the forehead; and the trembling hair which cheating love spreads as his golden nets; and the inviting cheeks, compared with which hyacinthine purple is poor, and the very blush, Adonis, of thy own flower! . . . But for me, while the forbearance of the blind boy allows it, I prepare as soon as possible to leave these happy walls, and, using the help of divine all-heal, to flee far from the infamous dwellings of the sorceress Circe. It is fixed that I do go back to the rushy marshes of Cam, and once more approach the murmur of the hoarse-murmuring school. Meanwhile accept the little gift of your faithful friend, and these few words forced into alternate measures.

To Alexander Gill, Jr. (*Familiar Letters*, No. III.)

. . . Indeed, every time I recollect your almost constant conversations with me (which even in this Athens, the University itself, I long after and miss), I think immediately, and not without grief, what a quantity of benefit my absence from you has cheated me of, — me who never left your company without a manifest increase and ἐπίδοσις of literary knowledge, just as if I had been to some emporium of learning. Truly, amongst us here, as far as I know, there are hardly one or two that do not fly off unfeathered to Theology while all but rude and uninitiated in either Philology or Philosophy, — content also with the slightest possible touch of Theology itself, just as much as may suffice for sticking together a little sermon anyhow, and stitching it over with worn patches obtained promiscuously: a fact giving reason for the dread that by degrees there may break in among our clergy the priestly ignorance of a former age. For myself, finding almost no real companions in study here, I should certainly be looking straight back to London, were I not meditating a retirement during this summer vacation into a deep literary leisure and a period of hiding, so to speak, in the bowers of the Muses.

But, as this is your own daily practice, I think it almost a crime to interrupt you longer with my din at present. Farewell.

CAMBRIDGE, July 2, 1628.

To Thomas Young. (*Familiar Letters*, No. IV.)

. . . Having been invited to your part of the country, as soon as spring is a little advanced, I will gladly come, to enjoy the delights of the season, and not less of your conversation, and will withdraw myself from the din of town for a while to your Stoa of the Iceni, as to that most celebrated Porch of Zeno or the Tusculan Villa of Cicero, where you, with moderate means but regal spirit, like some Serranus or Curius, placidly reign in your little farm, and, contemning fortune, hold, as it were, a triumph over riches, ambition, pomp, luxury, and whatever the herd of men admire and are marked by. . . .

CAMBRIDGE, July 21, 1628.

To Charles Diodati,

making a stay in the country, who, having written to the author on the 13th of December, and asked him to excuse his verses, if they were less good than usual, on the ground that, in the midst of the festivities with which he had been received by his friends, he was unable to give a sufficiently prosperous attention to the Muses, had the following reply :

. . . You seem to be enjoying yourself rarely. How well you describe the feasts, and the merry December and preparations for Christmas, and the cups of French wine round the gay hearth ! Why do you complain that poesy is absent from these festivities? Festivity and poetry are surely not incompatible. . . . One sees the triple influence of Bacchus, Apollo, and Ceres, in the verses you have sent me. And, then, have you not music — the harp lightly touched by nimble hands, and the lute giving time to the fair ones as they dance in the old tapestried room? Believe me, where the ivory keys leap, and the accompanying dance goes round the perfumed hall, there will the Song-god be. But let me not go too far. Light Elegy is the care of many gods, and calls any one of them by turns to her assistance — Bacchus, Erato, Ceres, Venus, and little Cupid besides. To poets of this order, therefore, conviviality is allowable; and they may often indulge in draughts of good old wine. *But the man who speaks of high matters — the heaven of the full-grown Jove, and pious heroes, and demigod leaders of men, the man who now sings the holy counsels of the gods above, and now the subterranean realms guarded by the fierce dog — let him live sparely, after the manner of the Samian master; let herbs afford him his innocent diet, let clear water in a beechen cup stand near him, and let him drink sober draughts from a pure fountain!* To this be there added a youth chaste and free from guilt, and rigid morals, and hands without stain. Being such, thou shalt rise up, glittering in sacred raiment and purified by lustral waters, an augur about to go into the presence of the unoffended gods. So is wise Tiresias said to have lived, after he had been deprived of his sight; and Theban Linus; and Calchas the exile; and old Orpheus. So did the scantily-eating, water-drinking Homer carry his hero Ulysses through the monster-teeming hall of Circe, and the straits insidious with the voices of the Syrens, and through thy courts, too, O infernal King, where he is said to have held the troops of shades enthralled by libations of black blood. For the poet is sacred and the priest of the gods; and his breast and his mouth breathe the indwelling Jove.

And now, if you will know what I am myself doing (if indeed

you think it is of so much consequence to know if I am doing anything), here is the fact: we are engaged in singing the heavenly birth of the King of Peace, and the happy age promised by the holy books, and the infant cries and cradling in a manger under a poor roof of that God who rules, with his Father, the Kingdom of Heaven, and the sky with the new-sprung star in it, and the ethereal choirs of hymning angels, and the gods of the heathen suddenly fleeing to their endangered fanes. This is the gift which we have presented to Christ's natal day. On that very morning, at daybreak, it was first conceived. The verses, which are composed in the vernacular, await you in close keeping; you shall be the judge to whom I shall recite them.

Prolusiones quædam Oratoriæ

Some University Latin Oratorical Exercises, seven in number, first published in 1674, the year of Milton's death, along with his Familiar Letters (Epistolæ Familiares), 'as a make-weight to counterbalance the paucity of the Letters,' have an autobiographic value; but, with the exception of a small bit, space does not allow the admission of them here. 'They throw light,' says Masson, 'upon Milton's career at Cambridge. They illustrate the extent and nature of his reading, his habits and tastes as a student, the relation in which he stood to the University system of his time, and to the new intellectual tendencies which were gradually affecting that system. They also settle in the most conclusive manner the fact that Milton passed through two stages in his career at the University, — a stage of decided unpopularity, in his own College at least, which lasted till about 1628, and a final stage of triumph, when his powers were recognized.'

Masson characterizes the seventh oratorical exercise as
D

'one of the finest pieces of Latin prose ever penned by an Englishman.'

The following is a passage, in Masson's close translation, from this exercise, which exhibits what continued to be Milton's attitude through life:

'I regard it, my hearers, as known and accepted by all, that the great Maker of the Universe, when he had constituted all things else as fleeting and corruptible, did mingle up with Man, in addition to that of him which is mortal, a certain divine breath, as it were part of Himself, immortal, indestructible, free from death and extinction; which, after it had sojourned purely and holily for some time in the earth as a heavenly guest, should flutter aloft to its native heaven, and return to its proper home and fatherland: accordingly, that *nothing can deservedly be taken into account as among the causes of our happiness that does not somehow or other regard both that everlasting life and this civil life below.*'

'When his earlier writings,' says Masson, 'are compared with those of his coevals at the University, what strikes one most, next to their vastly greater merit altogether, is their more ideal tone. As, more than any of them, he was conscious of the *os magna soniturum*, the mouth formed for great utterances, so all that he does utter has a certain character and form of magnitude.'

Milton's Latin poem, 'Ad Patrem' (To Father), was occasioned, as may be seen in the poem, by an expressed dissatisfaction on the part of his father with his continued devotion, after leaving the University, to his favorite studies and the Muses, to the exclusion of all consideration of a profession. He had, while yet at the University, fully decided that the Church, for which he was destined by his parents, was not for him, bowing, as it was, beneath the galling 'yoke of prelaty'; and to the legal profession he must have been equally, if not more, averse.

Such a tribute of filial affection and gratitude, as is this poem, certainly overcame all objections the father may have expressed in regard to his course of life at the time.

We learn from this poem, which was no doubt composed soon after Milton's final return to his father's house at Horton, in 1632, he being then in his twenty-fourth year, that, along with the Latin and the Greek, he had acquired, and by his father's advice, a knowledge of the French, Italian, and Hebrew. We also learn of the father's musical genius, both instrumental and vocal, and of the son's lofty estimate of the power of poesy. He ascribes to it a divine nature which evidences man's heavenly origin, and bespeaks him illuminated from above.

I give the translation by the poet Cowper, which, while being somewhat free, is, I think, altogether the best and most poetical that has been made. That by Masson, in hexameters, is closer to the original, but has in it a dactylic dance which is not so much in harmony with the tone of the original as is Cowper's blank-verse translation.

To Father

Oh, that Pieria's spring would thro' my breast
Pour its inspiring influence, and rush
No rill, but rather an o'erflowing flood !
That, for my venerable father's sake,
All meaner themes renounced, my muse, on wings   5
Of duty borne, might reach a loftier strain.
For thee, my father ! howsoe'er it please,
She frames this slender work, nor know I aught
That may thy gifts more suitably requite ;
Though to requite them suitably would ask   10
Returns much nobler, and surpassing far

The meagre stores of verbal gratitude;
But, such as I possess, I send thee all.
This page presents thee in their full amount
With thy son's treasures, and the sum is nought;   15
Nought, save the riches that from airy dream
In secret grottos and in laurel bowers
I have, by golden Clio's gift, acquired.

Verse is a work divine; despise not thou
Verse, therefore, which evinces (nothing more)   20
Man's heavenly source, and which, retaining still
Some scintillations of Promethean fire,
Bespeaks him animated from above.
The gods love verse; the infernal Powers themselves
Confess the influence of verse, which stirs   25
The lowest deep, and binds in triple chains
Of adamant both Pluto and the Shades.
In verse the Delphic priestess, and the pale
Tremulous Sibyl make the future known;
And he who sacrifices, on the shrine   30
Hangs verse, both when he smites the threatening bull,
And when he spreads his reeking entrails wide
To scrutinize the Fates enveloped there.
We, too, ourselves, what time we seek again
Our native skies, and one eternal now   35
Shall be the only measure of our being,
Crowned all with gold, and chaunting to the lyre
Harmonious verse, shall range the courts above,
And make the starry firmament resound;
And, even now, the fiery spirit pure   40
That wheels yon circling orbs, directs, himself,
Their mazy dance with melody of verse
Unutterable, immortal, hearing which

Huge Ophiuchus holds his hiss suppressed,
Orion, softened, drops his ardent blade,   45
And Atlas stands unconscious of his load.
Verse graced of old the feasts of kings ere yet
Luxurious dainties, destined to the gulph
Immense of gluttony, were known, and ere
Lyæus deluged yet the temperate board.   50
Then sat the bard a customary guest
To share the banquet, and, his length of locks
With beechen honours bound, proposed in verse
The characters of heroes, and their deeds
To imitation, sang of Chaos old, sword, belt, and club;   55
Of nature's birth, of gods that crept in search
Of acorns fallen, and of the thunder bolt
Not yet produced from Etna's fiery cave.
And what avails, at last, tune without voice,
Devoid of matter? Such may suit perhaps   60
The rural dance, but such was ne'er the song
Of Orpheus, whom the streams stood still to hear
And the oaks followed. Not by chords alone
Well touched, but by resistless accents more
To sympathetic tears the ghosts themselves   65
He moved; these praises to his verse he owes.

Nor thou persist, I pray thee, still to slight
The sacred Nine, and to imagine vain
And useless, powers by whom inspired thyself
Art skilful to associate verse with airs   70
Harmonious, and to give the human voice
A thousand modulations, heir by right
Indisputable of Arion's fame.
Now say, what wonder is it if a son
Of thine delight in verse, if so conjoined   75

In close affinity, we sympathize
In social arts and kindred studies sweet?
Such distribution of himself to us
Was Phœbus' choice ; thou hast thy gift and I
Mine also ; and between us we receive, 80
Father and son, the whole inspiring god.
No ! howsoe'er the semblance thou assume
Of hate, thou hatest not the gentle Muse,
My Father ! for thou never bad'st me tread
The beaten path and broad that leads right on 85
To opulence, nor didst condemn thy son
To the insipid clamours of the bar,
To laws voluminous and ill observed ;
But, wishing to enrich me more, to fill
My mind with treasure, ledst me far away 90
From city din to deep retreats, to banks
And streams Aonian, and, with free consent,
Didst place me happy at Apollo's side.
I speak not now, on more important themes
Intent, of common benefits and such 95
As nature bids, but of thy larger gifts,
My Father ! who, when I had opened once
The stores of Roman rhetoric, and learned
The full-toned language of the eloquent Greeks,
Whose lofty music graced the lips of Jove, 100
Thyself didst counsel me to add the flowers
That Gallia boasts, those, too, with which the smooth
Italian his degenerate speech adorns,
That witnesses his mixture with the Goth ;
And Palestine's prophetic songs divine. 105
To sum the whole, whate'er the heaven contains,
The earth beneath it, and the air between,
The rivers and the restless deep, may all

Prove intellectual gain to me, my wish
Concurring with thy will; Science herself,   110
All cloud removed, inclines her beauteous head,
And offers me the lip, if, dull of heart,
I shrink not and decline her gracious boon.

Go now and gather dross, ye sordid minds
That covet it; what could my Father more?   115
What more could Jove himself, unless he gave
His own abode, the heaven, in which he reigns?
More eligible gifts than these were not
Apollo's to his son, had they been safe,
As they were insecure, who made the boy   120
The world's vice-luminary, bade him rule
The radiant chariot of the day, and bind
To his young brows his own all-dazzling wreath.
I, therefore, although last and least, my place
Among the learned in the laurel grove   125
Will hold, and where the conqueror's ivy twines,
Henceforth exempt from the unlettered throng
Profane, nor even to be seen by such.
Away then, sleepless Care, Complaint away,
And Envy, with thy 'jealous leer malign!'   130
Nor let the monster Calumny shoot forth
Her venomed tongue at me. Detested foes!
Ye all are impotent against my peace,
For I am privileged, and bear my breast
Safe, and too high for your viperean wound.   135
But thou, my Father! since to render thanks
Equivalent, and to requite by deeds
Thy liberality, exceeds my power,
Suffice it that I thus record thy gifts,
And bear them treasured in a grateful mind!   140

> Ye, too, the favourite pastime of my youth,
> My voluntary numbers, if ye dare
> To hope longevity, and to survive
> Your master's funeral, not soon absorbed
> In the oblivious Lethæan gulph   145
> Shall to futurity perhaps convey
> This theme, and by these praises of my sire
> Improve the Fathers of a distant age!

An English letter to a friend (unknown), who, it appears, had been calling him to account for his apparent indifference as to his work in life

This letter has an exceptional autobiographic value. The sonnet, which is inserted, appears to have been independently written some time before, and was originally published in 1645, with the heading 'On his having arrived at the age of twenty-three.'

'Sir, — Besides that in sundry respects I must acknowledge me to profit by you whenever we meet, you are often to me, and were yesterday especially, as a good watchman to admonish that the hours of the night pass on (for so I call my life, as yet obscure and unserviceable to mankind), and that the day with me is at hand, wherein Christ commands all to labor, while there is light. Which, because I am persuaded you do to no other purpose than out of a true desire that God should be honoured in every one, I therefore think myself bound, though unasked, to give you an account, as oft as occasion is, of this my tardy moving, according to the precept of my conscience, which I firmly trust is not without God. Yet now I will not strain for any set apology, but only refer myself to what my mind shall have at any time to declare herself at her best ease.

But if you think, as you said, that too much love of learning is in fault, and that I have given up myself to dream away my years in the arms of studious retirement, like Endymion with the moon, as the tale of Latmus goes, yet consider that, if it were no more but the mere love of learning, whether it proceed from a principle bad, good, or natural, it could not have held out thus long against so strong opposition on the other side of every kind. For, if it be bad, why should not all the fond hopes that forward youth and vanity are fledge with, together with gain, pride, and ambition, call me forward more powerfully than a poor, regardless, and unprofitable sin of curiosity should be able to withhold me; whereby a man cuts himself off from all action, and becomes the most helpless, pusillanimous, and unweaponed creature in the world, the most unfit and unable to do that which all mortals most aspire to, either to be useful to his friends or to offend his enemies? Or, if it be to be thought a natural proneness, there is against that a much more potent inclination inbred, which about this time of a man's life solicits most — the desire of house and family of his own; to which nothing is esteemed more helpful than the early entering into credible employment, and nothing hindering than this affected solitariness. And, though this were enough, yet there is another act, if not of pure, yet of refined nature, no less available to dissuade prolonged obscurity — a desire of honour and repute and immortal fame, seated in the breast of every true scholar; which all make haste to by the readiest ways of publishing and divulging conceived merits — as well those that shall, as those that never shall, obtain it. Nature, therefore, would presently work the more prevalent way, if there were nothing but this inferior bent of herself to restrain her. Lastly, the love of learning, as it is the pursuit of something good, it would sooner follow the more excellent and supreme good

known and presented, and so be quickly diverted from the
empty and fantastic chase of shadows and notions, to the
solid good flowing from due and timely obedience to that
command in the Gospel set out by the terrible feasing of him
that hid the talent.

It is more probable, therefore, that not the endless delight
of speculation, but this very consideration of that great com-
mandment, does not press forward, as soon as many do, to
undergo, but keeps off, with a sacred reverence and religious
advisement how *best* to undergo, not taking thought of being
late, so it give advantage to be more *fit;* for those that were
latest lost nothing when the master of the vineyard came to
give each one his hire. And here I am come to a stream-
head, copious enough to disburden itself, like Nilus, at seven
mouths into an ocean. But then I should also run into a
reciprocal contradiction of ebbing and flowing at once, and
do that which I excuse myself for not doing — preach and not
preach. Yet, that you may see that I am something suspicious
of myself, and do take notice of a certain belatedness in me,
I am the bolder to send you some of my nightward thoughts
some while since, because they come in not altogether unfitly,
made up in a Petrarchian stanza, which I told you of:

> How soon hath Time, the subtle thief of youth,
>   Stolen on his wing my three-and-twentieth year!
>   My hasting days fly on with full career;
> But my late spring no bud or blossom shew'th.
> Perhaps my semblance might deceive the truth   5
>   That I to manhood am arrived so near;
>   And inward ripeness doth much less appear,
> That some more timely-happy spirits indu'th.
> Yet be it less or more, or soon or slow,
>   It shall be still in strictest measure even   10

> To that same lot, however mean or high,
> Toward which Time leads me, and the will of Heaven.
> All is, if I have grace to use it so,
> As ever in my great Task-Master's eye.

By this I believe you may well repent of having made mention at all of this matter; for, if I have not all this while won you to this, I have certainly wearied you of it. This, therefore, alone may be a sufficient reason for me to keep me as I am, lest, having thus tired you singly, I should deal worse with a whole congregation and spoil all the patience of a parish; for I myself do not only see my own tediousness, but now grow offended with it, that has hindered me thus long from coming to the last and best *period* of my letter, and that which must now chiefly work my pardon, — that I am

> Your true and unfeigned friend, etc.'

To Alexander Gill, Jr. (*Familiar Letters*, No. V.)

If you had presented to me a gift of gold, or of preciously embossed vases, or whatever of that sort mortals admire, it were certainly to my shame not to have some time or other made you a remuneration in return, as far as my faculties might serve. Your gift of the day before yesterday, however, having been such a sprightly and elegant set of Hendecasyllabics, you have, just in proportion to the superiority of that gift to anything in the form of gold, made us the more anxious to find some dainty means by which to repay the kindness of so pleasant a favour. We had, indeed, at hand some things of our own of this same kind, but such as I could nowise deem fit to be sent in contest of equality of gift with yours. I send, therefore, what is not exactly mine, but belongs also to the truly divine poet, this ode of whom, only last week, with no deliberate intention certainly, but from I know not what sudden impulse before daybreak, I adapted, almost in bed, to the rule of Greek heroic verse: with the effect, it seems, that, relying on this coadjutor, who surpasses you no less in his subject than you surpass me in art, I should have something that might have a resemblance of approach to a balancing of accounts. Should anything meet you in it not coming up to your usual opinion of our productions, understand that, since I left your school, this is the first and only thing I have composed in Greek,— employing myself, as you know, more willingly in Latin and English matters; inasmuch as whoever spends study and pains in this age on Greek composition runs a risk of singing mostly to the deaf. . . .

From our suburban residence (*E nostro suburbano*), December 4, 1634.

To Charles Diodati. (*Familiar Letters*, No. VI.)

Now at length I see plainly that what you are driving at is to vanquish me sometimes in the art of obstinate silence; and, if it is so, bravo! have that little glory over us, for behold! we write first. All the same, if ever the question should come into contention why neither has written to the other for so long, do not think but that I shall stand by many degrees the more excused of the two,—manifestly so indeed, as being one by nature slow and lazy to write, as you well know; while you, on the other hand, whether by nature or by habit, are wont without difficulty to be drawn into epistolary correspondence of this sort. It makes also for my favour that I know your method of studying to be so arranged that you frequently take breath in the middle, visit your friends, write much, sometimes make a journey, whereas my genius is such that no delay, no rest, no care or thought almost of anything, holds me aside until I reach the end I am making for, and round off, as it were, some great period of my studies. . . .

LONDON, September 2, 1637.

To Charles Diodati. (*Familiar Letters*, No. VII.)

. . . What besides God has resolved concerning me I know not, but this at least : *He has instilled into me, if into any one, a vehement love of the beautiful.* Not with so much labour, as the fables have it, is Ceres said to have sought her daughter Proserpina as it is my habit day and night to seek for this *idea of the beautiful,* as for a certain image of supreme beauty, through all the forms and faces of things (*for many are the shapes of things divine*), and to follow it as it leads me on by some sure traces which I seem to recognize. Hence it is that, when any one scorns what the vulgar opine in their depraved estimation of things, and dares to feel and speak and be that which the highest wisdom throughout all ages has taught to be best, to that man I attach myself forthwith by a kind of real necessity, wherever I find him. If, whether by nature or by my fate, I am so circumstanced that by no effort or labour of mine can I myself rise to such an honour and elevation, yet that I should always worship and look up to those who have attained that glory, or happily aspire to it, neither gods nor men, I reckon, have bidden nay.

But now I know you wish to have your curiosity satisfied. You make many anxious inquiries, even as to what I am at present thinking of. Hearken, Theodotus, but let it be in your private ear, lest I blush ; and allow me for a little to use big language with you. You ask what I am thinking of ? So may the good Deity help me, of immortality ! And what am I doing ? *Growing my wings* and meditating flight ; but as yet our Pegasus raises himself on very tender pinions. Let us be lowly wise!

* * * * * * * *

I have by continuous reading brought down the affairs of the Greeks as far as the time when they ceased to be Greeks. I have been long engaged in the obscure business of the state of Italians under the Longobards, the Franks, and the Germans, down to the time when liberty was granted them by Rodolph, King of Germany: from that period it will be better to read separately what each City did by its own wars. . . .

LONDON, September 23, 1637.

To Benedetto Bonmattei of Florence. (*Familiar Letters,* No. VIII.)

. . . I, certainly, who have not wet merely the tips of my lips with both those tongues, but have, as much as any, to the full allowance of my years, drained their deeper draughts, can yet sometimes willingly and eagerly go for a feast to that Dante of yours, and to Petrarch, and a good few more; nor has Attic Athens herself, with her pellucid Ilissus, nor that old Rome with her bank of the Tiber, been able so to hold me but that I love often to visit your Arno and these hills of Fæsule. See now, I entreat, whether it has not been with enough of providential cause that *I* have been given to you for these few days, as your latest guest from the ocean, who am so great a lover of your nation that, as I think, there is no other more so. . . .

FLORENCE, September 10, 1638.

Mansus

Milton's Latin poem addressed to Manso, Marquis of Villa, in grateful acknowledgment of the distinguished attention which had been shown him by the aged Marquis, during his stay in Naples, contains the first intimation in his writings of his contemplating an epic poem to be based on the legendary or mythical history of Britain, with King Arthur for its hero.

The following is Masson's quite literal prose translation of vv. 70-100:

... 'Oh that my lot might yield me such a friend, one who should know as well how to decorate Apollo's children, if perchance I shall ever call back into verse our native kings, and Arthur stirring wars even under the earth that hides him, or speak of the great-souled heroes, the knights of the unconquered Table, bound in confederate brotherhood, and (Oh may the spirit be present to me!) break the Saxon phalanxes under the British Mars. Then, when, having measured out the period of a not silent life, and full of years, I shall leave the dust its due, he would stand by my bed with wet eyes; it would be enough if I said to him standing by "Let me be thy charge;" he would see that my limbs, slacked in livid death, were softly laid in the narrow coffin; perchance he would bring out from the marble our features, wreathing the hair either with the leaf of Paphian myrtle or with that of Parnassian laurel; but I should repose in secure peace. Then, too, if faith is aught, if there are assured rewards of the good, I myself, withdrawn into the ether of the heaven-housed gods, whither labour and the pure mind and the fire of virtue carry us, shall behold these things from some part of the unseen world, as far as the fates allow, and, smiling serene, with soul entire, shall feel my face suffused with the purple light, and applaud myself the while in the joy of ethereal Olympus.'

From the 'Areopagitica: a speech for the liberty of unlicensed printing. To the Parliament of England'

And lest some should persuade ye, lords and commons, that these arguments of learned men's discouragement at this your order are mere flourishes, and not real, I could recount what I have seen and heard in other countries, where this kind of inquisition tyrannizes; when I have sat among their learned men, (for that honour I had,) and been counted happy to be born in such a place of philosophic freedom, as they supposed England was, while themselves did nothing but bemoan the servile condition into which learning amongst them was brought; that this was it which had damped the glory of Italian wits; that nothing had been there written now these many years but flattery and fustian. There it was that I found and visited the famous Galileo, grown old, a prisoner to the Inquisition, for thinking in astronomy otherwise than the Franciscan and Dominican licensers thought. And though I knew that England then was groaning loudest under the prelatical yoke, nevertheless I took it as a pledge of future happiness, that other nations were so persuaded of her liberty.

Yet was it beyond my hope, that those worthies were then breathing in her air, who should be her leaders to such a deliverance, as shall never be forgotten by any revolution of time that this world hath to finish. When that was once begun, it was as little in my fear, that what words of complaint I heard among learned men of other parts uttered against the Inquisition, the same I should hear, by as learned men at home, uttered in time of parliament against an order of licensing; and that so generally, that when I had disclosed myself a companion of their discontent, I might say, if without envy, that he whom an honest quæstorship had endeared to the Sicilians, was not more by them importuned against Verres, than the favourable opinion

which I had among many who honour ye, and are known and
respected by ye, loaded me with entreaties and persuasions, that
I would not despair to lay together that which just reason
should bring into my mind, towards the removal of an unde-
served thraldom upon learning.

To Lucas Holstenius in the Vatican at Rome. (*Familiar
Letters*, No. IX.)

Although I both can and often do remember many courteous
and most friendly acts done me by many in this my passage
through Italy, yet, for so brief an acquaintance, I do not know
whether I can justly say that from any one I have had greater
proofs of goodwill than those which have come to me from you.
For, when I went up to the Vatican for the purpose of meeting
you, though a total stranger to you, — unless perchance anything
had been previously said about me to you by Alexander Cheru-
bini, — you received me with the utmost courtesy. Admitted
at once with politeness into the Museum, I was allowed to be-
hold the superb collection of books, and also very many manu-
script Greek authors set forth with your explanations, — some
of whom, not yet seen in our age, seemed now, in their array,
like Virgil's

penitus convalle virenti
Inclusæ animæ superumque ad lumen ituræ, (vi. 679)

to demand the active hands of the printer, and a delivery into
the world, while others, already edited by your care, are eagerly
received everywhere by scholars : — dismissed, too, richer than
I came, with two copies of one of these last presented to me
by yourself. Then, I could not but believe that it was in con-
sequence of the mention you made of me to the most excellent
Cardinal Francesco Barberini that, when he, a few days after,

gave that public musical entertainment with truly Roman magnificence (ἀκρόαμα illud musicum magnificentiâ vere Romanâ publice exhiberet), he himself, waiting at the doors, and seeking me out in so great a crowd, almost seizing me by the hand, indeed, admitted me within in a truly most honourable manner. Further, when, on this account, I went to pay my respects to him next day, you again were the person that both made access for me and obtained me an opportunity of leisurely conversation with him — an opportunity such as, with so great a man, — than whom, on the topmost summit of dignity, nothing more kind, nothing more courteous, — was truly, place and time considered, too ample rather than too sparing. . . .

FLORENCE, March 30, 1639.

Epitaphium Damonis

The ' Epitaphium Damonis ' is a pastoral elegy, occasioned by the death of Charles Diodati, which occurred in the summer or autumn of 1638, while Milton was on his continental tour As an expression of the poet's grief for the loss of his boyhood's and early manhood's dearest, most intimate, and sympathetic friend, it has a general autobiographic character; but it contains one passage (vv. 161-178), having a special interest of the kind, in which he again alludes to his contemplated epic poem, to be based on the legendary history of Britain.

The following is Masson's translation of the Argument and of vv. 161-178 :

'Thyrsis and Damon, shepherds of the same neighbourhood, following the same pursuits, were friends from their boyhood, in the highest degree of mutual attachment. Thyrsis, having set out to travel for mental improvement, received news when abroad of Damon's death. Afterwards at length returning, and finding the matter to be so, he deplores himself and his solitary condition in the following poem. Under the guise of Damon, however, is here understood Charles Diodati, tracing his descent on the father's side from the Tuscan city of Lucca, but otherwise English — a youth remarkable, while he lived, for his genius, his learning, and other most shining virtues.'

'Go unpastured, my lambs: your master now heeds not your bleating.
I have a theme of the Trojans cruising our southern headlands
Shaping to song, and the realm of Imogen, daughter of Pandras,
Brennus and Arvirach, dukes, and Bren's bold brother, Belinus;
Then the Armorican settlers under the laws of the Britons,
Ay, and the womb of Igraine fatally pregnant with Arthur,
Uther's son, whom he got disguised in Gorlois' likeness,
All by Merlin's craft. Oh then, if life shall be spared me,
Thou shalt be hung, my pipe, far off on some brown dying pine tree,
Much forgotten of me; or else your Latian music
Changed for the British war-screech! What then? For one to do all things,
One to hope all things, fits not! Prize sufficiently ample
Mine, and distinction great (unheard of ever thereafter
Though I should be, and inglorious, all through the world of the stranger),
If but yellow-haired Ouse shall read me, the drinker of Alan,
Humber, which whirls as it flows, and Trent's whole valley of orchards,
Thames, my own Thames, above all, and Tamar's western waters,
Tawny with ores, and where the white waves swinge the far Orkneys.'

From 'Of Reformation in England'

Oh, sir, I do now feel myself inwrapped on the sudden into those mazes and labyrinths of dreadful and hideous thoughts, that which way to get out, or which way to end, I know not, unless I turn mine eyes, and with your help lift up my hands to that eternal and propitious Throne, where nothing is readier than grace and refuge to the distresses of mortal suppliants: and it were a shame to leave these serious thoughts less piously than the heathen were wont to conclude their graver discourses.

Thou, therefore, that sittest in light and glory unapproachable, Parent of angels and men! next, thee I implore, omnipotent King, Redeemer of that lost remnant whose nature thou didst assume, ineffable and everlasting Love! and thou, the third subsistence of divine infinitude, illumining Spirit, the joy and solace of created things! one Tripersonal godhead! look upon this thy poor and almost spent and expiring church, leave her not thus a prey to these importunate wolves, that wait and think long till they devour thy tender flock; these wild boars that have broke into thy vineyard, and left the print of their polluting hoofs on the souls of thy servants. Oh! let them not bring about their damned designs, that stand now at the entrance of the bottomless pit, expecting the watchword to open and let out those dreadful locusts and scorpions, to reinvolve us in that pitchy cloud of infernal darkness, where we shall never more see the sun of thy truth again, never hope for the cheerful dawn, never more hear the bird of morning sing. Be moved with pity at the afflicted state of this our shaken monarchy, that now lies labouring under her throes, and struggling against the grudges of more dreaded calamities.

O thou, that, after the impetuous rage of five bloody inundations, and the succeeding sword of intestine war, soaking the land in her own gore, didst pity the sad and ceaseless revolution of our swift and thick-coming sorrows; when we were quite breathless, of thy free grace didst motion peace, and terms of covenant with us; and having first well nigh freed us from antichristian thraldom, didst build up this Britannic empire to a glorious and enviable height, with all her daughter-islands about her; stay us in this felicity, let not the obstinacy of our half-obedience and will-worship bring forth that viper of sedition, that for these fourscore years hath been breeding to eat through the entrails of our peace; but let her cast her abortive spawn without the danger of this travailing and throbbing kingdom: that we may still remember in our solemn thanksgivings, how for us, the northern ocean even to the frozen Thule was scattered with the proud shipwrecks of the Spanish armada, and the very maw of hell ransacked, and made to give up her concealed destruction, ere she could vent it in that horrible and damned blast.

Oh how much more glorious will those former deliverances appear, when we shall know them not only to have saved us from greatest miseries past, but to have reserved us for greatest happiness to come! Hitherto thou hast but freed us, and that not fully, from the unjust and tyrannous claim of thy foes; now unite us entirely, and appropriate us to thyself, tie us everlastingly in willing homage to the prerogative of thy eternal throne.

And now we know, O thou our most certain hope and defence, that thine enemies have been consulting all the sorceries of the great whore, and have joined their plots with that sad intelligencing tyrant that mischiefs the world with his mines of Ophir, and lies thirsting to revenge his naval ruins that have larded our seas: but let them all take counsel together, and let it come to nought; let them decree, and do thou cancel it; let them gather themselves, and be scattered; let them embattle themselves, and be broken ; let them embattle, and be broken, for thou art with us.

Then, amidst the hymns and hallelujahs of saints, some one may perhaps be heard offering at high strains in new and lofty measures, to sing and celebrate thy divine mercies and marvellous judgments in this land throughout all ages; whereby this great and warlike nation, instructed and inured to the fervent and continual practice of truth and righteousness, and casting far from her the rags of her old vices, may press on hard to that high and happy emulation to be found the soberest, wisest, and most Christian people at that day, when thou, the eternal and shortly-expected King, shalt open the clouds to judge the several kingdoms of the world, and distributing national honours and rewards to religious and just commonwealths, shalt put an end to all earthly tyrannies, proclaiming thy universal and mild monarchy through heaven and earth ; where they undoubtedly, that by their labours, counsels, and prayers, have been earnest for the common good of religion and their country, shall receive above the inferior orders of the blessed, the regal addition of principalities, legions, and thrones into their glorious titles, and in supereminence of beatific vision, progressing the dateless and irrevoluble circle of eternity, shall clasp inseparable hands with joy and bliss, in overmeasure for ever.

From 'Animadversions upon the Remonstrant's Defence,' etc.

O thou the ever-begotten Light and perfect Image of the Father ! thou hast opened our difficult and sad times, and given us an unexpected breathing after our long oppressions : thou hast done justice upon those that tyrannized over us, while some men wavered and admired a vain shadow of wisdom in a tongue nothing slow to utter guile, though thou hast taught us to admire only that which is good, and to count that only praiseworthy, which is grounded upon thy divine precepts. Thou hast discovered the plots, and frustrated the hopes, of all the wicked in the land, and put to shame the persecutors of thy church: thou hast made our false prophets to be found a lie in the sight of all the people, and chased them with sudden confusion and amazement before the redoubled brightness of thy descending cloud, that now covers thy tabernacle. Who is there that cannot trace thee now in thy beamy walk through the midst of thy sanctuary, amidst those golden candlesticks, which have long suffered a dimness amongst us through the violence of those that had seized them, and were more taken with the mention of their gold than of their starry light; teaching the doctrine of Balaam, to cast a stumbling-block before thy servants, commanding them to eat things sacrificed to idols, and forcing them to fornication? Come, therefore, O thou that hast the seven stars in thy right hand, appoint thy chosen priests according to their orders and courses of old, to minister before thee, and duly to press and pour out the consecrated oil into thy holy and ever-burning lamps. Thou has sent out the spirit of prayer upon thy servants over all the land to this effect, and stirred up their vows as the sound of many waters about thy throne. Every one can say, that now certainly thou hast visited this land, and hast not forgotten the utmost corners of the earth, in a time when men had thought that thou wast gone up from us to the furthest end of the heavens, and hadst left to do marvellously among the sons of these last ages. Oh perfect and accomplish thy glorious acts! for men may leave their works unfinished, but thou art a God, thy nature is perfection: shouldst thou bring us thus far onward from Egypt to destroy us in this wilderness, though we deserve, yet thy great name would suffer in the rejoicing of thine enemies, and the deluded hope of all thy servants. When thou hast settled peace in the church, and righteous judgment in the kingdom, then shall all thy saints address their voices of joy and triumph to thee, standing on the shore of that Red Sea into which our enemies had almost driven us. *And he that now for haste snatches up a plain ungarnished present as a thank-offering to thee, which could not be deferred in regard of thy so many late deliverances wrought for us one upon another, may then perhaps take up a harp, and sing thee an elaborate song to generations.* In that day it shall no more be said as in scorn, this or that was never held so till this present age, when men have better learnt that the times and seasons pass along under thy feet to go and come at thy bidding : and as thou didst dignify our fathers' days with many revelations above all the foregoing ages, since thou tookest the flesh ; so thou canst vouchsafe to us (though unworthy) as large a portion of thy Spirit as thou pleasest : for who shall prejudice thy all-governing will? seeing the power of thy grace is not passed away with the primitive times, as fond and faithless men imagine, but thy kingdom is now at hand, and thou standing at the door. Come forth out of thy royal chambers, O Prince of all the kings of the earth ! put on the visible robes of thy imperial majesty, take up that unlimited sceptre which thy Almighty Father hath bequeathed thee ; for now the voice of thy bride calls thee, and all creatures sigh to be renewed.

From 'The Reason of Church Government urged against Prelaty'

For me, I have determined to lay up as the best treasure and solace of a good old age, if God vouchsafe it me, the honest liberty of free speech from my youth, where I shall think it available in so dear a concernment as the church's good. For if I be, either by disposition or what other cause, too inquisitive, or suspicious of myself and mine own doings, who can help it? But this I foresee, that should the church be brought under heavy oppression, and God have given me ability the while to reason against that man that should be the author of so foul a deed; or should she, by blessing from above on the industry and courage of faithful men, change this her distracted estate into better days, without the least furtherance or contribution of those few talents, which God at that present had lent me; I foresee what stories I should hear within myself, all my life after, of discourage and reproach. Timorous and ungrateful, the church of God is now again at the foot of her insulting enemies, and thou bewailest. What matters it for thee, or thy bewailing? When time was, thou couldst not find a syllable of all that thou hast read, or studied, to utter in her behalf. Yet ease and leisure was given thee for thy retired thoughts, out of the sweat of other men. Thou hast the diligence, the parts, the language of a man, if a vain subject were to be adorned or beautified; but when the cause of God and his church was to be pleaded, for which purpose that tongue was given thee which thou hast, God listened if he could hear thy voice among his zealous servants, but thou wert dumb as a beast; from henceforward be that which thine own brutish silence hath made thee. Or else I should have heard on the other ear: Slothful, and ever to be set light by, the church hath now overcome her late distresses after the unwearied labours of many her true servants that stood up in her defence; thou also wouldst take upon thee to share amongst them of their joy: but wherefore thou? Where canst thou shew any word or deed of thine which might have hastened her peace? Whatever thou dost now talk, or write, or look, is the alms of other men's active prudence and zeal. Dare not now to say or do anything better than thy former sloth and infancy; or if thou darest, thou dost impudently to make a thrifty purchase of boldness to thyself, out of the painful merits of other men;

what before was thy sin is now thy duty, to be abject and worthless. These, and such-like lessons as these, I know would have been my matins duly, and my even-song. But now by this little diligence, mark what a privilege I have gained with good men and saints, to claim my right of lamenting the tribulations of the church, if she should suffer, when others, that have ventured nothing for her sake, have not the honour to be admitted mourners. But if she lift up her drooping head and prosper, among those that have something more than wished her welfare, I have my charter and freehold of rejoicing to me and my heirs. Concerning therefore this wayward subject against prelaty, the touching whereof is so distasteful and disquietous to a number of men, as by what hath been said I may deserve of charitable readers to be credited, that neither envy nor gall hath entered me upon this controversy, but the enforcement of conscience only, and a preventive fear lest the omitting of this duty should be against me, when I would store up to myself the good provision of peaceful hours : so, lest it should be still imputed to me, as I have found it hath been, that some self-pleasing humour of vain-glory hath incited me to contest with men of high estimation, now while green years are upon my head ; from this needless surmisal I shall hope to dissuade the intelligent and equal auditor, if I can but say successfully that which in this exigent behoves me ; although I would be heard only, if it might be, by the elegant and learned reader, to whom principally for a while I shall beg leave I may address myself. To him it will be no new thing, though I tell him that if I hunted after praise, by the ostentation of wit and learning, I should not write thus out of mine own season when I have neither yet completed to my mind the full circle of my private studies, although I complain not of any insufficiency to the matter in hand ; or were I ready to my wishes, it were a folly to commit anything elaborately composed to the careless and interrupted listening of these tumultuous times. Next, if I were wise only to my own ends, I would certainly take such a subject as of itself might catch applause, whereas this hath all the disadvantages on the contrary, and such a subject as the publishing whereof might be delayed at pleasure, and time enough to pencil it over with all the curious touches of art, even to the perfection of a faultless picture; whenas in this argument the not deferring is of great moment to the good speeding, that if solidity have leisure to do her office, art cannot have much. Lastly, I should not choose this manner of writing, wherein knowing myself inferior to myself, led by the genial power of nature to another task, I have the use, as I may account, but of my left hand. And though I shall be foolish in saying more to this purpose, yet, since it will be such a folly, as wisest men go about to commit, having only confessed and so committed, I may trust with more reason, because with more folly, to have courteous pardon. For although a poet, soaring in the high reason of his fancies, with his garland and singing robes about him, might, without apology, speak more of himself than I mean to do; yet for me sitting here below in the cool element of prose, a mortal thing among many readers of no empyreal conceit, to venture and divulge unusual things of myself, I shall petition to the gentler sort, it may not be envy to me. I must say, therefore, that after I had for my first years, by the ceaseless diligence and care of my father, (whom God recompense!) been exercised to the tongues, and some sciences, as my age would suffer, by sundry masters and teachers, both at home and at the schools, it was found that whether aught was imposed me by them that had the overlooking, or betaken to of mine own choice in English, or other tongue, prosing or versing, but chiefly by this latter, the style, by certain vital signs it had, was likely to live. But much latelier in the private academies of Italy, whither I

was favoured to resort, perceiving that some trifles which I
had in memory, composed at under twenty or thereabout, (for
the manner is, that every one must give some proof of his wit
and reading there,) met with acceptance above what was
looked for; and other things, which I had shifted in scarcity of
books and conveniences to patch up amongst them, were re-
ceived with written encomiums, which the Italian is not forward
to bestow on men of this side the Alps; I began thus far to
assent both to them and divers of my friends here at home,
and not less to an inward prompting which now grew daily
upon me, that by labour and intense study, (which I take to be
my portion in this life,) joined with the strong propensity of
nature, I might perhaps leave something so written to aftertimes,
as they should not willingly let it die. These thoughts at once
possessed me, and these other; that if I were certain to write
as men buy leases, for three lives and downward, there ought
no regard be sooner had than to God's glory, by the honour
and instruction of my country. For which cause, and not only
for that I knew it would be hard to arrive at the second rank
among the Latins, I applied myself to that resolution, which
Ariosto followed against the persuasions of Bembo, to fix all the
industry and art I could unite to the adorning of my native
tongue; not to make verbal curiosities the end, (that were a
toilsome vanity,) but to be an interpreter and relater of the
best and sagest things among mine own citizens throughout
this island in the mother dialect. That what the greatest and
choicest wits of Athens, Rome, or modern Italy, and those
Hebrews of old did for their country, I, in my proportion, with
this over and above, of being a Christian, might do for mine:
not caring to be once named abroad, though perhaps I could
attain to that, but content with these British islands as my
world; whose fortune hath hitherto been, that if the Athenians,
as some say, made their small deeds great and renowned by

their eloquent writers, England hath had her noble achievements made small by the unskilful handling of monks and mechanics.

Time serves not now, and perhaps I might seem too profuse to give any certain account of what the mind at home, in the spacious circuits of her musing, hath liberty to propose to herself, though of highest hope and hardest attempting; whether that epic form whereof the two poems of Homer, and those other two of Virgil and Tasso, are a diffuse, and the book of Job a brief model: or whether the rules of Aristotle herein are strictly to be kept, or nature to be followed, which in them that know art, and use judgment, is no transgression, but an enriching of art: and lastly, what king or knight, before the conquest, might be chosen in whom to lay the pattern of a Christian hero. And as Tasso gave to a prince of Italy his choice whether he would command him to write of Godfrey's expedition against the Infidels, or Belisarius against the Goths, or Charlemagne against the Lombards; if to the instinct of nature and the emboldening of art aught may be trusted, and that there be nothing adverse in our climate, or the fate of this age, it haply would be no rashness, from an equal diligence and inclination, to present the like offer in our own ancient stories; or whether those dramatic constitutions, wherein Sophocles and Euripides reign, shall be found more doctrinal and exemplary to a nation. The Scripture also affords us a divine pastoral drama in the Song of Solomon, consisting of two persons, and a double chorus, as Origen rightly judges. And the Apocalypse of St. John is the majestic image of a high and stately tragedy, shutting up and intermingling her solemn scenes and acts with a sevenfold chorus of hallelujahs and harping symphonies: and this my opinion the grave authority of Pareus, commenting that book, is sufficient to confirm. Or if occasion shall lead, to imitate those magnific odes and hymns, wherein Pindarus and Callimachus are in most things worthy, some others in their frame judicious, in their matter most an end faulty. But those frequent songs throughout the law and prophets beyond all these, not in their divine argument alone, but in the very critical art of composition, may be easily made appear over all the kinds of lyric poesy to be incomparable. These abilities, wheresoever they be found, are the inspired gift of God, rarely bestowed, but yet to some (though most abuse) in every nation; and are of power, beside the office of a pulpit, to imbreed and cherish in a great people the seeds of virtue and public civility, to allay the perturbations of the mind, and set the affections in right tune; to celebrate in glorious and lofty hymns the throne and equipage of God's almightiness, and what he works, and what he suffers to be wrought with high providence in his church; to sing victorious agonies of martyrs and saints, the deeds and triumphs of just and pious nations, doing valiantly through faith against the enemies of Christ; to deplore the general relapses of kingdoms and states from justice and God's true worship. Lastly, whatsoever in religion is holy and sublime, in virtue amiable or grave, whatsoever hath passion or admiration in all the changes of that which is called fortune from without, or the wily subtleties and refluxes of man's thoughts from within; all these things with a solid and treatable smoothness to paint out and describe. Teaching over the whole book of sanctity and virtue, through all the instances of example, with such delight to those especially of soft and delicious temper, who will not so much as look upon truth herself, unless they see her elegantly dressed; that whereas the paths of honesty and good life appear now rugged and difficult, though they be indeed easy and pleasant, they will then appear to all men both easy and pleasant, though they were rugged and difficult indeed. And what a benefit this would be to our youth and gentry, may be soon guessed by what we know of the corruption and bane which they suck in daily from the writings and interludes of libidinous and ignorant poetasters, who having scarce ever heard of that which is the main consistence of a true poem, the choice of such persons as they ought to introduce, and what is moral and decent to each one; do for the most part lay up vicious principles in sweet pills to be swallowed down, and make the taste of virtuous documents harsh and sour. But because the spirit of man cannot demean itself lively in this body, without some recreating intermission of labour and serious things, it were happy for the commonwealth, if our magistrates, as in those famous governments of old, would take into their care, not only the deciding of our contentious law-cases and brawls, but the managing of our public sports and festival pastimes; that they might be, not such as were authorized a while since, the provocations of drunkenness and lust, but such as may inure and harden our bodies by martial exercises to all warlike skill and performance; and may civilize, adorn, and make discreet our minds by the learned and affable meeting of frequent academies, and the procurement of wise and artful recitations, sweetened with eloquent and graceful enticements to the love and practice of justice, temperance, and fortitude, instructing and bettering the nation at all opportunities, that the call of wisdom and virtue may be heard everywhere, as Solomon saith : ' She crieth without, she uttereth her voice in the streets, in the top of high places, in the chief concourse, and in the openings of the gates.' Whether this may not be, not only in pulpits, but after another persuasive method, at set and solemn paneguries, in theatres, porches, or what other place or way may win most upon the people to receive at once both recreation and instruction, let them in authority consult. The thing which I had to say and those intentions which have lived within me ever since I could conceive myself anything worth to my country,

I return to crave excuse that urgent reason hath plucked from me, by an abortive and foredated discovery. And the accomplishment of them lies not but in a power above man's to promise; but that none hath by more studious ways endeavoured, and with more unwearied spirit that none shall, that I dare almost aver of myself, as far as life and free leisure will extend; and that the land had once enfranchised herself from this impertinent yoke of prelaty, under whose inquisitorious and tyrannical duncery, no free and splendid wit can flourish. Neither do I think it shame to covenant with any knowing reader, that for some years yet I may go on trust with him toward the payment of what I am now indebted, as being a work not to be raised from the heat of youth, or the vapours of wine; like that which flows at waste from the pen of some vulgar amourist, or the trencher fury of a rhyming parasite; nor to be obtained by the invocation of dame Memory and her Siren daughters, but by devout prayer to that eternal Spirit, who can enrich with all utterance and knowledge, and sends out his seraphim, with the hallowed fire of his altar, to touch and purify the lips of whom he pleases: to this must be added industrious and select reading, steady observation, insight into all seemly and generous arts and affairs; till which in some measure be compassed, at mine own peril and cost, I refuse not to sustain this expectation from as many as are not loth to hazard so much credulity upon the best pledges that I can give them. Although it nothing content me to have disclosed thus much beforehand, but that I trust hereby to make it manifest with what small willingness I endure to interrupt the pursuit of no less hopes than these, and leave a calm and pleasing solitariness, fed with cheerful and confident thoughts, to embark in a troubled sea of noises and hoarse disputes, put from beholding the bright countenance of truth in the quiet and still air of delightful studies, to come into the dim reflection of hollow antiquities sold by the seeming bulk, and there be fain to club quotations with men whose learning and belief lies in marginal stuffings, who, when they have, like good sumpters, laid ye down their horse-loads of citations and fathers at your door, with a rhapsody of who and who were bishops here or there, ye may take off their packsaddles, their day's work is done, and episcopacy, as they think, stoutly vindicated. Let any gentle apprehension, that can distinguish learned pains from unlearned drudgery imagine what pleasure or profoundness can be in this, or what honour to deal against such adversaries. But were it the meanest under-service, if God by his secretary conscience enjoin it, it were sad for me if I should draw back; for me especially, now when all men offer their aid to help, ease, and lighten the difficult labours of the church, to whose service, by the intentions of my parents and friends, I was destined of a child, and in mine own resolutions: till coming to some maturity of years, and perceiving what tyranny had invaded the church, that he who would take orders must subscribe slave, and take an oath withal, which, unless he took with a conscience that would retch, he must either straight perjure, or split his faith; I thought it better to prefer a blameless silence before the sacred office of speaking, bought and begun with servitude and forswearing. Howsoever, thus church-outed by the prelates, hence may appear the right I have to meddle in these matters, as before the necessity and constraint appeared.

From 'Apology for Smectymnuus'

If, readers, to that same great difficulty of well-doing what we certainly know, were not added in most men as great a carelessness of knowing what they and others ought to do, we had been long ere this, no doubt but all of us, much further on our way to some degree of peace and happiness in this kingdom. But since our sinful neglect of practising that which we know to be undoubtedly true and good, hath brought forth among us, through God's just anger, so great a difficulty now to know that which otherwise might be soon learnt, and hath divided us by a controversy of great importance indeed, but of no hard solution, which is the more our punishment; I resolved (of what small moment soever I might be thought) to stand on that side where I saw both the plain authority of scripture leading, and the reason of justice and equity persuading; with this opinion, which esteems it more unlike a Christian to be a cold neuter in the cause of the church, than the law of Solon made it punishable after a sedition in the state.

And because I observe that fear and dull disposition, lukewarmness and sloth, are not seldomer wont to cloak themselves under the affected name of moderation, than true and lively zeal is customably disparaged with the term of indiscretion, bitterness, and choler; I could not to my thinking honour a good cause more from the heart, than by defending it earnestly, as oft as I could judge it to behove me, notwithstanding any false name that could be invented to wrong or undervalue an honest meaning. Wherein although I have not doubted to single forth more than once such of them as were thought the chief and most nominated opposers on the other side, whom no man else undertook; if I have done well either to be confident of the truth, whose force is best seen against the ablest resistance, or to be jealous and tender of the hurt that might be done among the weaker by the entrapping authority of great names titled to false opinions; or that it be lawful to attribute somewhat to gifts of God's imparting, which I boast not, but thankfully acknowledge, and fear also lest at my certain account they be reckoned to me rather many than few; or if lastly it be but justice not to defraud of due esteem the wearisome labours and studious watchings, wherein I have spent and tired out almost a whole youth, I shall not distrust to be acquitted of presumption: knowing, that if heretofore all ages have received with favour and good acceptance the early industry of him that hath been hopeful, it were but hard measure now if the freedom of any timely spirit should be oppressed merely by the big and blunted fame of his elder adversary; and that his sufficiency must be now sentenced, not by pondering the reason he shews, but by calculating the years he brings.

However, as my purpose is not, nor hath been formerly, to look on my adversary abroad, through the deceiving glass of other men's great opinion of him, but at home, where I may find him in the proper light of his own worth, so now against the rancour of an evil tongue, from which I never thought so absurdly, as that I of all men should be exempt, I must be forced to proceed from the unfeigned and diligent inquiry of my own conscience at home, (for better way I know not, readers,) to give a more true account of myself abroad than this modest confuter, as he calls himself, hath given of me. Albeit, that in doing this I shall be sensible of two things which to me will be nothing pleasant; the one is, that not unlikely I shall be thought too much a party in mine own cause, and therein to see least: the other, that I shall be put unwillingly to molest the public view with the vindication of a private name; as if it were worth the while that the people should care whether such a one were thus, or thus. Yet those I entreat who have found the leisure to read that name, however of small repute, unworthily defamed, would be so good and so patient as to hear the same person not unneedfully defended.

I will not deny but that the best apology against false accusers is silence and sufferance, and honest deeds set against dishonest words. And that I could at this time most easily and securely, with the least loss of reputation, use no other defence, I need not despair to win belief; whether I consider both the foolish contriving and ridiculous aiming of these his slanderous bolts, shot so wide of any suspicion to be fastened on me, that I have oft with inward contentment perceived my friends congratulating themselves in my innocence, and my enemies ashamed of their partner's folly : or whether I look at these present times, wherein most men, now scarce permitted the liberty to think over their own concernments, have removed the seat of their thoughts more outward to the expectation of public events: or whether the examples of men, either noble or religious, who have sat down lately with a meek silence and sufferance under many libellous endorsements, may be a rule to others, I might well appease myself to put up any reproaches in such an honourable society of fellow-sufferers, using no other defence.

And were it that slander would be content to make an end where it first fixes, and not seek to cast out the like infamy upon each thing that hath but any relation to the person traduced, I should have pleaded against this confuter by no other advocates than those which I first commended, silence and sufferance, and speaking deeds against faltering words. But when I discerned his intent was not so much to smite at me, as through me to render odious the truth which I had written, and to stain with ignominy that evangelic doctrine which opposes the tradition of prelacy, I conceived myself to be now not as mine own person, but as a member incorporate into that truth whereof I was persuaded, and whereof I had declared openly to be a partaker. Whereupon I thought it my duty, if not to myself, yet to the religious cause I had in hand, not to leave on my garment the least spot or blemish in good name, so long as

God should give me to say that which might wipe it off; lest those disgraces which I ought to suffer, if it so befall me, for my religion, through my default religion be made liable to suffer for me. And, whether it might not something reflect upon those reverent men, whose friend I may be thought in writing the Animadversions, was not my last care to consider: if I should rest under these reproaches, having the same common adversary with them, it might be counted small credit for their cause to have found such an assistant, as this babbler hath devised me. What other thing in his book there is of dispute or question, in answering thereto I doubt not to be justified; except there be who will condemn me to have wasted time in throwing down that which could not keep itself up. As for others, who notwithstanding what I can allege have yet decreed to misinterpret the intents of my reply, I suppose they would have found as many causes to have misconceived the reasons of my silence.

* * * * * * * * *

Thus having spent his first onset, not in confuting, but in a reasonless defaming of the book, the method of his malice hurries him to attempt the like against the author; not by proofs and testimonies, but 'having no certain notice of me,' as he professes, 'further than what he gathers from the Animadversions,' blunders at me for the rest, and flings out stray crimes at a venture, which he could never, though he be a serpent, suck from anything that I have written, but from his own stuffed magazine and hoard of slanderous inventions, over and above that which he converted to venom in the drawing. To me, readers, it happens as a singular contentment; and let it be to good men no light satisfaction, that the slanderer here confesses he has 'no further notice of me than his own conjecture.' Although it had been honest to have inquired, before he uttered such infamous words, and I am credibly informed he did inquire; but finding small comfort from the intelligence which he received, whereon to ground the falsities which he had provided, thought it his likeliest course, under a pretended ignorance, to let drive at random, lest he should lose his odd ends, which from some penurious book of characters he had been culling out and would fain apply. Not caring to burden me with those vices, whereof, among whom my conversation hath been, I have been ever least suspected; perhaps not without some subtlety to cast me into envy, by bringing on me a necessity to enter into mine own praises. In which argument I know every wise man is more unwillingly drawn to speak, than the most repining ear can be averse to hear.

Nevertheless, since I dare not wish to pass this life unpersecuted of slanderous tongues, for God hath told us that to be generally praised is woeful, I shall rely on his promise to free the innocent from causeless aspersions: whereof nothing sooner can assure me, than if I shall feel him now assisting me in the just vindication of myself, which yet I could defer, it being more meet, that to those other matters of public debatement in this book I should give attendance first, but that I fear it would but harm the truth for me to reason in her behalf, so long as I should suffer my honest estimation to lie unpurged from these insolent suspicions. And if I shall be large, or unwonted in justifying myself to those who know me not, for else it would be needless, let them consider that a short slander will ofttimes reach further than a long apology; and that he who will do justly to all men, must begin from knowing how, if it so happen, to be not unjust to himself. I must be thought, if this libeller (for now he shows himself to be so) can find belief, after an inordinate and riotous youth spent at the university, to have been at length 'vomited out thence.' For which commodious lie, that he may be encouraged in the trade another time, I thank him; for it hath given me an apt occasion to acknowledge publicly with all grateful mind, that more than ordinary favour and respect, which I found above any of my equals at the hands of those courteous and learned men, the fellows of that college wherein I spent some years: who, at my parting, after I had taken two degrees, as the manner is, signified many ways how much better it would content them that I would stay; as by many letters full of kindness and loving respect, both before that time, and long after, I was assured of their singular good affection towards me. Which being likewise propense to all such as were for their studious and civil life worthy of esteem, I could not wrong their judgments and upright intentions, so much as to think I had that regard from them for other cause, than that I might be still encouraged to proceed in the honest and laudable courses, of which they apprehended I had given good proof. And to those ingenuous and friendly men, who were ever the countenancers of virtuous and hopeful wits, I wish the best and happiest thing that friends in absence wish one to another.

As for the common approbation or dislike of that place, as now it is, that I should esteem or disesteem myself, or any other the more for that, too simple and too credulous is the confuter, if he think to obtain with me, or any right discerner. Of small practice were that physician, who could not judge by what both she and her sister hath of long time vomited, that the worser stuff she strongly keeps in her stomach, but the better she is ever kecking at, and is queasy. She vomits now out of sickness; but ere it will be well with her, she must vomit by strong physic. In the meantime, that suburb sink, as this rude scavenger calls it, and more than scurrilously taunts it with the plague, having a worse plague in his middle entrail, that suburb wherein I dwell shall be in my account a more honourable place than his university. Which as in the time of her better health, and mine own younger judgment, I never greatly admired, so now much less. But he follows me to the city, still usurping and forging beyond his book notice, which only *he* affirms to have had; 'and where my morning haunts are, he wisses not.' It is wonder that, being so rare an alchymist of slander, he could not extract that, as well as the university vomit, and the suburb sink which his art could distil so cunningly; but because his lembec fails him, to give him and envy the more vexation, I will tell him.

Those morning haunts are where they should be, at home; not sleeping, or concocting the surfeits of an irregular feast, but up and stirring, in winter often ere the sound of any bell awake men to labour or to devotion; in summer as oft with the bird that first rouses, or not much tardier, to read good authors, or cause them to be read, till the attention be weary, or memory have its full fraught: then, with useful and generous labours preserving the body's health and hardiness to render lightsome, clear, and not lumpish obedience to the mind, to the cause of religion, and our country's liberty, when it shall require firm hearts in sound bodies to stand and cover their stations, rather than to see the ruin of our protestation, and the inforcement of a slavish life.

These are the morning practices: proceed now to the afternoon; 'in playhouses,' he says, 'and the bordelloes.' Your intelligence, unfaithful spy of Canaan? He gives in his evidence, that 'there he hath traced me.' Take him at his word, readers; but let him bring good sureties ere ye dismiss him, that while he pretended to dog others, he did not turn in for his own pleasure: for so much in effect he concludes against himself, not contented to be caught in every other gin, but he must be such a novice as to be still hampered in his own hemp. In the Animadversions, saith he, I find the mention of old cloaks, false beards, night-walkers, and salt lotion; therefore, the animadverter haunts playhouses and bordelloes; for if he did not, how could he speak of such gear? Now that he may know what it is to be a child, and yet to meddle with edged tools, I turn his antistrophon upon his own head; the confuter knows that these things are the furniture of playhouses and bordelloes, therefore, by the same reason, 'the confuter himself hath been traced in those places.' Was it such a dissolute speech, telling of some politicians who were wont to eavesdrop in disguises, to say they were often liable to a night-walking cudgeller, or the emptying of a urinal? What if I had writ, as your friend the author of the aforesaid mime, 'Mundus alter et idem,' to have been ravished like some young Cephalus or Hylas, by a troop of camping housewives in Viraginea, and that he was there forced to swear himself an uxorious varlet; then after a long servitude to have come into Aphrodisia, that pleasant country, that gave such a sweet smell to his nostrils among the shameless courtezans of Desvergonia? Surely he would have then concluded me as constant at the bordello, as the galley-slave at his oar.

But since there is such necessity to the hearsay of a tire, a periwig, or a vizard, that plays must have been seen, what difficulty was there in that? when in the colleges so many of the young divines, and those in next aptitude to divinity, have been seen so often upon the stage, writhing and unboning their clergy limbs to all the antic and dishonest gestures of Trinculoes, buffoons, and bawds; prostituting the shame of that ministry, which either they had, or were nigh having, to the eyes of courtiers and court ladies, with their grooms and mademoiselles. There, while they acted and overacted, among other young scholars, I was a spectator; they thought themselves gallant men, and I thought them fools; they made sport, and I laughed; they mispronounced, and I misliked; and, to make up the Atticism, they were out, and I hissed. Judge

now whether so many good textmen were not sufficient to
instruct me of false beards and vizards, without more expositors; and how can this confuter take the face to object to
me the seeing of that which his reverend prelates allow, and
incite their young disciples to act? For if it be unlawful to
sit and behold a mercenary comedian personating that which
is least unseemly for a hireling to do, how much more blameful is it to endure the sight of as vile things acted by persons
either entered, or presently to enter, into the ministry; and
how much more foul and ignominious for them to be the
actors!

But because as well by this upbraiding to me the bordelloes,
as by other suspicious glancings in his book, he would seem
privily to point me out to his readers, as one whose custom of
life were not honest, but licentious, I shall entreat to be borne
with, though I digress; and in a way not often trod, acquaint
ye with the sum of my thoughts in this matter, through the
course of my years and studies: although I am not ignorant
how hazardous it will be to do this under the nose of the envious, as it were in skirmish to change the compact order, and
instead of outward actions, to bring inmost thoughts into front.
And I must tell ye, readers, that by this sort of men I have
been already bitten at; yet shall they not for me know how
slightly they are esteemed, unless they have so much learning
as to read what in Greek ἀπειροκαλία is, which, together
with envy, is the common disease of those who censure books
that are not for their reading. With me it fares now, as with
him whose outward garment hath been injured and ill-bedighted; for having no other shift, what help but to turn the
inside outwards, especially if the lining be of the same, or, as
it is sometimes, much better? So if my name and outward demeanour be not evident enough to defend me, I must make trial
if the discovery of my inmost thoughts can: wherein of two

purposes, both honest and both sincere, the one perhaps I shall not miss; although I fail to gain belief with others, of being such as my perpetual thoughts shall here disclose me, I may yet not fail of success in persuading some to be such really themselves, as they cannot believe me to be more than what I feign.

I had my time, readers, as others have, who have good learning bestowed upon them, to be sent to those places where, the opinion was, it might be soonest attained; and as the manner is, was not unstudied in those authors which are most commended. Whereof some were grave orators and historians, whose matter methought I loved indeed, but as my age then was, so I understood them; others were the smooth elegiac poets, whereof the schools are not scarce, whom both for the pleasing sound of their numerous writing, which in imitation I found most easy, and most agreeable to nature's part in me, and for their matter, which what it is, there be few who know not, I was so allured to read, that no recreation came to me better welcome. For that it was then those years with me which are excused, though they be least severe, I may be saved the labour to remember ye. Whence having observed them to account it the chief glory of their wit, in that they were ablest to judge, to praise, and by that could esteem themselves worthiest to love those high perfections, which under one or other name they took to celebrate; I thought with myself by every instinct and presage of nature, which is not wont to be false, that what emboldened them to this task, might with such diligence as they used embolden me; and that what judgment, wit, or elegance was my share, would herein best appear, and best value itself, by how much more wisely, and with more love of virtue I should choose (let rude ears be absent) the object of not unlike praises. For albeit these thoughts to some will seem virtuous and commendable, to others only pardonable, to a third sort perhaps idle; yet the mentioning of them now will end in serious.

Nor blame it, readers, in those years to propose to themselves such a reward, as the noblest dispositions above other things in this life have sometimes preferred: whereof not to be sensible when good and fair in one person meet, argues both a gross and shallow judgment, and withal an ungentle and swainish breast. For by the firm settling of these persuasions, I became, to my best memory, so much a proficient, that if I found those authors anywhere speaking unworthy things of themselves, or unchaste of those names which before they had extolled; this effect it wrought with me, from that time forward their art I still applauded, but the men I deplored; and above them all, preferred the two famous renowners of Beatrice and Laura, who never write but honour of them to whom they devote their verse, displaying sublime and pure thoughts, without transgression. And long it was not after, when I was confirmed in this opinion, *that he who would not be frustrate of his hope to write well hereafter in laudable things, ought himself to be a true poem; that is, a composition and pattern of the best and honourablest things; not presuming to sing high praises of heroic men, or famous cities, unless he have in himself the experience and the practice of all that which is praiseworthy.* These reasonings, together with a certain niceness of nature, an honest haughtiness, and self-esteem either of what I was, or what I might be, (which let envy call pride,) and lastly that modesty, whereof, though not in the title-page, yet here I may be excused to make some beseeming profession; all these uniting the supply of their natural aid together, kept me still above those low descents of mind, beneath which he must deject and plunge himself, that can agree to saleable and unlawful prostitutions.

Next, (for hear me out now, readers,) that I may tell ye

whither my younger feet wandered; I betook me among those lofty fables and romances, which recount in solemn cantos the deeds of knighthood founded by our victorious kings, and from hence had in renown over all Christendom. There I read it in the oath of every knight, that he should defend to the expense of his best blood, or of his life, if it so befell him, the honour and chastity of virgin or matron; from whence even then I learned what a noble virtue chastity sure must be, to the defence of which so many worthies, by such a dear adventure of themselves, had sworn. And if I found in the story afterward, any of them, by word or deed, breaking that oath, I judged it the same fault of the poet, as that which is attributed to Homer, to have written indecent things of the gods. Only this my mind gave me, that every free and gentle spirit, without that oath, ought to be born a knight, nor needed to expect the guilt spur, or the laying of a sword upon his shoulder to stir him up both by his counsel and his arms, to secure and protect the weakness of any attempted chastity. So that even these books, which to many others have been the fuel of wantonness and loose living, I cannot think how, unless by divine indulgence, proved to me so many incitements, as you have heard, to the love and steadfast observation of that virtue which abhors the society of bordelloes.

Thus, from the laureat fraternity of poets, riper years and the ceaseless round of study and reading led me to the shady spaces of philosophy; but chiefly to the divine volumes of Plato, and his equal Xenophon: where, if I should tell ye what I learnt of chastity and love, I mean that which is truly so, whose charming cup is only virtue, which she bears in her hand to those who are worthy; (the rest are cheated with a thick intoxicating potion, which a certain sorceress, the abuser of love's name, carries about;) and how the first and chiefest office of love begins and ends in the soul, producing those happy twins of her divine generation, knowledge and virtue. With such abstracted sublimities as these, it might be worth your listening, readers, as I may one day hope to have ye in a still time, when there shall be no chiding; not in these noises, the adversary, as ye know, barking at the door, or searching for me at the bordelloes, where it may be he has lost himself, and raps up without pity the sage and rheumatic old prelatess with all her young Corinthian laity, to inquire for such a one.

Last of all, not in time, but as perfection is last, that care was ever had of me, with my earliest capacity, not to be negligently trained in the precepts of the Christian religion : this that I have hitherto related, hath been to show, that though Christianity had been but slightly taught me, yet a certain reservedness of natural disposition, and moral discipline, learnt out of the noblest philosophy, was enough to keep me in disdain of far less incontinences than this of the bordello. But having had the doctrine of holy scripture unfolding those chaste and high mysteries, with timeliest care infused, that 'the body is for the Lord, and the Lord for the body;' thus also I argued to myself, that if unchastity in a woman, whom St. Paul terms the glory of man, be such a scandal and dishonour, then certainly in a man, who is both the image and glory of God, it must, though commonly not so thought, be much more deflouring and dishonourable; in that he sins both against his own body, which is the perfecter sex, and his own glory, which is in the woman; and, that which is worst, against the image and glory of God, which is in himself. Nor did I slumber over that place expressing such high rewards of ever accompanying the Lamb with those celestial songs to others inapprehensible, but not to those who were not defiled with women, which doubtless means fornication ; for marriage must not be called a defilement.

Thus large I have purposely been, that if I have been justly taxed with this crime, it may come upon me, after all this my confession, with a tenfold shame: but if I have hitherto deserved no such opprobious word, or suspicion, I may hereby engage myself now openly to the faithful observation of what I have professed.

* * * * * * * * *

I had said, that because the Remonstrant was so much offended with those who were tart against the prelates, sure he loved toothless satires, which I took were as improper as a toothed sleekstone. This champion from behind the arras cries out, that those toothless satires were of the Remonstrant's making; and arms himself here tooth and nail, and horn, to boot, to supply the want of teeth, or rather of gums in the satires; and for an onset tells me, that the simile of a sleekstone 'shows I can be as bold with a prelate as familiar with a laundress.' But does it not argue rather the lascivious promptness of his own fancy, who, from the harmless mention of a sleekstone, could neigh out the remembrance of his old conversation among the viragian trollops? For me, if he move me, I shall claim his own oath, the oath *ex officio*, against any priest or prelate in the kingdom, to have ever as much hated such pranks as the best and chastest of them all. That exception which I made against toothless satires, the confuter hopes I had from the satirist, but is far deceived: neither have I ever read the hobbling distich which he means.

For this good hap I had from a careful education, to be inured and seasoned betimes with the best and elegantest authors of the learned tongues, and thereto brought an ear that could measure a just cadence, and scan without articulating: rather nice and humorous in what was tolerable, than patient to read every drawling versifier. Whence lighting upon this title of 'toothless satires,' I will not conceal ye what I thought, readers, that sure this must be some sucking satyr, who might have done better to have used his coral, and made an end of teething, ere he took upon him to wield a satire's whip. But when I heard him talk of 'scouring the rusty swords of elvish knights,' do not blame me if I changed my thought, and concluded him some desperate cutler.

* * * * * * * * *

But now, readers, we have the port within sight; his last section, which is no deep one, remains only to be forded, and then the wished shore. And here first it pleases him much, that he had descried me, as he conceives, to be unread in the councils. Concerning which matter it will not be unnecessary to shape him this answer: that some years I had spent in the stories of those Greek and Roman exploits, wherein I found many things both nobly done, and worthily spoken: when, coming in the method of time to that age wherein the church had obtained a Christian emperor, I so prepared myself, as being now to read examples of wisdom and goodness among those who were foremost in the church, not elsewhere to be paralleled; but to the amazement of what I expected I found it all quite contrary: excepting in some very few, nothing but ambition, corruption, contention, combustion; insomuch that I could not but love the historian, Socrates, who, in the proem to his fifth book professes, 'he was fain to intermix affairs of state; for that it would be else an extreme annoyance to hear, in a continued discourse, the endless brabbles and counterplottings of the bishops.'

Finding, therefore, the most of their actions in single to be weak, and yet turbulent, full of strife and yet flat of spirit; and the sum of their best council there collected, to be most commonly in questions either trivial or vain, or else of short and easy decision, without that great bustle which they made; I concluded that if their single ambition and ignorance was such, then certainly united in a council it would be much more; and if the compendious recital of what they there did was so tedious and unprofitable, then surely to set out the whole extent of their tattle in a dozen volumes would be a loss of time irrecoverable. Besides that which I had read of St. Martin, who for his last sixteen years could never be persuaded to be at any council of the bishops. And Gregory Nazianzen betook him to the same resolution, affirming to Procopius, 'that of any council or meeting of bishops he never saw good end; nor any remedy thereby of evil in the church, but rather an increase. For,' saith he, 'their contentions and desire of lording no tongue is able to express.'

I have not, therefore, I confess, read more of the councils, save here and there; I should be sorry to have been such a prodigal of my time; but, that which is better, I can assure this confuter, I have read into them all. And if I want anything yet I shall reply something toward that which in the defence of Murena was answered by Cicero to Sulpitius the lawyer. 'If ye provoke me (for at no hand else will I undertake such a frivolous labour) I will in three months be an expert councilist.' For, be not deceived, readers, by men that would overawe your ears with big names and huge tomes that contradict and repeal one another, because they can cram a margin with citations. Do but winnow their chaff from their wheat, ye shall see their great heap shrink and wax thin, past belief.

* * * * * * * * *

But this which comes next in view, I know not what good vein or humour took him when he let drop into his paper; I that was erewhile the ignorant, the loiterer, on the sudden by his permission am now granted 'to know something.' And that 'such a volley of expressions' he hath met withal, 'as he would never desire to have them better clothed.' For me, readers, although I cannot say that I am utterly untrained in those rules which best rhetoricians have given, or unacquainted with those examples which the prime authors of eloquence have written in any learned tongue; yet true eloquence I find to be none, but the serious and hearty love of truth: and that whose mind soever is fully possessed with a fervent desire to know good things, and with the dearest charity to infuse the knowledge of them into others, when such a man would speak, his words, (by what I can express,) like so many nimble and airy servitors, trip about him at command, and in well-ordered files, as he would wish, fall aptly into their own places.

To Carlo Dati, Nobleman of Florence. (*Familiar Letters,* No. X.)

When I came upon that passage where you write that you had sent me three letters before, which I now know to have been lost, then, in the first place, that sincere gladness of mine at the receipt of this one began to be infected and troubled with a sad regret, and presently a something heavier creeps in upon me, to which I am accustomed in very frequent grievings over my own lot: the sense, namely, that those whom the mere necessity of neighbourhood, or something else of a useless kind, has closely conjoined with me, whether by accident or by the tie of law (sive casu, sive lege, conglutinavit), they are the persons, though in no other respect commendable, who sit daily in my company, weary me, nay, by heaven, all but plague me to death whenever they are jointly in the humour for it, whereas those whom habits, disposition, studies, had so handsomely made my friends, are now almost all denied me either by death or by most unjust separation of place, and are so for the most part snatched from my sight that I have to live well nigh in a perpetual solitude. As to what you say that from the time of my departure from Florence you have been anxious about my health and always mindful of me, I truly congratulate myself that a feeling has been equal and mutual in both of us, the existence of which on my side only I was perhaps claiming to my credit. Very sad to me also, I will not conceal from you, was that departure, and it planted stings in my heart which now rankle there deeper, as often as I think with myself of my reluctant parting, my separation as by a wrench, from so many companions at once, such good friends as they were, and living so pleasantly with each other in one city, far off indeed, but to me most dear. I call to witness that tomb of Damon, ever to be sacred and solemn to me, whose adornment with every tribute of grief was my weary task, till I betook myself at length to what comforts I could, and desired again to breathe a little — I call that sacred grave to witness that I have had no greater delight all this while than in recalling to my mind the most pleasant memory of all of you, and of yourself especially. This you must have read for yourself long ere now, if that poem reached you, as now first I hear from you it did. I had carefully caused it to be sent, in order that, however small a proof of talent, it might, even in those few lines introduced into it emblem-wise, be no obscure proof of my love towards you. My idea was that by this means I should lure either yourself or some of the others to write to me; for, if I wrote first, either I had to write to all, or I feared that, if I gave the preference to any one, I should incur the reproach of such others as came to know it, hoping as I do that very many are yet there alive who might certainly have a claim to this attention from me. Now, however, you first of all, both by this most friendly call of your letter, and by your thrice repeated attention of writing before, have freed the reply for which I have been somewhile since in your debt from any expostulation from the others. There was, I confess, an additional cause for my silence in that most turbulent state of our Britain, subsequent to my return home, which obliged me to divert my mind shortly afterwards from the prosecution of my studies to the defence anyhow of life and fortune. What safe retirement for literary leisure could you suppose given one among so many battles of a civil war, slaughters, flights, seizures of goods? Yet, even in the midst of these evils, since you desire to be informed about my studies, know that we have published not a few things in our native tongue; which, were they not written in English, I would willingly send to you, my friends in Florence, to whose opinions, I attach very much value. The part of the Poems which is in Latin I will send shortly, since you wish it; and I would have done so spontaneously long ago, but that, on account of the rather harsh sayings against the Pope of Rome in some of the pages, I had a suspicion they would not be quite agreeable to your ears. Now I beg of you that the indulgence you were wont to give, I say not to your own Dante and Petrarch in the same case, but with singular politeness to my own former freedom of speech, as you know, among you, the same you, Dati, will obtain (for of yourself, I am sure) from my other friends whenever I may be speaking of your religion in our peculiar way.

London, April 21, 1647.

On his Blindness

When I consider how my light is spent
 Ere half my days in this dark world and wide,
 And that one talent which is death to hide

Lodged with me useless, though my soul more bent
To serve therewith my Maker, and present
    My true account, lest He, returning, chide;
    'Doth God exact day labour, light denied?'
I fondly ask. But Patience, to prevent
That murmur, soon replies, 'God doth not need
Either man's work or his own gifts. Who best
    Bear his mild yoke, they serve Him best. His state
    Is kingly: thousands at his bidding speed,
And post o'er land and ocean without rest;
They also serve who only stand and wait.'

To the most distinguished Leonard Philaras, of Athens, Ambassador from the Duke of Parma to the King of France. (*Familiar Letters*, No. XII.)

Your good will toward me, most honoured Leonard Philaras, as well as your high opinion of our *Defence for the English People*, I learnt from your letters, written partly on that subject, to Mr. Augier, a man illustrious among us for his remarkable fidelity in diplomatic business for this republic: after which I received, through the same, your kind greeting, with your portrait, and the accompanying eulogium, certainly most worthy of your virtues,—and then, finally, a most polite letter from yourself. Be assured that I, who am not in the habit of despising the genius of the Germans, or even of the Danes or Swedes, cannot but value very much such an opinion of me from. *you*, a native of Attic Athens, who have besides, after happily finishing a course of literary studies among the Italians, reached such ample honours by great handling of affairs. For, as the great Alexander himself, when carrying on war in the remotest parts of the earth, declared that he had undergone such great labours *for the sake of the good opinion of the Athe-*

nians, why should not I congratulate myself, and think myself honoured to the highest, in having received praises from one in whom singly at this day the Arts of the old Athenians and all their celebrated excellencies appear, after so long an interval, to revive and rebloom? Remembering how many men of supreme eloquence were produced by that city, I have pleasure in confessing that whatever literary advance I have made I owe chiefly to steady intimacy with their writings from my youth upwards. But, were there in me, by direct gift from them, or a kind of transfusion, such a power of pleading that I could rouse our armies and fleets for the deliverance of Greece, the land of eloquence, from her Ottoman oppressor,— to which mighty act you seem almost to implore our aid — truly there is nothing which it would be more or sooner in my desire to do. For what did even the bravest men of old, or the most eloquent, consider more glorious or more worthy of them than, whether by pleading or by bravely acting, to make the Greeks free and self-governing? There is, however, something else besides to be tried, and in my judgment far the most important : namely, that some one should, if possible, arouse and rekindle in the minds of the Greeks, by the relation of that old story, the old Greek valour itself, the old industry, the old patience of labour. Could some one do *that*— and from no one more than yourself ought we to expect it, looking to the strength of your feeling for your native land, and the combination of the same with the highest prudence, skill in military affairs, and a powerful passion for the recovery of the ancient political liberty — then, I am confident, neither would the Greeks be wanting to themselves, nor any other nation wanting to the Greeks. Farewell.

LONDON, June, 1652.

To Henry Oldenburg, agent for the city of Bremen in Lower Saxony with the Commonwealth. (Familiar Letters, No. XIV.)

Your former letter, Honoured Sir, was given to me when your messenger, I was told, was on the point of return ; whence it happened that there was no opportunity of reply at that time. While I was afterwards purposing an early reply, some unexpected business took me off ; but for which I should certainly not have sent you my book, Defence though it is called, in such a naked condition, without accompanying excuse. And now I have your second letter, in which your thanks are quite disproportioned to the slenderness of the gift. It was in my mind, too, more than once, to send you back English for your Latin, in order that, as you have learnt to speak our language more accurately and happily than any other foreigner of my acquaintance, you should not lose any opportunity of writing the same ; which I believe you could do with equal accuracy. But in this, just as henceforward the impulse may be, let your own choice regulate. As to the substance of your communication, you plainly think with me that a 'Cry' of that kind 'to Heaven' transcends all bounds of human sense ; the more impudent, then, must be he who declares so boldly he has heard it. You throw in a scruple after all as to who he is : but, formerly, whenever we talked on this subject, just after you had come hither from Holland, you seemed to have no doubt whatever but Morus was the author, inasmuch as that was the common report in those parts and no one else was named. If, then, you have now at last any more certain information on the point, be so good as to inform me. As to the treatment of the argument, I should wish (why should I dissemble?) not to differ from you, if only because I would fain know what there is to which one would more readily yield than the sincere judgment of friendly men, like yourself, and praise free from all flattery. To prepare myself, as you suggest, for other labours, — whether nobler or more useful I know not, for what can be nobler or more useful in human affairs than the vindication of Liberty? — truly, if my health shall permit, and this blindness of mine, a sorer affliction than old age, and lastly the 'cries' of such brawlers as there have been about me, I shall be induced to that easily enough. An idle ease has never had charms for me, and this unexpected contest with the Adversaries of Liberty took me off against my will when I was intent on far different and altogether pleasanter studies: not that in any way I repent of what I have done, since it was necessary; for I am far from thinking that I have spent any toil, as you seem to hint, on matters of inferior consequence. But of this at other time: meanwhile, learned Sir, not to detain you too long, farewell, and reckon me among your friends.

WESTMINSTER, July 6, 1654.

To Leonard Philaras, Athenian. (*Familiar Letters*, No. XV.)

Though from boyhood I have ever been devoted to all things Greek, and especially to your native city, Athens, yet, in addition to this, I have ever cherished the conviction that sometime that city would make a fair return to me for my devotion; and in very truth that ancient genius of your most glorious land has fulfilled my prophecy; for it has given me *you*, a genuine son of Attica, and a true friend of mine; who, though I was known to you only by my writings, yet addressed me most kindly by letter when separated by long distance, and later, coming unexpectedly to London, visited me in my blindness, and, in that misfortune which has made me to no one more distinguished, to many less so, you honour me still with the same kindness.

Inasmuch as you urge me not to abandon all hope of recovering my sight, and write that you have at Paris a friend and relative who is a physician, Thevenot by name, a man of special eminence in treating eyes, whom you propose to consult with regard to mine, if you only learn from me enough to enable him to understand the causes and symptoms of the disease; — in view of this I will do what you suggest, in order that I may not seem to reject the possibility of any help that may come from God's hand.

It is now, I should say, ten years, more or less, since I found my sight growing dim and weak; at the same time my spleen was affected and my internal organs were troubled with flatulency; in the morning whenever I began to read anything in accordance with my usual custom, my eyes at once began to pain me and to shrink from the task, though they would experience relief after a brief period of bodily exercise; whenever I looked at a lamp, a halo would seem to encircle it. Not long after this, at the left extremity of the left eye (for that eye lost its sight some years before the other), there gradually came on a dimness, which took from my view all objects situated on that side; objects directly in front of it, too, were seen less clearly whenever I happened to close the right eye. During the last three years the other eye has gradually lost its sight; but some months before my blindness became complete, everything that I saw, even though I was perfectly still, seemed to swim about, moving now to the right, now to the left. My forehead and temples suffer from constant burning sensations. This often affects my eyes with a certain drowsiness, from breakfast till evening; so that I often think of the words of Phineus the seer of Salmydessus, in the *Argonautica*:

κάρος δέ μιν ἀμφεκάλυψεν
Πορφύρεος · γαῖαν δὲ πέριξ ἐδόκησε φέρεσθαι
νειόθεν, ἀβληχρῷ δ' ἐπὶ κώματι κέκλιτ' ἄναυδος.

But I must not omit to say that, while there still remained some little sense of sight, whenever I lay down in bed, and reclined on either side, bright lights in abundance would flash from my eyes even when closed; subsequently, as my power of sight grew daily less, dull colours would dart forth in the same way, accompanied with throbbings and noises within my head. But now the brightness seems to be dispelled, and, at times, absolute blackness, or blackness veined with an ashy grayness, as it were, is often wont to spread over my eyes. Yet the dimness which is there, both night and day, seems always more like something white than like anything black, which, as the eye turns, allows the merest particle of light to enter, as through a tiny crack. But even though from this circumstance the physician might gather some little hope, yet I am resigned as to an absolutely incurable affliction; and I often reflect that, though to each one of us are allotted many days of darkness, as the Wise Man reminds us, my darkness as yet, by God's special grace, passed, as it is, amid leisure and studies, and the voices of friends and their greetings, is far pleasanter than the darkness of death. But if, as it is written, 'man shall not live by bread alone, but by every word that proceedeth out of the mouth of God,' what reason is there why any one should not find comfort also in the reflection that one sees not by the eyes only, but by the light of God's guidance and providence. So long, at least, as He himself looks out for me, and provides for me, as He does, and so long as He leads and guides me with His hand through all the ways of life, I shall gladly bid my eyes keep their long holiday, since it has so seemed best to Him. But you, my dear Philaras, whatever be the issue, I greet with as stout and firm a heart as if I were Lynceus himself.

WESTMINSTER, September 28, 1654.

To Cyriac Skinner

Cyriack, this three years' day, these eyes, though clear
  To outward view, of blemish or of spot,
  Bereft of light, their seeing have forgot;
  Nor to their idle orbs doth sight appear
Of sun, or moon, or star, throughout the year,   5
  Or man or woman. Yet I argue not
    Against Heaven's hand or will, nor bate a jot
  Of heart or hope, but still bear up and steer
Right onward. What supports me, dost thou ask?
  The conscience, friend, to have lost them overplied   10
  In Liberty's defence, my noble task,
Of which all Europe talks from side to side,
  This thought might lead me through the world's vain mask
  Content, though blind, had I no better guide.

On his deceased wife

  Methought I saw my late espoused saint
  Brought to me like Alcestis from the grave,
  Whom Jove's great son to her glad husband gave,
  Rescued from Death by force, though pale and faint.
  Mine, as whom washed from spot of child-bed taint   5
  Purification in the Old Law did save,
  And such as yet once more I trust to have
  Full sight of her in Heaven without restraint,
  Came vested all in white, pure as her mind.
  Her face was veiled; yet to my fancied sight   10
  Love, sweetness, goodness, in her person shined
  So clear as in no face with more delight.
  But, oh! as to embrace me she inclined,
  I waked, she fled, and day brought back my night.

To the most accomplished Emeric Bigot. (*Familiar Letters*, No. XXI.)

. . . Many have made a figure by their published writings whose living voice and daily conversation have presented next to nothing that was not low and common : if then, I can attain the distinction of seeming myself equal in mind and manners to any writings of mine that have been tolerably to the purpose, there will be the double effect that I shall so have added weight personally to my writings, and shall receive back by way of reflection from them credit, how small soever it may be, yet greater in proportion. For, in that case, whatever is right and laudable in them, that same I shall seem not more to have derived from authors of high excellence than to have fetched forth pure and sincere from the inmost feelings of my own mind and soul. I am glad, therefore, to know that you are assured of my tranquillity of spirit in this great affliction of loss of sight, and also of the pleasure I have in being civil and attentive in the reception of visitors from abroad. Why, in truth, should I not bear gently the deprivation of sight, when I may hope that it is not so much lost as revoked and retracted inwards, for the sharpening rather than the blunting of my mental edge? Whence it is that I neither think of books with anger, nor quite intermit the study of them, grievously though they have mulcted me, — were it only that I am instructed against such moroseness by the example of King Telephus of the Mysians, who refused not to be cured in the end by the weapon that had wounded him. . . .

WESTMINSTER, March 24, 1658.

To Henry Oldenburg. (*Familiar Letters*, No. XXIX.)

... Of any such work as compiling the history of our political troubles, which you seem to advise, I have no thought whatever [longe absum] : they are worthier of silence than of commemoration. What is needed is not one to compile a good history of our troubles, but one who can happily end the troubles themselves; for, with you, I fear lest, amid these our civil discords, or rather sheer madnesses, we shall seem to the lately confederated enemies of Liberty and Religion a too fit object of attack, though in truth, they have not yet inflicted a severer wound on Religion than we ourselves have been long doing by our crimes. But God, as I hope, on His own account, and for His own glory, now in question, will not allow the counsels and onsets of the enemy to succeed as they themselves wish, whatever convulsions Kings and Cardinals meditate and design. ...

WESTMINSTER, December 20, 1659.

The following extract from the Prefatory address to the Parliament (the restored Rump) shows no misgivings, on the part of Milton, in regard to the stability of the Commonwealth. But he must have been secretly hopeless. Cromwell had died the previous year, on September 3, and his son Richard, his successor, had abdicated on the 25th of the following May. A state of things little short of anarchy had set in before the publication of Milton's pamphlet. But as late as near the end of February, 1660, he published 'The Ready and Easy Way to Establish a Free Commonweaith,' still, as it appears, unable to believe, desperate as was the state of things, that the Commonwealth was in its death throes. On the 29th of the following May, Charles II. entered London amid the wildest acclamations of the people; and the commonwealth, for which Milton had fought to the bitter end, was no more, and he himself was in concealment. But he must have been assured that the principles for which he had fought would sooner or later assert themselves in spite of all opposition that could be brought against them, though he could hardly have thought that these principles would assert themselves so soon as they did. Fourteen years after his death, James II. was driven from the throne, and the constitutional basis of the monarchy underwent a quite radical change — a change largely, if not wholly, due to the work of Puritanism, which, it was generally supposed, at the Restoration of Charles II., had been completely undone. 'It was,' says John Richard Green, 'from the moment of its (Puritanism's) seeming fall that its real victory began.'

From 'Considerations touching the Likeliest Means to remove Hirelings out of the Church.' (August, 1659)

Owing to your protection, Supreme Senate! this liberty of writing, which I have used these eighteen years on all occasions to assert the just rights and freedoms both of church and state, and so far approved, as to have been trusted with the representment and defence of your actions to all Christendom against an adversary of no mean repute; to whom should I address what I still publish on the same argument, but to you, whose magnanimous councils first opened and unbound the age from a double bondage under prelatical and regal tyranny; above our own hopes heartening us to look up at last, like men and Christians, from the slavish dejection, wherein from father to son we were bred up and taught; and thereby deserving of these nations, if they be not barbarously ingrateful, to be acknowledged, next under God, the authors and best patrons of religious and civil liberty, that ever these islands brought forth? The care and tuition of whose peace and safety, after a short but scandalous night of interruption, is now again, by a new dawning of God's miraculous providence among us, revolved upon your shoulders. And to whom more appertain these considerations, which I propound, than to yourselves, and the debate before you, though I trust of no difficulty, yet at present of great expectation, not whether ye will gratify, were it no more than so, but whether ye will hearken to the just petition of many thousands best affected both to religion and to this your return, or whether ye will satisfy, which you never can, the covetous pretences and demands of insatiable hirelings, whose disaffection ye well know both to yourselves and your resolutions? That I, though among many others in this common concernment, interpose to your deliberations what my thoughts also are; your own judgment and the success thereof hath given me the confidence: which requests but this, that if I have prosperously, God so favouring me, defended the public cause of this commonwealth to foreigners, ye would not think the reason and ability, whereon ye trusted once (and repent not) your whole reputation to the world, either grown less by more maturity and longer study, or less available in English than in another tongue; but that if it sufficed some years past to convince and satisfy the unengaged of other nations in the justice of your doings, though then held paradoxal, it may as well suffice now against weaker opposition in matters, except here in England with a spirituality of men devoted to their temporal gain, of no controversy else among protestants. Neither do I doubt, seeing daily the acceptance which they find who in their petitions venture to bring advice also, and new models of a commonwealth, but that you will interpret it much more the duty of a Christian to offer what his conscience persuades him may be of moment to the freedom and better constituting of the church : since it is a deed of highest charity to help undeceive the people, and a work worthiest your authority, in all things else authors, assertors, and now recoverers of our liberty, to deliver us, the only people of all protestants left still undelivered, from the oppressions of a simonious decimating clergy, who shame not, against the judgment and practice of all other churches reformed, to maintain, though very weakly, their popish and oft-refuted positions ; not in a point of conscience wherein they might be blameless, but in a point of covetousness and unjust claim to other men's goods ; a contention foul and odious in any man, but most of all in ministers of the gospel, in whom contention, though for their own right, scarce is allowable. Till which grievances be removed, and religion set free from the monopoly of hirelings, I dare affirm that no model whatsoever of a commonwealth will prove successful or undisturbed ; and so persuaded, implore divine assistance on your pious counsels and proceedings to unanimity in this and all other truth.

—John Milton.

Autobiographic passages in the 'Paradise Lost'

'Hail, holy Light, offspring of Heaven first-born !
Or of the Eternal coeternal beam
May I express thee unblamed ? since God is light,
And never but in unapproachèd light
Dwelt from eternity — dwelt then in thee,   5
Bright effluence of bright essence, increate !
Or hearest thou rather pure Ethereal stream,
Whose fountain who shall tell ? Before the Sun,
Before the Heavens, thou wert, and at the voice

Of God, as with a mantle, didst invest 10
The rising World of waters dark and deep,
Won from the void and formless Infinite!
Thee I revisit now with bolder wing,
Escaped the Stygian Pool, though long detained
In that obscure sojourn, while in my flight, 15
Through utter and through middle Darkness borne,
With other notes than to the Orphéan lyre
I sung of Chaos and eternal Night,
Taught by the Heavenly Muse to venture down
The dark descent, and up to reascend, 20
Though hard and rare. Thee I revisit safe,
And feel thy sovran vital lamp; but thou
Revisit'st not these eyes, that roll in vain
To find thy piercing ray, and find no dawn;
So thick a drop serene hath quenched their orbs, 25
Or dim suffusion veiled. Yet not the more
Cease I to wander where the Muses haunt
Clear spring, or shady grove, or sunny hill,
Smit with the love of sacred song; but chief
Thee, Sion, and the flowery brooks beneath, 30
That wash thy hallowed feet, and warbling flow,
Nightly I visit : nor sometimes forget
Those other two equalled with me in fate,
So were I equalled with them in renown,
Blind Thamyris and blind Mæonides, 35
And Tiresias and Phineus, prophets old :
Then feed on thoughts that voluntary move
Harmonious numbers ; as the wakeful bird
Sings darkling, and, in shadiest covert hid,
Tunes her nocturnal note. Thus with the year 40
Seasons return ; but not to me returns
Day, or the sweet approach of even or morn,

Or sight of vernal bloom, or summer's rose,
Or flocks, or herds, or human face divine;
But cloud instead and ever-during dark   45
Surrounds me, from the cheerful ways of men
Cut off, and, for the book of knowledge fair,
Presented with a universal blank
Of Nature's works, to me expunged and rased,
And wisdom at one entrance quite shut out.   50
So much the rather thou, Celestial Light,
Shine inward and the mind through all her powers
Irradiate; there plant eyes; all mist from thence
Purge and disperse, that I may see and tell
Of things invisible to mortal sight.'   55
        —*Paradise Lost*, Book iii. 1-55.

'Descend from Heaven, Urania, by that name
If rightly thou art called, whose voice divine
Following, above the Olympian hill I soar,
Above the flight of Pegasean wing!
The meaning, not the name, I call; for thou   5
Nor of the Muses nine, nor on the top
Of old Olympus dwell'st; but, heavenly-born,
Before the hills appeared or fountain flowed,
Thou with Eternal Wisdom didst converse,
Wisdom thy sister, and with her didst play   10
In presence of the Almighty Father, pleased
With thy celestial song. Up led by thee,
Into the Heaven of Heavens I have presumed,
An earthly guest, and drawn empyreal air,
Thy tempering. With like safety guided down, 15
Return me to my native element;
Lest, from this flying steed unreined (as once
Bellerophon, though from a lower clime)

Dismounted, on the Aleian field I fall,
Erroneous there to wander and forlorn.   20
Half yet remains unsung, but narrower bound
Within the visible Diurnal Sphere.
Standing on Earth, not rapt above the pole,
More safe I sing with mortal voice, unchanged
To hoarse or mute, though fallen on evil days,   25
On evil days though fallen, and evil tongues,
In darkness, and with dangers compassed round,
And solitude ; yet not alone, while thou
Visit'st my slumbers nightly, or when Morn
Purples the East. Still govern thou my song,   30
Urania, and fit audience find, though few.
But drive far off the barbarous dissonance
Of Bacchus and his revellers, the race
Of that wild rout that tore the Thracian bard
In Rhodope, where woods and rocks had ears   35
To rapture, till the savage clamour drowned
Both harp and voice ; nor could the Muse defend
Her son. So fail not thou who thee implores ;
For thou art heavenly, she an empty dream.'
          —*Paradise Lost*, Book vii. 1-39.

'No more of talk where God or Angel Guest
With Man, as with his friend, familiar used
To sit indulgent, and with him partake
Rural repast, permitting him the while
Venial discourse unblamed. I now must change   5
Those notes to tragic — foul distrust, and breach
Disloyal, on the part of man, revolt
And disobedience ; on the part of Heaven,
Now alienated, distance and distaste,
Anger and just rebuke, and judgment given,   10

That brought into this World a world of woe,
Sin and her shadow Death, and Misery,
Death's harbinger. Sad task! yet argument
Not less but more heroic than the wrath
Of stern Achilles on his foe pursued   15
Thrice fugitive about Troy wall; or rage
Of Turnus for Lavinia disespoused;
Or Neptune's ire, or Juno's, that so long
Perplexed the Greek, and Cytherea's son;
If answerable style I can obtain   20
Of my celestial Patroness, who deigns
Her nightly visitation unimplored,
And dictates to me slumbering, or inspires
Easy my unpremeditated verse,
Since first this subject for heroic song   25
Pleased me, long choosing and beginning late,
Not sedulous by nature to indite
Wars, hitherto the only argument
Heroic deemed, chief mastery to dissect
With long and tedious havoc fabled knights   30
In battles feigned (the better fortitude
Of patience and heroic martyrdom
Unsung), or to describe races and games,
Or tilting furniture, emblazoned shields,
Impresses quaint, caparisons and steeds,   35
Bases and tinsel trappings, gorgeous knights
At joust and tournament; then marshalled feast
Served up in hall with sewers and seneshals:
The skill of artifice or office mean;
Not that which justly gives heroic name   40
To person or to poem / Me, of these
Nor skilled nor studious, higher argument
Remains, sufficient of itself to raise

> That name, unless an age too late, or cold
> Climate, or years, damp my intended wing 45
> Depressed; and much they may if all be mine,
> Not hers who brings it nightly to my ear.'
>
> —*Paradise Lost*, Book ix. 1-47.

The following verses addressed to the seraph Abdiel, Milton, at the time he wrote them, might justly have taken to himself:

> 'Servant of God, well done! Well hast thou fought
> The better fight, who single hast maintained
> Against revolted multitudes the cause
> Of truth, in word mightier than they in arms,
> And for the testimony of truth hast borne
> Universal reproach, far worse to bear
> Than violence; for this was all thy care—
> To stand approved in sight of God, though worlds
> Judged thee perverse.'
>
> —*Paradise Lost*, Book vi. 29-37.

Milton regarded himself as an Abdiel (*i.e.* as the name signifies in Hebrew, Servant of God), in the past struggle for civil and religious liberty; like Abdiel,

> 'Among innumerable false, unmoved,
> Unshaken, unseduced, unterrified,
> His loyalty he kept, his love, his zeal;
> Nor number nor example with him wrought
> To swerve from truth, or change his constant mind,
> Though single.'
>
> —*Paradise Lost*, Book v. 898-903.

The following, from 'Paradise Regained,' Book i. 196-208, Milton might have written of himself:

'Oh, what a multitude of thoughts at once
Awakened in me swarm, while I consider
What from within I feel myself, and hear
What from without comes often to my ears,
Ill sorting with my present state compared!
When I was yet a child, no childish play
To me was pleasing; *all my mind was set
Serious to learn and know, and thence to do,
What might be public good; myself I thought
Born to that end, born to promote all truth,
All righteous things.* Therefore, above my years,
The Law of God I read, and found it sweet;
Made it my whole delight.'

The following letter reveals the difficulties under which Milton, in his blindness, was, at times, obliged to write.

To the very distinguished Peter Heimbach, Councillor to the Elector of Brandenburg. (*Familiar Letters*, No. XXXI.)

Small wonder if, in the midst of so many deaths of my countrymen, in a year of such heavy pestilence, you believed, as you write you did, on the faith of some special rumour, that I also had been cut off. Such a rumour among your people is not displeasing, if it was the occasion of making known the fact that they were anxious for my safety, for then I can regard it as a sign of their good will to me. But, by the blessing of God, who had provided for my safety in a country retreat, I am still both alive and well, nor useless yet, I hope, for any duty that remains to be performed by me in this life.— That after so long an interval I should have come into your mind is very agreeable; although, from your exuberant expression of the matter, you seem to afford some ground for suspecting that you have rather forgotten me, professing as you do such an admiration of the marriage-union in me of so many different virtues. Truly, I should dread a too numerous progeny from so many forms of the marriage-union as you enumerate, were it not an established truth that virtues are nourished most and flourish most in straitened and hard circumstances; albeit I may say that one of the virtues of your list has not very handsomely requited me the hospitable reception she had. For what you call *policy*, but I would rather have you call *loyalty to one's country*,—this particular lass, after inveigling me with her fair name, has almost expatriated me, so to speak. The chorus of the rest, however, makes a very fine harmony. One's country is wherever it is well with one.— And now I will conclude, after first begging you, if you find anything incorrectly written or without punctuation here, to impute that to the boy who has taken it down from my dictation, and who is utterly ignorant of Latin, so that I was forced, while dictating, not without misery, to spell out the letters of the words one by one. Meanwhile, I am glad that the merits of one whom I knew as a young man of excellent hope have raised him to so honourable a place in his Prince's favour; and I desire and hope all prosperity for you otherwise. Farewell!

LONDON, August 15, 1666.

PASSAGES IN MILTON'S PROSE AND POETICAL WORKS IN WHICH HIS IDEA OF TRUE LIBERTY, INDIVIDUAL, DOMESTIC, CIVIL, POLITICAL, AND RELIGIOUS, IS EXPLICITLY SET FORTH

FROM an early period of his life Milton, as has been seen, looked forward to the production of a great poem which would embody his highest ideals of the true life of man and which 'after times would not willingly let die'; and all his studies and all his earliest efforts in poetry were, advisedly, preparations for this prospective creation. He estimated learning wholly as a means of building himself up for the work to which he felt himself dedicated. He cared not for learned lumber which he could not bring into relation with his intellectual or spiritual vitality, or make use of in his creative work. 'Learning for its own sake' was no part of his creed as a scholar. He may be said to speak for himself in the words which he gives to the Saviour in the 'Paradise Regained' (Book iv. 322 *et seq.*) :

> 'who reads
> Incessantly, and to his reading brings not
> A spirit and judgment equal or superior,
> — And what he brings, what needs he elsewhere seek? —
> Uncertain and unsettled still remains,
> Deep-versed in books and shallow in himself,
> Crude or intoxicate, collecting toys
> And trifles for choice matters, worth a spunge ;
> As children gathering pebbles on the shore.'

And so, too, in the words which he gives to the angel Raphael, in the 'Paradise Lost' (Book vii. 126 *et seq.*) :

> 'But knowledge is as food, and needs no less
> Her temperance over appetite, to know
> In measure what the mind may well contain ;
> Oppresses else with surfeit, and soon turns
> Wisdom to folly, as nourishment to wind.'

Wordsworth had as firm an assurance as Milton had, that he was a dedicated spirit; but he did not attach the importance which Milton did to great acquisitions of knowledge as a means to the fulfilment of his mission. But Wordsworth's sense of his mission as a poet called for an expression of his soul-experiences in *occasional* poems. The composition of a great epic would have shut him off from expressing, day by day, the relations of Nature to the soul, as those relations were revealed to him — relations with which wide learning had comparatively little to do.

Milton was constitutionally, as well as by his education and associations, a Puritan. And the state of the times in which he lived coöperated with his mental and moral constitution, and with his education, to make *the conflict of Good and Evil, the great fact, for him, of the world, and, indeed, of the Universe.* To picture in the most impressive way possible this great fact, and the sure triumph of Good over Evil, however long that triumph may be retarded, he early felt to be his mission as a poet. And he looked upon the acquisition of great stores of learning as part of the indispensable equipment for one, who, in this conflict, would range himself on the side of Good. All history and all literatures, all sciences, religions, mythologies, were to be explored, and made subservient, as far as might be, by him who would fight the good fight. The accumulated knowledge and wisdom of mankind was for him a part of that panoply of God which St. Paul, in his Epistle to the Ephesians (vi. 11), commands to put on, in order to 'be able to stand against the wiles of the devil.'

But learning was but a part, and however indispensable, an inferior part, of this panoply. The soul's essential self, as the medium of the divine, must give the prime efficacy to whatever is done in the mighty conflict of good with evil. In the words of Browning's 'Sordello,' 'a poet must be earth's essential king,' and he is that by virtue of his exerting, or shedding the influence of, his essential personality in his poetical creations. In his 'Apology for Smectymnuus,' he says, 'And long it was not after, when I was confirmed in this opinion, that he who would not be frustrate of his hope to write well hereafter in laudable things, *ought himself to be a true poem;* that is, a composition and pattern of the best and honourablest things; not presuming to sing high praises of heroic men, or famous cities, *unless he have in himself the experience and the practice of all that which is praiseworthy.*'

And in his 'Reason of Church Government urged against Prelaty,' he speaks of the great work which looms hazily up in the future, as one 'not to be obtained by the invocation of dame memory and her siren daughters, but *by devout prayer to that eternal Spirit, who can enrich with all utterance and knowledge, and sends out his Seraphim, with the hallowed fire of his altar, to touch and purify the lips of whom he pleases:* to this must be added industrious and select reading, steady observation, insight into all seemly and generous arts and affairs;' etc. In his invocation of the Holy Spirit, in the opening of the 'Paradise Lost,' he says:

> 'And chiefly thou, O Spirit that dost prefer
> Before all temples *the upright heart and pure*,
> Instruct me.'

And in the 'Paradise Regained' (Book i. 8-15):

'Thou Spirit, who ledst this glorious Eremite
Into the desert, his victorious field,
Against the spiritual foe, and broughtst him thence
By proof the undoubted Son of God, *inspire,*
As thou art wont, my prompted song, else mute,
And bear through highth or depth of Nature's bounds,
With prosperous wing full summed, to tell of deeds
Above heroic.'

Milton did not entertain the restricted view of inspiration which is still entertained by large numbers of good people, namely, that only the writers of the Old and New Testaments were inspired. With him, every soul, raised, by ardent faith and sanctified desire, to a high plane of spirituality, and thus brought into relationship with the highest spiritual forces, was, in a measure, inspired.

What follows the quotation just made, from St. Paul's Epistle to the Ephesians (vi. 12-18), is the best expression which may be given of Milton's actuating creed:

'We wrestle not against flesh and blood, but against principalities, against powers, against the rulers of the darkness of this world, against spiritual wickedness in high places. Wherefore take unto you the whole armour of God, that ye may be able to withstand in the evil day, and having done all, to stand. Stand therefore, having your loins girt about with truth, and having on the breastplate of righteousness; and your feet shod with the preparation of the gospel of peace; above all, taking the shield of faith, wherewith ye shall be able to quench all the fiery darts of the wicked. And take the helmet of salvation, and the sword of the Spirit, which is the word of God: praying always with all prayer and supplication in the Spirit, and watching thereunto with all perseverance and supplication for all saints.'

It would seem that this grand passage from the Apostle must occur to every reader of Milton as the best expression of the law according to which he lived and wrote.

The intellectual and spiritual preparation which Milton felt necessary, and was making, with an undivided devotion, for the production of a great poem, determined his idea of liberty when, bidding farewell, for a time (he could not have thought that it would be for so long a time), to the loved haunts of the Muses, he engaged as a polemic prose writer, in the struggle for domestic, civil, political, and religious liberty. This idea, which may be said to be the informing principle of his prose works, is that *inward liberty is the condition of true outward liberty*. The latter cannot exist without the former. What is often miscalled liberty is license; which only leads to a more degraded inward servitude. For, in the absence of wholesome restraint, and of discipline either self-imposed, or imposed by those in authority, men in their weakness become more and more subjected to their lower nature. This idea is beautifully presented in the following passage:

From 'The Reason of Church Government urged against Prelaty.' Chap. I.

'There is not that thing in the world of more grave and urgent importance throughout the whole life of man, than is DISCIPLINE. What need I instance? He that hath read with judgment of nations and commonwealths, of cities and camps, of peace and war, sea and land, will readily agree that the flourishing and decaying of all civil societies, all the moments and turnings of human occasions, are moved to and fro as upon the axle of discipline. So that whatsoever power or sway in mortal things weaker men have attributed to Fortune, I durst with more confidence (the honour of Divine Providence ever saved) ascribe either to the vigour or the slackness of discipline. Nor is there any sociable perfection in this life, civil or sacred, that can be above discipline; but she is that which with her musical chords preserves and holds all the parts thereof together. Hence in those perfect armies of Cyrus in Xenophon, and Scipio in the Roman stories, the excellence of military skill was esteemed, not by the not needing, but by the readiest submitting to the edicts of their commander. And certainly discipline is not only the removal of disorder; but if any visible shape can be given to divine things, the very visible shape and image of Virtue, whereby she is not only seen in the regular gestures and motions of her heavenly paces, as she walks, but also makes the harmony of her voice audible to mortal ears. Yea, the angels themselves, in whom no disorder is feared, as the apostle that saw them in his rapture describes, are distinguished and quaternioned into their celestial princedoms and satrapies, according as God himself has writ his imperial decrees through the great provinces of heaven. The state also of the blessed in paradise, though never so perfect, is not therefore left without discipline, whose golden surveying reed marks out and measures every quarter and circuit of New Jerusalem. Yet is it not to be conceived, that those eternal effluences of sanctity and love in the glorified saints should by this means be confined and cloyed with repetition of that which is prescribed, but that our happiness may orb itself into a thousand vagancies of glory and delight, and with a kind of eccentrical equation be, as it were, an invariable planet of joy and felicity; how much less can we believe that God would leave his frail and feeble, though not less beloved church here below, to the perpetual stumble of conjecture

and disturbance in this our dark voyage, without the card
and compass of discipline? Which is so hard to be of man's
making, that we may see even in the guidance of a civil state
to worldly happiness, it is not for every learned, or every wise
man, though many of them consult in common, to invent or
frame a discipline : but if it be at all the work of man, it must
be of such a one as is a true knower of himself, and in whom
contemplation and practice, wit, prudence, fortitude, and
eloquence must be rarely met, both to comprehend the
hidden causes of things, and span in his thoughts all the
various effects that passion or complexion can work in man's
nature ; and hereto must his hand be at defiance with gain,
and his heart in all virtues heroic ; so far is it from the ken
of these wretched projectors of ours, that bescrawl their
pamphlets every day with new forms of government for our
church. And therefore all the ancient lawgivers were either
truly inspired, as Moses, or were such men as with authority
enough might give it out to be so, as Minos, Lycurgus, Numa,
because they wisely forethought that men would never quietly
submit to such a discipline as had not more of God's hand in
it than man's. To come within the narrowness of house-
hold government, observation will show us many deep
counsellors of state and judges to demean themselves in-
corruptly in the settled course of affairs, and many worthy
preachers, upright in their lives, powerful in their audience :
but look upon either of these men when they are left to
their own disciplining at home, and you shall soon perceive,
for all their single knowledge and uprightness, how deficient
they are in the regulating of their own family ; not only in
what may concern the virtuous and decent composure of
their minds in their several places, but, that which is of a
lower and easier performance, the right possessing of the
outward vessel, their body, in health or sickness, rest or

labour, diet or abstinence, whereby to render it more pliant to the soul, and useful to the commonwealth; which if men were but as good to discipline themselves, as some are to tutor their horses and hawks, it could not be so gross in most households. If then it appear so hard, and so little known how to govern a house well, which is thought of so easy discharge, and for every man's undertaking, what skill of man, what wisdom, what parts can be sufficient to give laws and ordinances to the elect household of God? If we could imagine that he had left it at random without his provident and gracious ordering, who is he so arrogant, so presumptuous, that durst dispose and guide the living ark of the Holy Ghost, though he should find it wandering in the field of Bethshemesh, without the conscious warrant of some high calling? But no profane insolence can parallel that which our prelates dare avouch, to drive outrageously, and shatter the holy ark of the church, not borne upon their shoulders with pains and labour in the word, but drawn with rude oxen, their officials, and their own brute inventions. Let them make shows of reforming while they will, so long as the church is mounted upon the prelatical cart, and not, as it ought, between the hands of the ministers, it will but shake and totter; and he that sets to his hand, though with a good intent to hinder the shogging of it, in this unlawful waggonry wherein it rides, let him beware it be not fatal to him, as it was to Uzza.'

The following are some of the many explicit statements of Milton's idea of Liberty, which occur in his Prose Works. They may be said to be variations on the saying of the Saviour (John viii. 31, 32), 'If ye abide in my word, then are ye truly my disciples; and ye shall know the truth, and the truth shall make you free':

'What though the brood of Belial, the draff of men, to whom no liberty is pleasing, but unbridled and vagabond lust without

pale or partition, will laugh broad perhaps, to see so great a strength of scripture mustering up in favour, as they suppose, of their debaucheries; they will know better when they shall hence learn, that honest liberty is the greatest foe to dishonest licence.'
— *The Doctrine and Discipline of Divorce.*

'Real and substantial liberty is rather to be sought from within than from without; its existence depends, not so much on the terror of the sword, as in sobriety of conduct and integrity of life.'
— *Second Defence of the People of England.*

'The exposition here alleged is neither new nor licentious, as some now would persuade the commonalty, although it be nearer truth that nothing is more new than these teachers themselves, and nothing more licentious than some known to be, whose hypocrisy yet shames not to take offence at this doctrine for licence, whereas indeed they fear it would remove licence, and leave them few companions.'
— *Tetrachordon.*

'In every commonwealth, when it decays, corruption makes two main steps: first, when men cease to do according to the inward and uncompelled actions of virtue, caring only to live by the outward constraint of law, and turn this simplicity of real good into the craft of seeming so by law. To this hypocritical honesty was Rome declined in that age wherein Horace lived, and discovered it to Quinctius':

'Whom do we count a good man, whom but he
Who keeps the laws and statutes of the Senate?
Who judges in great suits and controversies?
Whose witness and opinion wins the cause?
But his own house, and the whole neighbourhood
Sees his foul inside through his whited skin.'

'The next declining is, when law becomes now too strait for the secular manners, and those too loose for the cincture of law. This brings in false and crooked interpretations to eke out law, and invents the subtle encroachments of obscure traditions hard to be disproved.'
— *Tetrachordon.*

'If men within themselves would be governed by reason, and not generally give up their understanding to a double tyranny of custom from without, and blind affections within, ⋅ ⋅ ⋅ they would discern better what it is to favour and uphold the tyrant of a nation. But, being slaves within doors, no wonder that they strive so much to have the public state conformably governed to the inward vicious rule by which they govern themselves. For, indeed, none can love freedom heartily but good men; the rest love not freedom but licence, which never hath more scope or more indulgence than under tyrants. Hence is it that tyrants are not oft offended, nor stand much in doubt of bad men, as being all naturally servile; but in whom virtue and true worth most is eminent, them they fear in earnest, as by right their masters; against them lies all their hatred and suspicion. Consequently, neither do bad men hate tyrants, but have been always readiest, with the falsified names of loyalty and obedience, to colour over their base compliances.'
— *The Tenure of Kings and Magistrates.*

'He who reigns within himself, and rules passions, desires, and fears, is more than a king.'

'For stories teach us, that liberty sought out of season, in a corrupt and degenerate age, brought Rome itself to a further slavery; for liberty hath a sharp and double edge, fit only to be handled by just and virtuous men; to bad and dissolute, it becomes a mischief unwieldy in their own hands: neither is it completely given, but by them who have the happy skill to know what is grievance and unjust to a people, and how to remove it wisely; what good laws are wanting, and how to frame them substantially, that good men may enjoy the freedom which they merit, and the bad, the curb which they need. But to do this, and to know these exquisite proportions, the heroic wisdom which is required, surmounted far the principles of these narrow politicians: what wonder then if they sunk as these unfortunate Britons before them, entangled and oppressed with things too hard and generous, above their strain and temper?'

—*The History of Britain*, Book iii.

'But when God hath decreed servitude on a sinful nation, fitted by their own vices for no condition but servile, all estates of government are alike unable to avoid it.'

— *The History of Britain*, Book v.

Peroration of 'The Second Defence of the People of England'

'It is of no little consequence, O citizens, by what principles you are governed, either in acquiring liberty, or in retaining it when acquired. And unless that liberty which is of such a kind as arms can neither procure nor take away, which alone is the fruit of piety, of justice, of temperance, and unadulterated virtue, shall have taken deep root in your minds and hearts, there will not long be wanting one who will snatch from you by treachery what you have acquired by arms. War has made many great whom peace makes small. If after being released from the toils of war, you neglect the arts of peace, if your peace and your liberty be a state of warfare, if war be your only virtue, the summit of your praise, you will, believe me, soon find peace the most adverse to your interests. Your peace will be only a more distressing war; and that which you imagined liberty will prove the worst of slavery. Unless by the means of piety, not frothy and loquacious, but operative, unadulterated, and sincere, you clear the horizon of the mind from those mists of superstition which arise from the ignorance of true religion, you will always have those who will bend your necks to the yoke as if you were brutes, who, notwithstanding all your triumphs, will put you up to the highest bidder, as if you were mere booty made in war; and will find an exuberant source of wealth in your ignorance and superstition. Unless you will subjugate the propensity to avarice, to ambition, and sensuality, and expel all luxury from yourselves and your families, you will find that you have cherished a more stubborn and intractable despot at home, than you ever encountered in the field; and even your very bowels will be continually teeming with an intolerable progeny of tyrants. Let these be the first enemies whom you subdue; this constitutes the campaign of peace; these are triumphs, difficult indeed, but bloodless; and far more honourable than those trophies which are purchased only by slaughter and by rapine. Unless you are victors in this service, it is in vain that you have been victorious over the despotic enemy in the field. For if you think that it is a more grand, a more beneficial, or a more wise policy, to invent subtle expedients for increasing the revenue, to multiply our naval and military force, to rival in craft the ambassadors of foreign states, to form skilful treaties and alliances, than to administer unpolluted justice to the people, to redress the injured and to succour the distressed, and speedily to restore to every one his own, you are involved in a cloud of error; and too late will you perceive, when the illusion of those mighty benefits has vanished, that in neglecting these, which you now think inferior considerations, you have only been precipitating your own ruin and despair. The fidelity of enemies and allies is frail and perishing, unless it be cemented by the principles of justice; that wealth and those honours, which most covet, readily change masters; they forsake the idle, and repair where virtue, where industry, where patience flourish most. Thus nation precipitates the downfall of nation; thus the more sound part of one people subverts the more corrupt; thus you obtained the ascendant over the royalists. If you plunge into the same depravity, if you imitate their excesses, and hanker after the same vanities, you will become royalists as well as they, and liable to be subdued by the same enemies, or by others in your turn; who, placing their reliance on the same religious principles, the same patience, the same integrity and discretion which made you strong, will deservedly triumph over you who are immersed in debauchery, in the luxury and the sloth of kings. Then, as if God was weary of protecting you, you will be seen to have passed through the fire that you might perish in the smoke; the contempt which you will then experience will be great as the admiration which you now enjoy; and, what may in future profit others, but cannot benefit yourselves, you will leave a salutary proof what great things the solid reality of virtue and of piety might have effected, when the mere counterfeit and varnished resemblance could attempt such mighty achievements, and make such considerable advances towards the execution. For, if either through your want of knowledge, your want of constancy, or your want of virtue, attempts so noble, and actions so glorious, have had an issue so unfortunate, it does not therefore follow that better men should be either less daring in their projects or less sanguine in their hopes. But from such an abyss of corruption into which you so readily fall, no one, not even Cromwell himself, nor a whole nation of Brutuses, if they were alive, could deliver you if they would, or would deliver you if they could. For who would vindicate your right of unrestrained suffrage, or of choosing what representatives you liked best, merely that you might elect the creatures of your own faction, whoever they might be, or him, however small might be his worth, who would give you the most lavish feasts, and enable you to drink to the greatest excess? Thus not wisdom and authority, but turbulence and gluttony, would soon exalt the vilest miscreants from our taverns and our brothels, from our towns and villages, to the rank and dignity of senators. For should the management of the republic be entrusted to persons to whom no one would willingly entrust the management of his private concerns; and the treasury of the state be left to the care of those who had lavished their own fortunes in an infamous prodigality? Should they have the charge of the public purse, which they would soon convert into a private, by their unprincipled peculations? Are they fit to be the legislators of a whole people who themselves know not what law, what reason, what right and wrong, what crooked and straight, what licit and illicit means? who think that all power consists in outrage, all dignity in the parade of insolence? who neglect every other consideration for the corrupt qualification of their friendships, or the prosecution of their resentments? who disperse their own relations and creatures through the provinces, for the sake of levying taxes and confiscating goods; men, for the greater part, the most profligate and vile, who buy up for themselves what they pretend to expose to sale, who thence collect an exorbitant mass of wealth, which they fraudulently divert from the public service; who thus spread their pillage through the country, and in a moment emerge from penury and rags to a state of splendour and of wealth? Who could endure such thievish servants, such vicegerents of their lords? Who could believe that the masters and the patrons of a banditti could be the proper guardians of liberty? or who would suppose that he should ever be made one hair more free by such a set of public functionaries, (though they might amount to five hundred elected in this manner from the counties and boroughs,) when among them who are the very guardians of liberty, and to whose custody it is committed, there must be so many, who know not either how to use or to enjoy liberty, who neither understand the principles nor merit the possession? But, what is worthy of remark, those who are the most unworthy of liberty are wont to behave most ungratefully towards their deliverers. Among such persons, who would be willing either to fight for liberty, or to encounter the least peril in its defence? It is not agreeable to the nature of things that such persons ever should be free. However much they may brawl about liberty, they are slaves, both at home and abroad, but without perceiving it; and when they do perceive it, like unruly horses that are impatient of the bit, they will endeavour to throw off the yoke, not from the love of genuine liberty, (which a good man only loves and knows how to obtain,) but from the impulses of pride and little passions. But though they often attempt it by arms, they will make no advances to the execution; they may change their masters, but will never be able to get rid of their servitude. This often happened to the ancient Romans, wasted by excess, and enervated by luxury: and it has still more so been the fate of the moderns; when, after a long interval of years, they aspired, under the auspices of Crescentius Nomentanus, and afterwards of Nicolas Rentius, who had assumed the title of Tribune of the People, to restore the splendour and reëstablish the government of ancient Rome. For, instead of fretting with vexation, or thinking that you can lay the blame on any one but yourselves, know that to be free is the same thing as to be pious, to be wise, to be temperate and just, to be frugal and abstinent, and, lastly, to be magnanimous and brave; so to be the opposite of all these is the same as to be a slave; and it usually happens, by the appointment, and as it were retributive justice, of the Deity, that that people which cannot govern themselves, and moderate their passions, but crouch under the slavery of their lusts, should be delivered up to the sway of those whom they abhor, and made to submit to an involuntary servitude. It is also sanctioned by the dictates of justice and by the constitution of nature, that he who from the imbecility or derangement of his intellect, is incapable of governing himself, should, like a minor, be committed to the government of another; and least of all should he be appointed to superintend the affairs of others or the interest of the state. You, therefore, who wish to remain free, either instantly be wise, or, as soon as possible, cease to be fools; if you think slavery an intolerable evil, learn obedience to reason and the government of yourselves; and, finally, bid adieu to your dissensions, your jealousies, your superstitions, your outrages, your rapine, and your lusts. Unless you will spare no pains to effect this, you must be judged unfit, both by God and mankind, to be entrusted with the possession of liberty and the administration of the government; but will rather, like a nation in a state of pupilage, want some active and courageous guardian to undertake the management of your affairs. With respect to myself, whatever turn things may take, I thought that my exertions on the present occasion would be serviceable to my country; and, as they have been cheerfully bestowed, I hope that they have not been bestowed in vain. And I have not circumscribed my defence of liberty within any petty circle around me, but have made it so general and comprehensive, that the justice and the reasonableness of such uncommon occurrences, explained and defended, both among my countrymen and among foreigners, and which all good men cannot but approve, may serve to exalt the glory of my country, and to excite the imitation of posterity. If the conclusion do not answer to the beginning, that is their concern; I have delivered my testimony, I would almost say, have erected a monument, that will not readily be destroyed, to the reality of those singular and mighty achievements which were above all praise. As the epic poet, who adheres at all to the rules of that species of composition, does not profess to describe the whole life of the hero whom he celebrates, but only some particular action of his life, as the resentment of Achilles at Troy, the return of Ulysses, or the coming of Æneas into Italy; so it will be sufficient, either for my justification or apology, that I have heroically celebrated at least one exploit of my countrymen; I pass by the rest, for who could recite the achievements of a whole people? If, after such a display of courage and of vigour, you basely relinquish the path of virtue, if you do anything unworthy of yourselves, posterity will sit in judgment on your conduct. They will see that the foundations were well laid; that the beginning (nay, it was more than a beginning) was glorious; but with deep emotions of concern will they regret, that those were wanting who might have completed the structure. They will lament that perseverance was not conjoined with such exertions and such virtues. They will see that there was a rich harvest of glory, and an opportunity afforded for the greatest achievements, but that men only were wanting for the execution; while they were not wanting who could rightly counsel, exhort, inspire, and bind an unfading wreath of praise round the brows of the illustrious actors in so glorious a scene.'

This informing idea of the Prose Works comes out explicitly in the second of the sonnets,

On the Detraction which followed upon my Writing Certain Treatises

'I did but prompt the age to quit their clogs
By the known rules of ancient liberty,
When straight a barbarous noise environs me

Of owls and cuckoos, asses, apes, and dogs:
As when those hinds that were transformed to frogs   5
Railed at Latona's twin-born progeny,
Which after held the sun and moon in fee.
But this is got by casting pearl to hogs,
That bawl for freedom in their senseless mood,
And still revolt when truth would set them free.   10
Licence they mean when they cry liberty;
For who loves that must first be wise and good;
But from that mark how far they rove we see,
For all this waste of wealth, and loss of blood.'

Again it appears, and in the most explicit form, in the 'Paradise Lost,' Book xii. 82–101. The angel Michael, in his discourse with Adam, on the mount of speculation, says:

'yet know withal,
Since thy original lapse, true liberty
Is lost, which always with right reason dwells
Twinned, and from her hath no dividual being.   85
Reason in man obscured, or not obeyed,
Immediately inordinate desires
And upstart passions catch the government
From Reason, and to servitude reduce
Man, till then free. Therefore, since he permits   90
Within himself unworthy powers to reign
Over free reason, God, in judgment just,
Subjects him from without to violent lords,
Who oft as undeservedly enthral
His outward freedom. Tyranny must be,   95
Though to the tyrant thereby no excuse.
Yet sometimes nations will decline so low
From virtue, which is reason, that no wrong,

> But justice and some fatal curse annexed,
> Deprives them of their outward liberty,   100
> Their inward lost.'

In the 'Samson Agonistes,' Samson says to the Chorus (vv. 268-276, and here Milton may be said virtually to speak, as he does throughout the drama, in *propria personâ*) :

> ' But what more oft, in nations grown corrupt
> And by their vices brought to servitude,
> Than to love bondage more than liberty,   270
> Bondage with ease than strenuous liberty ;
> And to despise, or envy, or suspect
> Whom God hath of his special favour raised
> As their deliverer? if he aught begin,
> How frequent to desert him, and at last   275
> To heap ingratitude on worthiest deeds?'

In the 'Paradise Regained,' Book ii. 410-486, Satan says to the Saviour :

> 'all thy heart is set on high designs,   410
> High actions ; but wherewith to be achieved ?
> Great acts require great means of enterprise ;
> Thou art unknown, unfriended, low of birth,
> A carpenter thy father known, thyself
> Bred up in poverty and straits at home,   415
> Lost in a desert here, and hunger-bit.
> Which way, or from what hope, dost thou aspire
> To greatness? whence authority derivest?
> What followers, what retinue canst thou gain?
> Or at thy heels the dizzy multitude,   420
> Longer than thou canst feed them on thy cost?

Money brings honour, friends, conquest, and realms.
What raised Antipater, the Edomite,
And his son Herod placed on Judah's throne —
Thy throne — but gold that got him puissant friends? 425
Therefore, if at great things thou wouldest arrive,
Get riches first, get wealth, and treasure heap, —
Not difficult, if thou hearken to me.
Riches are mine, fortune is in my hand;
They whom I favour thrive in wealth amain, 430
While virtue, valour, wisdom, sit in want.'
To whom thus Jesus patiently replied:
'Yet wealth without these three is impotent
To gain dominion, or to keep it gained;
Witness those ancient empires of the earth, 435
In highth of all their flowing wealth dissolved.
But men endued with these have oft attained
In lowest poverty to highest deeds;
Gideon, and Jephtha, and the shepherd-lad,
Whose offspring on the throne of Judah sat 440
So many ages, and shalt yet regain
That seat, and reign in Israel without end.
Among the Heathen — for throughout the world
To me is not unknown what hath been done
Worthy of memorial — canst thou not remember 445
Quintius, Fabricius, Curius, Regulus?
For I esteem those names of men so poor,
Who could do mighty things, and could contemn
Riches, though offered from the hand of kings.
And what in me seems wanting, but that I 450
May also in this poverty as soon
Accomplish what they did? perhaps and more.
Extol not riches then, the toil of fools,
The wise man's cumbrance, if not snare; more apt

To slacken Virtue, and abate her edge, 455
Than prompt her to do aught may merit praise.
What, if with like aversion I reject
Riches and realms! yet not, for that a crown,
Golden in shew, is but a wreath of thorns,
Brings dangers, troubles, cares, and sleepless nights, 460
To him who wears the regal diadem,
When on his shoulders each man's burden lies;
For therein stands the office of a king,
His honour, virtue, merit, and chief praise,
That for the public all this weight he bears. 465
Yet he who reigns within himself, and rules
Passions, desires, and fears, is more a king;
Which every wise and virtuous man attains:
And who attains not, ill aspires to rule
Cities of men, or headstrong multitudes, 470
Subject himself to anarchy within,
Or lawless passions in him, which he serves.
But to guide nations in the way of truth
By saving doctrine, and from error lead
To know, and knowing, worship God aright, 475
Is yet more kingly: this attracts the soul,
Governs the inner man, the nobler part;
That other o'er the body only reigns,
And oft by force, which to a generous mind
So reigning can be no sincere delight. 480
Besides, to give a kingdom hath been thought
Greater and nobler done, and to lay down
Far more magnanimous, than to assume.
Riches are needless then, both for themselves,
And for thy reason why they should be sought, 485
To gain a sceptre, oftest better missed.'

All this, it may be truly said, is nothing more than the old teaching of Solomon, 'He that ruleth his spirit is better than he that taketh a city' (Prov. xvi. 32). There has always been truth enough in the world which, if realized in men's lives, would soon bring about the millennium. But, unfortunately, it has only been born in their brains.

Great writers owe their power among men, not necessarily so much to a wide range of ideas or to the originality of their ideas, as to the vitality which they are able to impart to some one comprehensive fructifying idea with which, through constitution of mind, or circumstances, they have become *possessed*. It is only when a man is really possessed with an idea (that is, if it does not run away with him), that he can express it with a quickening power, and ring all possible changes upon it.

The passages quoted sufficiently show the *kind* of liberty which Milton estimated above all others, and to the advancement of which he devoted his best powers, for twenty years, and those years the best, generally, of a man's life, for intellectual and creative work, namely, from thirty-two to fifty-two. The last eight of those years he worked in total darkness, not bating a jot of heart or hope, sustained by the consciousness of having lost his eyes 'overplied in Liberty's defence'—'the glorious liberty,' more especially, 'of the children of God,' 'the liberty wherewith Christ hath made us free,' without which, outward liberty he regarded as a temptation and a snare.

In addition to the absolute merit attaching to his labors in the cause of liberty, it must not be forgotten that he turned aside with a heroic self-denial, during all those years of his manhood's prime, from what he had, from his early years up, felt himself dedicated to, and toward fitting himself for the accomplishment of which, he had, with an unflagging ardor, trained and marshalled all his faculties.

COMUS

A Masque presented at Ludlow Castle, 1634, before the Earl of Bridgewater, then President of Wales

MASQUES, in the reigns of Elizabeth, James I., and Charles I., were generally written for the entertainment of royalty and nobility. They were, besides, in most cases, presented by royal and noble persons. In their setting, they were in strong contrast to the public drama of the day, got up, as they were, with great magnificence of architecture, scenery, and 'appareling' (Ben Jonson's word for the apparatus of the scene), and frequently at an enormous expense. They were generally offset by grotesque and comic antimasques, which were played by common actors, dancers, and buffoons, from the public theatres. Shakespeare's 'A Midsummer Night's Dream' was probably not written as a regular drama for the public stage, but as a masque, on the occasion of some noble marriage. 'The most lamentable comedy and most cruel death of Pyramus and Thisbe' presented by the 'rude mechanicals,' 'hard-handed men,' in the fifth act, is the antimasque. It offsets the Masque in a special way. The Masque makes great demands on the imagination in its presentation of the fairy world; the antimasque is absurdly realistic — nothing is left by the 'rude mechanicals' to the imagination.

The Masque of 'Comus' is the last notable, if not entirely the last, composition of the kind in English literature, and the loftiest and loveliest. It is a glorification of the power of purity and chastity over the impure and the unchaste; and the poet no doubt meant it as a reflection upon the license and excesses and revelries (of which Comus is a personification) of the profligate and extravagant court of the time, imported from

'Celtic and Iberian fields.' The now obvious attitude of the composition was perhaps not at all suspected when it was performed at Ludlow Castle.

There is nothing in the Masque of 'Comus' that is even suggestive of the antimasque of the earlier masques, unless it be where the Country Dancers come in before the entrance of the Attendant Spirit with the two Brothers and the Lady, who catch the dancers at their sport. The Attendant Spirit addresses them in the song (vv. 958-965):

> 'Back, shepherds, back! Enough your play
> Till next sunshine holiday.
> Here be, without duck or nod,
> Other trippings to be trod
> Of lighter toes,' etc.

The subject of 'Comus' was too serious to be offset or parodied in any way by an antimasque; and, furthermore, Milton was not the man for anything of the kind. His theme excluded all humor, even if he had had any to expend upon it. Its seriousness must have been deepened for him by what he no doubt already felt in regard to the Court and the Church, that both were corrupt, and that both were leagued in their despotic tendencies, or rather in their actual despotic characters.

The traditional story that the two sons of the Earl of Bridgewater, the Lord Brackley and Mr. Thomas Egerton, and their sister, the Lady Alice Egerton, were lost in Haywood Forest on their way to Ludlow Castle from Herefordshire, where they had been visiting their relatives, the Egertons, and that the Lady Alice was for a time separated from her brothers, they having gone to discover the right path, may have had its origin in the Masque. This seems more likely than that the Masque had its origin in the story.

In the talk of the two Brothers in regard to their lost sister, the idea of the Masque is explicitly presented by the elder Brother. He had said :

> ' My sister is not so defenceless left
> As you imagine ; she has a hidden strength
> Which you remember not.'

The second Brother replies :

> ' What hidden strength,
> Unless the strength of Heaven, if you mean that?'

And then the elder Brother gives expression, in a long speech, the gem of the Masque (vv. 418–475), to the power of chastity and purity over the unchaste and the impure.

In the service of this idea, the poet started, no doubt, with Comus, the personification of unchaste and impure revelry (κῶμος), and therefrom constructed his plot, in which a pure maiden is brought within range of the wiles and temptations of the enchanter. And as the daughter of the noble family for which the Masque was written was to play the part of the tempted maiden, in the presentation of the Masque, the incident of her being temporarily and necessarily left alone by her brothers in the forest, would be readily suggested to the poet. It afforded him, too, an opportunity of paying a high compliment to the children of the Earl of Bridgewater.

The traditional story may therefore be safely regarded as a figment.

Henry Lawes, the most prominent music teacher of the time, in noble and wealthy families, and with a high reputation as a musical composer, furnished the music for the Masque, and took the part of the Attendant Spirit, first appearing as such, and afterward in the guise of the old and faithful shepherd Thyrsis. It is not known by whom the parts of Comus and Sabrina were taken.

Lawes had been one of Milton's musical friends from early boyhood.

Milton addressed the following sonnet to him, which was prefixed to 'Choice Psalmes . . . by Henry and William Lawes, brothers, 1648.' In Milton's volume of poems published in 1645, Lawes is represented as 'Gentleman of the king's chapel and one of His Majesty's private music.'

To Mr. H. Lawes, on his Airs (1646)

' Harry, whose tuneful and well-measured song
  First taught our English music how to span
  Words with just note and accent, not to scan
  With Midas' ears, committing short and long,
Thy worth and skill exempts thee from the throng,   5
  With praise enough for envy to look wan;
  To after-age thou shalt be writ the man,
  That with smooth air could humour best our tongue.
Thou honourest verse, and verse must lend her wing
  To honour thee, the priest of Phœbus' quire,   10
  That tunest their happiest lines in hymn or story.
Dante shall give fame leave to set thee higher
  Than his Casella, whom he wooed to sing,
  Met in the milder shades of Purgatory.'

THE PERSONS

THE ATTENDANT SPIRIT, afterward in the habit of THYRSIS.
COMUS, with his Crew.
THE LADY.
FIRST BROTHER.
SECOND BROTHER.
SABRINA, the Nymph.
  The Chief Persons which presented were:
    The Lord Brackley;
    Mr. Thomas Egerton, his Brother;
    The Lady Alice Egerton.

The First Scene discovers a Wild Wood.

The ATTENDANT SPIRIT *descends or enters.*

Before the starry threshold of Jove's court
My mansion is, where those immortal shapes
Of bright aerial spirits live insphered
In regions mild of calm and serene air,
Above the smoke and stir of this dim spot 5
Which men call Earth, and, with low-thoughted care,
Confined and pestered in this pinfold here,
Strive to keep up a frail and feverish being,
Unmindful of the crown that virtue gives,
After this mortal change, to her true servants, 10
Amongst the enthronèd Gods on sainted seats.
Yet some there be that by due steps aspire
To lay their just hands on that golden key
That opes the palace of eternity.
To such my errand is; and, but for such, 15
I would not soil these pure ambrosial weeds
With the rank vapours of this sin-worn mould.
　But to my task. Neptune, besides the sway
Of every salt flood and each ebbing stream,
Took in by lot, 'twixt high and nether Jove, 20
Imperial rule of all the sea-girt isles
That, like to rich and various gems, inlay
The unadornèd bosom of the deep;
Which he, to grace his tributary gods,
By course commits to several government, 25
And gives them leave to wear their sapphire crowns
And wield their little tridents. But this Isle,
The greatest and the best of all the main,

He quarters to his blue-haired deities;
And all this tract that fronts the falling sun   30
A noble Peer of mickle trust and power
Has in his charge, with tempered awe to guide
An old and haughty nation proud in arms:
Where his fair offspring, nursed in princely lore,
Are coming to attend their father's state,   35
And new-intrusted sceptre.   But their way
Lies through the perplexed paths of this drear wood,
The nodding horror of whose shady brows
Threats the forlorn and wandering passenger;
And here their tender age might suffer peril,   40
But that, by quick command from sovran Jove,
I was despatched for their defence and guard.
And listen why; for I will tell you now
What never yet was heard in tale or song,
From old or modern bard, in hall or bower.   45
   Bacchus, that first from out the purple grape
Crushed the sweet poison of misusèd wine,
After the Tuscan mariners transformed,
Coasting the Tyrrhene shore, as the winds listed,
On Circe's island fell. (Who knows not Circe,   50
The daughter of the Sun, whose charmed cup
Whoever tasted lost his upright shape,
And downward fell into a grovelling swine?)
This Nymph, that gazed upon his clustering locks,
With ivy berries wreathed, and his blithe youth,   55
Had by him, ere he parted thence, a son
Much like his father, but his mother more,
Whom therefore she brought up, and Comus named:
Who, ripe, and frolic of his full-grown age,
Roving the Celtic and Iberian fields,   60
At last betakes him to this ominous wood,

And, in thick shelter of black shades imbowered,
Excels his mother at her mighty art,
Offering to every weary traveller
His orient liquor in a crystal glass, 65
To quench the drouth of Phœbus; which as they taste
(For most do taste through fond intemperate thirst),
Soon as the potion works, their human count'nance,
The express resemblance of the gods, is changed
Into some brutish form of wolf or bear, 70
Or ounce, or tiger, hog, or bearded goat,
All other parts remaining as they were.
And they, so perfect is their misery,
Not once perceive their foul disfigurement,
But boast themselves more comely than before, 75
And all their friends and native home forget,
To roll with pleasure in a sensual sty.
Therefore, when any favoured of high Jove
Chances to pass through this adventurous glade,
Swift as the sparkle of a glancing star 80
I shoot from heaven, to give him safe convoy,
As now I do. But first I must put off
These my sky robes, spun out of Iris' woof,
And take the weeds and likeness of a swain
That to the service of this house belongs, 85
Who, with his soft pipe, and smooth-dittied song,
Well knows to still the wild winds when they roar,
And hush the waving woods; nor of less faith,
And in this office of his mountain watch
Likeliest, and nearest to the present aid 90
Of this occasion. But I hear the tread
Of hateful steps; I must be viewless now.

COMUS *enters, with a charming rod in one hand, his glass in the other; with him a rout of monsters, headed like sundry sorts of wild beasts, but otherwise like men and women, their apparel glistering. They come in making a riotous and unruly noise, with torches in their hands.*

 Comus. The star that bids the shepherd fold
Now the top of heaven doth hold;
And the gilded car of day   95
His glowing axle doth allay
In the steep Atlantic stream;
And the slope sun his upward beam
Shoots against the dusky pole,
Pacing toward the other goal   100
Of his chamber in the east.
Meanwhile, welcome joy and feast,
Midnight shout and revelry,
Tipsy dance and jollity.
Braid your locks with rosy twine,   105
Dropping odours, dropping wine.
Rigour now is gone to bed;
And Advice with scrupulous head,
Strict Age, and sour Severity,
With their grave saws, in slumber lie.   110
We, that are of purer fire,
Imitate the starry quire,
Who, in their nightly watchful spheres,
Lead in swift round the months and years.
The sounds and seas, with all their finny drove,   115
Now to the moon in wavering morrice move;
And on the tawny sands and shelves
Trip the pert fairies and the dapper elves.

By dimpled brook and fountain-brim,
The wood-nymphs, decked with daisies trim, 120
Their merry wakes and pastimes keep;
What hath night to do with sleep?
Night hath better sweets to prove;
Venus now wakes, and wakens Love.
Come, let us our rites begin, 125
— 'Tis only daylight that makes sin —
Which these dun shades will ne'er report.
Hail, goddess of nocturnal sport,
Dark-veiled Cotytto, to whom the secret flame
Of midnight torches burns! mysterious dame, 130
That ne'er art called but when the dragon womb
Of Stygian darkness spets her thickest gloom,
And makes one blot of all the air!
Stay thy cloudy ebon chair,
Wherein thou ridest with Hecat', and befriend 135
Us thy vowed priests, till utmost end
Of all thy dues be done, and none left out;
Ere the blabbing eastern scout,
The nice Morn on the Indian steep,
From her cabined loop-hole peep, 140
And to the tell-tale Sun descry
Our concealed solemnity.
Come, knit hands, and beat the ground
In a light fantastic round.

The Measure.

Break off, break off! I feel the different pace 145
Of some chaste footing near about this ground.
Run to your shrouds within these brakes and trees;
Our number may affright. Some virgin sure

For so I can distinguish by mine art)
Benighted in these woods! Now to my charms, 150
And to my wily trains: I shall ere long
Be well stocked with as fair a herd as grazed
About my mother Circe. Thus I hurl
My dazzling spells into the spungy air,
Of power to cheat the eye with blear illusion, 155
And give it false presentments, lest the place
And my quaint habits breed astonishment,
And put the damsel to suspicious flight;
Which must not be, for that's against my course.
I, under fair pretence of friendly ends, 160
And well-placed words of glozing courtesy,
Baited with reasons not unplausible,
Wind me into the easy-hearted man,
And hug him into snares. When once her eye
Hath met the virtue of this magic dust, 165
I shall appear some harmless villager
Whom thrift keeps up about his country gear.
But here she comes; I fairly step aside,
And hearken, if I may her business hear.

The LADY *enters.*

Lady. This way the noise was, if mine ear be true, 170
My best guide now. Methought it was the sound
Of riot and ill-managed merriment,
Such as the jocund flute or gamesome pipe
Stirs up among the loose unlettered hinds,
When, for their teeming flocks, and granges full, 175
In wanton dance they praise the bounteous Pan,
And thank the gods amiss. I should be loth
To meet the rudeness and swilled insolence

Of such late wassailers; yet, oh! where else
Shall I inform my unacquainted feet   180
In the blind mazes of this tangled wood?
My brothers, when they saw me wearied out
With this long way, resolving here to lodge
Under the spreading favour of these pines,
Stepped, as they said, to the next thicket-side   185
To bring me berries, or such cooling fruit
As the kind hospitable woods provide.
They left me then when the gray-hooded Even,
Like a sad votarist in palmer's weed,
Rose from the hindmost wheels of Phœbus' wain.   190
But where they are, and why they came not back,
Is now the labour of my thoughts. 'Tis likeliest
They had engaged their wandering steps too far;
And envious darkness, ere they could return,
Had stole them from me. Else, O thievish Night,   195
Why shouldst thou, but for some felonious end,
In thy dark lantern thus close up the stars
That Nature hung in heaven, and filled their lamps
With everlasting oil to give due light
To the misled and lonely traveller?   200
This is the place, as well as I may guess,
Whence even now the tumult of loud mirth
Was rife, and perfect in my listening ear;
Yet nought but single darkness do I find.
What might this be? A thousand fantasies   205
Begin to throng into my memory,
Of calling shapes, and beckoning shadows dire,
And airy tongues that syllable men's names
On sands and shores and desert wildernesses.
These thoughts may startle well, but not astound   210
The virtuous mind, that ever walks attended

By a strong siding champion, Conscience.
O, welcome, pure-eyed Faith, white-handed Hope,
Thou hovering angel girt with golden wings,
And thou unblemished form of Chastity! 215
I see ye visibly, and now believe
That He, the Supreme Good, to whom all things ill
Are but as slavish officers of vengeance,
Would send a glistering guardian, if need were,
To keep my life and honour unassailed. . . . 220
Was I deceived, or did a sable cloud
Turn forth her silver lining on the night?
I did not err: there does a sable cloud
Turn forth her silver lining on the night,
And casts a gleam over this tufted grove. 225
I cannot hallo to my brothers, but
Such noise as I can make to be heard farthest
I'll venture; for my new enlivened spirits
Prompt me, and they perhaps are not far off.

Song.

Sweet Echo, sweetest nymph, that liv'st unseen 230
    Within thy airy shell
By slow Meander's margent green,
And in the violet-embroidered vale,
    Where the love-lorn nightingale
Nightly to thee her sad song mourneth well: 235
Canst thou not tell me of a gentle pair
    That likest thy Narcissus are?
    Oh, if thou have
    Hid them in some flowery cave,
    Tell me but where, 240
Sweet Queen of Parley, Daughter of the Sphere!

So mayst thou be translated to the skies,
And give resounding grace to all Heaven's harmonies!

   Comus. Can any mortal mixture of earth's mould
Breathe such divine enchanting ravishment?   245
Sure something holy lodges in that breast,
And with these raptures moves the vocal air
To testify his hidden residence.
How sweetly did they float upon the wings
Of silence, through the empty-vaulted night,   250
At every fall smoothing the raven down
Of darkness till it smiled! I have oft heard
My mother Circe with the Sirens three,
Amidst the flowery-kirtled Naiades,
Culling their potent herbs and baleful drugs,   255
Who, as they sung, would take the prisoned soul,
And lap it in Elysium: Scylla wept,
And chid her barking waves into attention,
And fell Charybdis murmured soft applause.
Yet they in pleasing slumber lulled the sense,   260
And in sweet madness robbed it of itself;
But such a sacred and home-felt delight,
Such sober certainty of waking bliss,
I never heard till now. I'll speak to her,
And she shall be my queen.—Hail, foreign wonder!   265
Whom, certain, these rough shades did never breed,
Unless the goddess that in rural shrine
Dwell'st here with Pan or Sylvan, by blest song
Forbidding every bleak unkindly fog
To touch the prosperous growth of this tall wood.   270

   Lady. Nay, gentle shepherd, ill is lost that praise
That is addressed to unattending ears.
Not any boast of skill, but extreme shift

How to regain my severed company,
Compelled me to awake the courteous Echo 275
To give me answer from her mossy couch.
    Comus. What chance, good Lady, hath bereft you thus?
    Lady. Dim darkness and this leavy labyrinth.
    Comus. Could that divide you from near-ushering guides?
    Lady. They left me weary on a grassy turf. 280
    Comus. By falsehood, or discourtesy, or why?
    Lady. To seek i' the valley some cool friendly spring.
    Comus. And left your fair side all unguarded, Lady?
    Lady. They were but twain, and purposed quick return.
    Comus. Perhaps forestalling night prevented them. 285
    Lady. How easy my misfortune is to hit!
    Comus. Imports their loss, beside the present need?
    Lady. No less than if I should my brothers lose.
    Comus. Were they of manly prime, or youthful bloom?
    Lady. As smooth as Hebe's their unrazored lips. 290
    Comus. Two such I saw, what time the laboured ox
In his loose traces from the furrow came,
And the swinked hedger at his supper sat.
I saw them under a green mantling vine,
That crawls along the side of yon small hill, 295
Plucking ripe clusters from the tender shoots;
Their port was more than human, as they stood.
I took it for a faery vision
Of some gay creatures of the element,
That in the colours of the rainbow live, 300
And play i' the plighted clouds. I was awe-strook,
And, as I passed, I worshipped. If those you seek,
It were a journey like the path to Heaven
To help you find them.
    Lady.   Gentle villager,
What readiest way would bring me to that place? 305

Comus. Due west it rises from this shrubby point.
Lady. To find out that, good shepherd, I suppose,
In such a scant allowance of star-light,
Would overtask the best land-pilot's art,
Without the sure guess of well-practised feet. 310
   Comus. I know each lane, and every alley green,
Dingle, or bushy dell, of this wild wood,
And every bosky bourn from side to side,
My daily walks and ancient neighbourhood;
And, if your stray attendance be yet lodged, 315
Or shroud within these limits, I shall know
Ere morrow wake, or the low-roosted lark
From her thatched pallet rouse. If otherwise,
I can conduct you, Lady, to a low
But loyal cottage, where you may be safe 320
Till further quest.
   Lady.   Shepherd, I take thy word,
And trust thy honest-offered courtesy;
Which oft is sooner found in lowly sheds,
With smoky rafters, than in tapestry halls
And courts of princes, where it first was named, 325
And yet is most pretended. In a place
Less warranted than this, or less secure,
It cannot be, that I should fear to change it.
Eye me, blest Providence, and square my trial
To my proportioned strength! Shepherd, lead on. 330

Enter the TWO BROTHERS.

Eld. Bro. Unmuffle, ye faint stars; and thou, fair moon,
That wont'st to love the traveller's benison,
Stoop thy pale visage through an amber cloud,
And disinherit Chaos, that reigns here

In double night of darkness and of shades; 335
Or, if your influence be quite dammed up
With black usurping mists, some gentle taper,
Though a rush-candle from the wicker hole
Of some clay habitation, visit us
With thy long-levelled rule of streaming light, 340
And thou shalt be our Star of Arcady,
Or Tyrian Cynosure.
 Sec. Bro.   Or, if our eyes
Be barred that happiness, might we but hear
The folded flocks, penned in their wattled cotes,
Or sound of pastoral reed with oaken stops, 345
Or whistle from the lodge, or village cock
Count the night-watches to his feathery dames,
'Twould be some solace yet, some little cheering,
In this close dungeon of innumerous boughs.
But, oh, that hapless virgin, our lost sister! 350
Where may she wander now, whither betake her
From the chill dew, amongst rude burs and thistles?
Perhaps some cold bank is her bolster now,
Or 'gainst the rugged bark of some broad elm
Leans her unpillowed head, fraught with sad fears. 355
What if in wild amazement and affright,
Or, while we speak, within the direful grasp
Of savage hunger, or of savage heat!
 Eld. Bro. Peace, brother: be not over-exquisite
To cast the fashion of uncertain evils; 360
For, grant they be so, while they rest unknown,
What need a man forestall his date of grief,
And run to meet what he would most avoid?
Or, if they be but false alarms of fear,
How bitter is such self-delusion! 365
I do not think my sister so to seek,

Or so unprincipled in virtue's book,
And the sweet peace that goodness bosoms ever,
As that the single want of light and noise
(Not being in danger, as I trust she is not) 370
Could stir the constant mood of her calm thoughts,
And put them into misbecoming plight.
Virtue could see to do what Virtue would
By her own radiant light, though sun and moon
Were in the flat sea sunk. And Wisdom's self 375
Oft seeks to sweet retirèd solitude,
Where, with her best nurse, Contemplation,
She plumes her feathers, and lets grow her wings,
That, in the various bustle of resort,
Were all to-ruffled, and sometimes impaired. 380
He that has light within his own clear breast,
May sit i' the centre, and enjoy bright day:
But he that hides a dark soul and foul thoughts
Benighted walks under the mid-day sun;
Himself is his own dungeon.
 Sec. Bro.   'Tis most true 385
That musing meditation most affects
The pensive secrecy of desert-cell,
Far from the cheerful haunt of men and herds,
And sits as safe as in a senate-house;
For who would rob a hermit of his weeds, 390
His few books, or his beads, or maple dish,
Or do his grey hairs any violence?
But Beauty, like the fair Hesperian tree
Laden with blooming gold, had need the guard
Of dragon-watch with unenchanted eye, 395
To save her blossoms, and defend her fruit,
From the rash hand of bold Incontinence.
You may as well spread out the unsunned heaps

Of miser's treasure by an outlaw's den,
And tell me it is safe, as bid me hope 400
Danger will wink on Opportunity,
And let a single helpless maiden pass
Uninjured in this wild surrounding waste.
Of night or loneliness it recks me not;
I fear the dread events that dog them both, 405
Lest some ill-greeting touch attempt the person
Of our unownèd sister.
    Eld. Bro.   I do not, brother,
Infer as if I thought my sister's state
Secure without all doubt or controversy;
Yet, where an equal poise of hope and fear 410
Does arbitrate the event, my nature is
That I incline to hope rather than fear,
And gladly banish squint suspicion.
My sister is not so defenceless left
As you imagine; she has a hidden strength, 415
Which you remember not.
    Sec. Bro.   What hidden strength,
Unless the strength of Heaven, if you mean that?
    Eld. Bro. I mean that too, but yet a hidden strength,
Which, if Heaven gave it, may be termed her own.
'Tis chastity, my brother, chastity; 420
She that has that, is clad in complete steel,
And, like a quivered nymph with arrows keen,
May trace huge forests, and unharboured heaths,
Infámous hills, and sandy perilous wilds;
Where, through the sacred rays of chastity, 425
No savage fierce, bandite, or mountaineer,
Will dare to soil her virgin purity.
Yea, there where very desolation dwells,
By grots and caverns shagged with horrid shades,

She may pass on with unblenched majesty, 430
Be it not done in pride, or in presumption.
Some say no evil thing that walks by night,
In fog or fire, by lake or moorish fen,
Blue meagre hag, or stubborn unlaid ghost,
That breaks his magic chains at curfew time, 435
No goblin or swart faery of the mine,
Hath hurtful power o'er true virginity.
Do ye believe me yet, or shall I call
Antiquity from the old schools of Greece
To testify the arms of chastity? 440
Hence had the huntress Dian her dread bow,
Fair silver-shafted queen for ever chaste,
Wherewith she tamed the brinded lioness
And spotted mountain-pard, but set at nought
The frivolous bolt of Cupid; gods and men 445
Feared her stern frown, and she was queen o' the woods.
What was that snaky-headed Gorgon shield
That wise Minerva wore, unconquered virgin,
Wherewith she freezed her foes to congealed stone,
But rigid looks of chaste austerity, 450
And noble grace that dashed brute violence
With sudden adoration and blank awe?
So dear to Heaven is saintly chastity
That, when a soul is found sincerely so,
A thousand liveried angels lackey her, 455
Driving far off each thing of sin and guilt,
And in clear dream and solemn vision
Tell her of things that no gross ear can hear;
Till oft converse with heavenly habitants
Begin to cast a beam on the outward shape, 460
The unpolluted temple of the mind,
And turns it by degrees to the soul's essence,

Till all be made immortal. But, when lust,
By unchaste looks, loose gestures, and foul talk,
But most by lewd and lavish act of sin, 465
Lets in defilement to the inward parts,
The soul grows clotted by contagion,
Imbodies, and imbrutes, till she quite lose
The divine property of her first being.
Such are those thick and gloomy shadows damp 470
Oft seen in charnel-vaults and sepulchres,
Lingering and sitting by a new-made grave,
As loth to leave the body that it loved,
And linked itself by carnal sensuality
To a degenerate and degraded state. 475
   Sec. Bro. How charming is divine Philosophy!
Not harsh and crabbed, as dull fools suppose,
But musical as is Apollo's lute,
And a perpetual feast of nectared sweets,
Where no crude surfeit reigns.
   Eld. Bro.   List! list! I hear 480
Some far-off hallo break the silent air.
   Sec. Bro. Methought so too; what should it be?
   Eld. Bro.   For certain,
Either some one, like us, night-foundered here,
Or else some neighbour woodman, or, at worst,
Some roving robber calling to his fellows. 485
   Sec. Bro. Heaven keep my sister! Again, again, and near!
Best draw, and stand upon our guard.
   Eld. Bro.   I'll hallo.
If he be friendly, he comes well: if not,
Defence is a good cause, and Heaven be for us!

Enter the ATTENDANT SPIRIT, *habited like a shepherd.*

That hallo I should know. What are you? Speak! 490
Come not too near; you fall on iron stakes else.
   Spir. What voice is that? my young Lord? speak again.
   Sec. Bro. O brother, 'tis my father's shepherd, sure.
   Eld. Bro. Thyrsis! whose artful strains have oft delayed
The huddling brook to hear his madrigal, 495
And sweetened every musk-rose of the dale.
How camest thou here, good swain? hath any ram
Slipped from the fold, or young kid lost his dam,
Or straggling wether the pent flock forsook?
How couldst thou find this dark sequestered nook? 500
   Spir. O my loved master's heir, and his next joy,
I came not here on such a trivial toy
As a strayed ewe, or to pursue the stealth
Of pilfering wolf; not all the fleecy wealth
That doth enrich these downs is worth a thought 505
To this my errand, and the care it brought.
But, oh! my virgin Lady, where is she?
How chance she is not in your company?
   Eld. Bro. To tell thee sadly, Shepherd, without blame
Or our neglect, we lost her as we came. 510
   Spir. Ay me unhappy! then my fears are true.
   Eld. Bro. What fears, good Thyrsis? Prithee briefly shew.
   Spir. I'll tell ye. 'Tis not vain or fabulous
(Though so esteemed by shallow ignorance)
What the sage poets, taught by the heavenly Muse, 515
Storied of old in high immortal verse,
Of dire Chimeras and enchanted isles,
And rifted rocks whose entrance leads to Hell;
For such there be, but unbelief is blind.

Within the navel of this hideous wood, 520
Immured in cypress shades, a sorcerer dwells,
Of Bacchus and of Circe born, great Comus,
Deep skilled in all his mother's witcheries,
And here to every thirsty wanderer
By sly enticement gives his baneful cup, 525
With many murmurs mixed, whose pleasing poison
The visage quite transforms of him that drinks,
And the inglorious likeness of a beast
Fixes instead, unmoulding reason's mintage
Charáctered in the face. This have I learnt 530
Tending my flocks hard by i' the hilly crofts
That brow this bottom-glade; whence, night by night,
He and his monstrous rout are heard to howl
Like stabled wolves, or tigers at their prey,
Doing abhorrèd rites to Hecate 535
In their obscurèd haunts of inmost bowers.
Yet have they many baits and guileful spells
To inveigle and invite the unwary sense
Of them that pass unweeting by the way.
This evening late, by then the chewing flocks 540
Had ta'en their supper on the savoury herb
Of knot-grass dew-besprent, and were in fold,
I sat me down to watch upon a bank
With ivy canopied, and interwove
With flaunting honey-suckle, and began, 545
Wrapt in a pleasing fit of melancholy,
To meditate my rural minstrelsy,
Till fancy had her fill. But ere a close,
The wonted roar was up amidst the woods,
And filled the air with barbarous dissonance; 550
At which I ceased, and listened them a while,
Till an unusual stop of sudden silence

Gave respite to the drowsy-flighted steeds
That draw the litter of close-curtained Sleep.
At last a soft and solemn-breathing sound   555
Rose like a steam of rich distilled perfumes,
And stole upon the air, that even Silence
Was took ere she was ware, and wished she might
Deny her nature, and be never more,
Still to be so displaced.   I was all ear,   560
And took in strains that might create a soul
Under the ribs of Death.   But, oh! ere long
Too well I did perceive it was the voice
Of my most honoured Lady, your dear sister.
Amazed I stood, harrowed with grief and fear;   565
And "O poor hapless nightingale," thought I,
"How sweet thou sing'st, how near the deadly snare!"
Then down the lawns I ran with headlong haste,
Through paths and turnings often trod by day,
Till, guided by mine ear, I found the place   570
Where that damned wizard, hid in sly disguise
(For so by certain signs I knew), had met
Already, ere my best speed could prevent,
The aidless innocent lady, his wished prey,
Who gently asked if he had seen such two,   575
Supposing him some neighbour villager.
Longer I durst not stay, but soon I guessed
Ye were the two she meant; with that I sprung
Into swift flight, till I had found you here,
But further know I not.
   Sec. Bro.   O night and shades,   580
How are ye joined with Hell in triple knot
Against the unarmed weakness of one virgin,
Alone and helpless! Is this the confidence
You gave me, brother?

Eld. Bro.   Yes, and keep it still;
Lean on it safely; not a period   585
Shall be unsaid for me. Against the threats
Of malice or of sorcery, or that power
Which erring men call Chance, this I hold firm :
Virtue may be assailed, but never hurt,
Surprised by unjust force, but not enthralled;   590
Yea, even that which Mischief meant most harm
Shall in the happy trial prove most glory.
But evil on itself shall back recoil,
And mix no more with goodness, when at last,
Gathered like scum, and settled to itself,   595
It shall be in eternal restless change
Self-fed, and self-consumed. If this fail,
The pillared firmament is rottenness,
And earth's base built on stubble. But come, let's on !
Against the opposing will and arm of Heaven   600
May never this just sword be lifted up;
But for that damned magician, let him be girt
With all the grisly legions that troop
Under the sooty flag of Acheron,
Harpies and Hydras, or all the monstrous forms   605
'Twixt Africa and Ind, I'll find him out,
And force him to return his purchase back,
Or drag him by the curls to a foul death,
Cursed as his life.
    Spir.   Alas ! good venturous youth,
I love thy courage yet, and bold emprise ;   610
But here thy sword can do thee little stead.
Far other arms and other weapons must
Be those that quell the might of hellish charms.
He with his bare wand can unthread thy joints,
And crumble all thy sinews.

Eld. Bro. Why, prithee, Shepherd, 615
How durst thou then thyself approach so near
As to make this relation?
Spir. Care and utmost shifts
How to secure the Lady from surprisal
Brought to my mind a certain shepherd-lad,
Of small regard to see to, yet well skilled 620
In every virtuous plant and healing herb
That spreads her verdant leaf to the morning ray.
He loved me well, and oft would beg me sing;
Which when I did, he on the tender grass
Would sit, and hearken e'en to ecstasy, 625
And in requital ope his leathern scrip,
And show me simples of a thousand names,
Telling their strange and vigorous faculties.
Amongst the rest a small unsightly root,
But of divine effect, he culled me out. 630
The leaf was darkish, and had prickles on it,
But in another country, as he said,
Bore a bright golden flower, but not in this soil,
Unknown, and like esteemed, and the dull swain
Treads on it daily with his clouted shoon; 635
And yet more med'cinal is it than that Moly
That Hermes once to wise Ulysses gave.
He called it Hæmony, and gave it me,
And bade me keep it as of sovereign use
'Gainst all enchantments, mildew blast or damp, 640
Or ghastly Furies' apparitiön.
I pursed it up, but little reckoning made,
Till now that this extremity compelled.
But now I find it true; for by this means
I knew the foul enchanter, though disguised, 645
Entered the very lime-twigs of his spells,

And yet came off. If you have this about you
(As I will give you when we go), you may
Boldly assault the necromancer's hall ;
Where if he be, with dauntless hardihood   650
And brandished blade rush on him, break his glass,
And shed the luscious liquor on the ground ;
But seize his wand. Though he and his curst crew
Fierce sign of battle make, and menace high,
Or, like the sons of Vulcan, vomit smoke,   655
Yet will they soon retire, if he but shrink.
    Eld. Bro. Thyrsis, lead on apace ; I'll follow thee ;
And some good angel bear a shield before us !

The Scene changes to a stately palace, set out with all manner of deliciousness : soft music, tables spread with all dainties. COMUS *appears with his rabble, and the* LADY *set in an enchanted chair, to whom he offers his glass, which she puts by, and goes about to rise.*

    Comus. Nay, Lady, sit. If I but wave this wand,
Your nerves are all chained up in alabaster,   660
And you a statue, or as Daphne was,
Root-bound, that fled Apollo.
    Lady.   Fool, do not boast.
Thou canst not touch the freedom of my mind
With all thy charms, although this corporal rind
Thou hast immanacled, while Heaven sees good.   665
    Comus. Why are you vext, Lady? why do you frown?
Here dwell no frowns, nor anger ; from these gates
Sorrow flies far. See, here be all the pleasures
That fancy can beget on youthful thoughts,
When the fresh blood grows lively, and returns   670

Brisk as the April buds in primrose season.
And first behold this cordial julep here,
That flames and dances in his crystal bounds,
With spirits of balm and fragrant syrups mixed.
Not that Nepenthes, which the wife of Thone   675
In Egypt gave to Jove-born Helena,
Is of such power to stir up joy as this,
To life so friendly, or so cool to thirst.
Why should you be so cruel to yourself,
And to those dainty limbs which Nature lent   680
For gentle usage and soft delicacy?
But you invert the covenants of her trust,
And harshly deal, like an ill borrower,
With that which you received on other terms,
Scorning the unexempt conditiön   685
By which all mortal frailty must subsist,
Refreshment after toil, ease after pain,
That have been tired all day without repast,
And timely rest have wanted. But, fair virgin,
This will restore all soon.

   Lady.   'Twill not, false traitor!   690
'Twill not restore the truth and honesty
That thou hast banished from thy tongue with lies.
Was this the cottage and the safe abode
Thou told'st me of? What grim aspects are these,
These oughly-headed monsters? Mercy guard me!   695
Hence with thy brewed enchantments, foul deceiver!
Hast thou betrayed my credulous innocence
With vizored falsehood and base forgery?
And wouldst thou seek again to trap me here
With liquorish baits, fit to ensnare a brute?   700
Were it a draught for Juno when she banquets,
I would not taste thy treasonous offer. None

But such as are good men can give good things;
And that which is not good is not delicious
To a well-governed and wise appetite. 705
Comus. O foolishness of men! that lend their ears
To those budge doctors of the Stoic fur,
And fetch their precepts from the Cynic tub,
Praising the lean and sallow Abstinence!
Wherefore did Nature pour her bounties forth 710
With such a full and unwithdrawing hand,
Covering the earth with odours, fruits, and flocks,
Thronging the seas with spawn innumerable,
But all to please and sate the curious taste?
And set to work millions of spinning worms, 715
That in their green shops weave the smooth-haired silk,
To deck her sons; and that no corner might
Be vacant of her plenty, in her own loins
She hutched the all-worshiped ore and precious gems,
To store her children with. If all the world 720
Should, in a pet of temperance, feed on pulse,
Drink the clear stream, and nothing wear but frieze,
The All-giver would be unthanked, would be unpraised,
Not half his riches known, and yet despised;
And we should serve him as a grudging master, 725
As a penurious niggard of his wealth,
And live like Nature's bastards, not her sons,
Who would be quite surcharged with her own weight,
And strangled with her waste fertility;
The earth cumbered, and the winged air darked with
    plumes, 730
The herds would over-multitude their lords;
The sea o'erfraught would swell, and the unsought diamonds
Would so emblaze the forehead of the deep,
And so bestud with stars, that they below

Would grow inured to light, and come at last 735
To gaze upon the sun with shameless brows.
List, Lady; be not coy, and be not cozened
With that same vaunted name, Virginity.
Beauty is Nature's coin; must not be hoarded,
But must be current; and the good thereof 740
Consists in mutual and partaken bliss,
Unsavoury in the enjoyment of itself.
If you let slip time, like a neglected rose
It withers on the stalk with languished head.
Beauty is Nature's brag, and must be shown 745
In courts, at feasts, and high solemnities,
Where most may wonder at the workmanship.
It is for homely features to keep home;
They had their name thence; coarse complexions
And cheeks of sorry grain will serve to ply 750
The sampler, and to tease the huswife's wool.
What need a vermeil-tinctured lip for that,
Love-darting eyes, or tresses like the morn?
There was another meaning in these gifts;
Think what, and be advised; you are but young yet. 755
  Lady. I had not thought to have unlocked my lips
In this unhallowed air, but that this juggler
Would think to charm my judgment, as mine eyes,
Obtruding false rules pranked in reason's garb.
I hate when vice can bolt her arguments, 760
And virtue has no tongue to check her pride.
Impostor! do not charge most innocent Nature,
As if she would her children should be riotous
With her abundance. She, good cateress,
Means her provision only to the good, 765
That live according to her sober laws,
And holy dictate of spare Temperance.

If every just man, that now pines with want,
Had but a moderate and beseeming share
Of that which lewdly-pampered Luxury 770
Now heaps upon some few with vast excess,
Nature's full blessings would be well dispensed
In unsuperfluous even proportiön,
And she no whit encumbered with her store;
And then the Giver would be better thanked, 775
His praise due paid: for swinish Gluttony
Ne'er looks to Heaven amidst his gorgeous feast,
But with besotted base ingratitude
Crams, and blasphemes his Feeder. Shall I go on?
Or have I said enow? To him that dares 780
Arm his profane tongue with contemptuous words
Against the sun-clad power of Chastity,
Fain would I something say;—yet to what end?
Thou hast nor ear, nor soul, to apprehend
The sublime notion and high mystery 785
That must be uttered to unfold the sage
And serious doctrine of Virginity;
And thou art worthy that thou shouldst not know
More happiness than this thy present lot.
Enjoy your dear wit, and gay rhetoric, 790
That hath so well been taught her dazzling fence;
Thou art not fit to hear thyself convinced.
Yet should I try, the uncontrollèd worth
Of this pure cause would kindle my rapt spirits
To such a flame of sacred vehemence, 795
That dumb things would be moved to sympathize,
And the brute Earth would lend her nerves, and shake,
Till all thy magic structures, reared so high,
Were shattered into heaps o'er thy false head.
    Comus. She fables not. I feel that I do fear 800

Her words set off by some superior power;
And, though not mortal, yet a cold shuddering dew
Dips me all o'er, as when the wrath of Jove
Speaks thunder and the chains of Erebus
To some of Saturn's crew. I must dissemble,   805
And try her yet more strongly.— Come, no more!
This is mere moral babble, and direct
Against the canon-laws of our foundation.
I must not suffer this; yet 'tis but the lees
And settlings of a melancholy blood.   810
But this will cure all straight; one sip of this
Will bathe the drooping spirits in delight
Beyond the bliss of dreams. Be wise, and taste.

The BROTHERS *rush in with swords drawn, wrest his glass out of his hand, and break it against the ground; his rout make sign of resistance, but are all driven in. The* ATTENDANT SPIRIT *comes in.*

 Spir. What! have you let the false enchanter scape?
Oh, ye mistook; ye should have snatched his wand,   815
And bound him fast. Without his rod reversed,
And backward mutters of dissevering power,
We cannot free the Lady that sits here
In stony fetters fixed, and motionless.
Yet stay: be not disturbed; now I bethink me,   820
Some other means I have which may be used,
Which once of Melibœus old I learnt,
The soothest shepherd that e'er piped on plains.
 There is a gentle nymph not far from hence,
That with moist curb sways the smooth Severn stream: 825
Sabrina is her name: a virgin pure;

Whilom she was the daughter of Locrine,
That had the sceptre from his father Brute.
She, guiltless damsel, flying the mad pursuit
Of her enragèd stepdame, Guendolen,   830
Commended her fair innocence to the flood,
That stayed her flight with his cross-flowing course.
The water-nymphs, that in the bottom played,
Held up their pearlèd wrists, and took her in,
Bearing her straight to aged Nereus' hall;   835
Who, piteous of her woes, reared her lank head,
And gave her to his daughters to imbathe
In nectared lavers strewed with asphodil,
And through the porch and inlet of each sense
Dropt in ambrosial oils, till she revived,   840
And underwent a quick immortal change,
Made Goddess of the river. Still she retains
Her maiden gentleness, and oft at eve
Visits the herds along the twilight meadows,
Helping all urchin blasts, and ill-luck signs   845
That the shrewd meddling elf delights to make,
Which she with precious vialed liquors heals;
For which the shepherds at their festivals
Carol her goodness loud in rustic lays,
And throw sweet garland wreaths into her stream 850
Of pansies, pinks, and gaudy daffodils.
And, as the old swain said, she can unlock
The clasping charm, and thaw the numbing spell,
If she be right invoked in warbled song;
For maidenhood she loves, and will be swift   855
To aid a virgin, such as was herself,
In hard-besetting need. This will I try,
And add the power of some adjuring verse.

Song.

Sabrina fair,
    Listen where thou art sitting   860
Under the glassy, cool, translucent wave,
    In twisted braids of lilies knitting
The loose train of thy amber-dropping hair;
    Listen for dear honour's sake,
    Goddess of the silver lake,   865
        Listen and save!

Listen and appear to us,
In name of great Oceanus.
By the earth-shaking Neptune's mace,
And Tethy's grave majestic pace;   870
By hoary Nereus' wrinkled look,
And the Carpathian wizard's hook;
By scaly Triton's winding shell,
And old soothsaying Glaucus' spell;
By Leucothea's lovely hands,   875
And her son that rules the strands;
By Thetis' tinsel-slippered feet,
And the songs of Sirens sweet;
By dead Parthenope's dear tomb,
And fair Ligea's golden comb,   880
Wherewith she sits on diamond rocks,
Sleeking her soft alluring locks;
By all the nymphs that nightly dance
Upon thy streams with wily glance;
Rise, rise, and heave thy rosy head   885
From thy coral-paven bed,
And bridle in thy headlong wave,
Till thou our summons answered have.
        Listen and save!

SABRINA *rises, attended by water-nymphs, and sings.*

<blockquote>

By the rushy-fringèd bank, 890
Where grows the willow and the osier dank,
  My sliding chariot stays,
Thick set with agate, and the azurn sheen
Of turkis blue, and emerald green,
  That in the channel strays; 895
Whilst, from off the waters fleet,
Thus I set my printless feet
O'er the cowslip's velvet head,
  That bends not as I tread.
Gentle swain, at thy request 900
  I am here!
  Spir. Goddess dear,
We implore thy powerful hand
To undo the charmèd band
Of true virgin here distrest 905
Through the force and through the wile
Of unblest enchanter vile.
  Sabr. Shepherd, 'tis my office blest
To help ensnarèd chastity.
Brightest Lady, look on me. 910
Thus I sprinkle on thy breast
Drops that from my fountain pure
I have kept of precious cure;
Thrice upon thy finger's tip,
Thrice upon thy rubied lip; 915
Next this marble venomed seat,
Smeared with gums of glutinous heat,
I touch with chaste palms moist and cold.
Now the spell hath lost his hold;
And I must haste ere morning hour 920
To wait in Amphitrite's bower.

</blockquote>

SABRINA *descends, and the* LADY *rises out of her seat.*

    Spir. Virgin, daughter of Locrine,
Sprung of old Anchises' line,
May thy brimmèd waves for this
Their full tribute never miss   925
From a thousand petty rills,
That tumble down the snowy hills;
Summer drouth, or singèd air
Never scorch thy tresses fair,
Nor wet October's torrent flood   930
Thy molten crystal fill with mud;
May thy billows roll ashore
The beryl, and the golden ore;
May thy lofty head be crowned
With many a tower and terrace round,   935
And here and there thy banks upon
With groves of myrrh and cinnamon.
    Come, Lady; while Heaven lends us grace,
Let us fly this cursed place,
Lest the sorcerer us entice   940
With some other new device.
Not a waste or needless sound,
Till we come to holier ground.
I shall be your faithful guide
Through this gloomy covert wide;   945
And not many furlongs thence
Is your Father's residence,
Where this night are met in state
Many a friend to gratulate
His wished presence, and beside   950
All the swains that there abide
With jigs, and rural dance resort.

We shall catch them at their sport,
And our sudden coming there
Will double all their mirth and cheer. 955
Come, let us haste; the stars grow high,
But Night sits monarch yet in the mid-sky.

The Scene changes, presenting Ludlow town and the President's castle; then come in country dancers; after them the ATTENDANT SPIRIT, *with the* TWO BROTHERS *and the* LADY.

Song.

Spir. Back, shepherds, back! enough your play,
Till next sunshine holiday.
Here be, without duck or nod, 960
Other trippings to be trod
Of lighter toes, and such court-guise
As Mercury did first devise
With the mincing Dryades
On the lawns and on the leas. 965

This second Song presents them to their Father and Mother.

Noble Lord, and Lady bright,
I have brought ye new delight.
Here behold so goodly grown
Three fair branches of your own.
Heaven hath timely tried their youth, 970
Their faith, their patience, and their truth,
And sent them here through hard assays
With a crown of deathless praise,
To triumph in victorious dance
O'er sensual folly and intemperance. 975

The dances ended, the SPIRIT *epiloguizes.*

Spir. To the ocean now I fly,
And those happy climes that lie
Where day never shuts his eye,
Up in the broad fields of the sky.
There I suck the liquid air, 980
All amidst the gardens fair
Of Hesperus, and his daughters three
That sing about the golden tree.
Along the crispèd shades and bowers
Revels the spruce and jocund Spring; 985
The Graces and the rosy-bosomed Hours
Thither all their bounties bring.
There eternal Summer dwells,
And west-winds with musky wing
About the cedarn alleys fling 990
Nard and cassia's balmy smells.
Iris there with humid bow
Waters the odorous banks, that blow
Flowers of more mingled hue
Than her purfled scarf can shew, 995
And drenches with Elysian dew
(List, mortals, if your ears be true)
Beds of hyacinth and roses,
Where young Adonis oft reposes,
Waxing well of his deep wound, 1000
In slumber soft, and on the ground
Sadly sits the Assyrian queen.
But far above, in spangled sheen,
Celestial Cupid, her famed son, advanced
Holds his dear Psyche, sweet entranced 1005
After her wandering labours long,

Till free consent the gods among
Make her his eternal bride,
And from her fair unspotted side
Two blissful twins are to be born, 1010
Youth and Joy; so Jove hath sworn.

But now my task is smoothly done,
I can fly, or I can run
Quickly to the green earth's end,
Where the bowed welkin slow doth bend, 1015
And from thence can soar as soon
To the corners of the moon.

Mortals, that would follow me,
Love Virtue; she alone is free.
She can teach ye how to climb 1020
Higher than the sphery chime;
Or, if Virtue feeble were,
Heaven itself would stoop to her.

LYCIDAS

THE poem of Lycidas was occasioned by the death of Milton's College friend, Edward King, son of Sir John King, Knight, Privy Councillor for Ireland, and Secretary to the Irish Government. King was admitted on the 9th of June, 1626, at the age of fourteen, to Christ's College, Cambridge, about sixteen months after Milton's admission. Milton left College after receiving his Master's degree in July, 1632; so that at this date, he and King had been at College together about six years. King was made a Fellow of his College in June, 1630, in conformity with a royal mandate, secured, it may have been, through Sir John's influence at court, due to his official position. He had also been Privy Councillor for the Kingdom of Ireland, to their majesties, Elizabeth and James.

Milton's claim, as a scholar, to the Fellowship must have been far superior to King's, and he was ahead of him in his College course. But Fellowships went a good deal by political and ecclesiastical influence; and, furthermore, it is not likely that Milton would have accepted a Fellowship at the time, if it had been offered to him, involving, as it did, the taking of orders, against which Milton's mind must already at that time have been decided, though he had been sent to the University with the Church in view.

King received his Master's degree in July, 1633, and continued his connection with the College as fellow, tutor, and, in 1634-35, as 'prælector.' He was noted for his amiability and purity of character and genuine piety; and Milton was probably drawn to him more by these qualities than by his intellectual and poetical abilities. He left numerous Latin compositions (published in various collections), which, according to Masson, have no remarkable poetical merit. But their subjects, all, with one exception, royal occasions, did not afford opportunities for the display of poetic genius, — the birth of the Princess Mary, the king's recovery from the smallpox, the king's safe return from Scotland, July, 1633, commendatory iambics prefixed to a Latin comedy, *Senile Odium*, performed in Queen's College, the birth of Prince James, Duke of York, the birth of the Princess Elizabeth, and the birth of the Princess Anne.

King was preparing himself for the Church; and it may be inferred from Milton's poem that he regarded him as worthy, in an eminent degree, to discharge the responsible duties of a Christian minister.

In the Long Vacation of 1637, King set out to visit his family and friends in Ireland. He embarked at Chester for Dublin. When but a short distance from the Welsh coast, the weather being at the time, as appears from Milton's poem, perfectly calm, the ship (it is alluded to as a 'fatal and perfidious bark') struck on a rock and soon went down, only a few of the passengers being rescued.

A volume of 'In Memoriam' poems, by members of different Colleges of the University, and others, twenty in Latin, three in Greek, and thirteen in English, was printed at the University Press and published early in the following year (1638). The Latin and Greek part of the volume bore the title, 'Justa Edovardo King naufrago, ab amicis mœrentibus, amoris et μνείας χάριν. *Si recte calculum ponas, ubique naufragium est.* Petron. Arb. Cantabrigiæ, apud Thomam Buck et Rogerum Daniel, celeberrimæ Academiæ typographos. 1638.'

The English part bore the title, 'Obsequies to the memorie of Mr. Edward King, Anno Dom. 1638. Printed by Th.

Buck and R. Daniel, printers to the Vniversitie of Cambridge, 1638.'

Prefixed to the volume is a brief Latin inscriptive panegyric, in which King's last moments are described: 'haud procul a littore Britannico, navi in scopulum allisa et rimis ex ictu fatiscente, dum alii vectores vitæ mortalis frustra satagerent, immortalem anhelans in genu provolutus oransque una cum navigio ab aquis absorptus, animam deo reddidit iiii eid. Sextilis anno Salutis MDCXXXVII, Ætatis xxv.'

The extracts given by Masson, from the English poems, have no poetic merit, nor merit of any kind, being clumsy tissues of far-fetched, cold-blooded conceits, of which the following, from three of the contributions, are not unfair specimens. There could not have been an excess of poetical ability in the University at the time.

> ' I am no poet here ; my pen's the spout
> Where the rain-water of my eyes runs out.
> In pity of that name whose fate we see
> Thus copied out in grief's Hydrographie.'

> 'Since first the waters gave
> A blessing to him which the soul did save,
> They loved the holy body still too much,
> And would regain some virtue from a touch.'

> ' Weep forth your tears, then ; pour out all your tide ;
> All waters are pernicious since King died.'

The writers must all have sat at the feet and learned of John Donne, whose coldly ingenious conceits had for some time been passing for poetry.

Milton might well lament, in the person of his bereaved shepherd, the sad decline of poetry, since the Elizabethan days.

'Alas! what boots it with uncessant care
To tend the homely, slighted, shepherd's trade,
And strictly meditate the thankless Muse?
Were it not better done, as others use,
To sport with Amaryllis in the shade,
Or with the tangles of Neæra's hair?'

Milton's poem comes last in the collection, without title, and with simply the initials I. M. appended. It presents a strange contrast to the worthless productions which precede it. Unless the other writers' poetic appreciation was very far in advance of their poetic power, as exhibited in their several contributions, they could have had but little appreciation of the merits of Milton's poem. There is no reason for supposing that King's death caused Milton a deep personal grief, such as that which was caused by the death of Charles Diodati, and to which the *Epitaphium Damonis* bears testimony.

Milton had no doubt cherished for King a deep regard, as one exceptionally fitted, by his purity of character, and sincere piety, for the sacred office. And the presentation, in his elegiac ode, of these qualities, afforded an occasion for giving an expression to what was evidently a greater grief to him than the death of his College friend, namely, the condition of the Church, which he regarded as corrupt in itself, and as in league with the despotic tendencies of the political power. All the 'higher strains' of the ode are inspired by a holy indignation toward the time-serving ecclesiastics, whose unworthiness, as shepherds of Christ's flock, he sets forth in the burning denunciations attributed to St. Peter, as the type of true episcopal power, — denunciations which are prophetic of those he is destined to pronounce in a few years, in his polemic prose works, against the more developed ecclesiastical and political abuses of the time, as one specially commissioned by God, so to do, in the words delivered to the prophet: 'Cry aloud, spare not, lift up thy voice like a trumpet, and declare unto my people their transgression, and to the house of Jacob their sins.'

When the poem was republished with the author's full name, in 1645, it had the following heading: 'In this Monody the author bewails a learned friend, unfortunately drowned in his passage from Chester on the Irish seas, 1637; and, by occasion, foretells the ruin of our corrupted Clergy, then in their height.'

This heading would, no doubt, have caused the rejection of the poem by the Cambridge authorities. Milton's hostility to the hierarchy of England was little suspected then: he was no doubt regarded as a loyal and dutiful son of his *Alma Mater*, and, besides, it is not likely that the several contributions to the King Memorial were looked into very closely by the Committee of Examination.

The death of the Shepherd Lycidas is made to image forth the death of a pure priesthood. It is possible that Milton may have seen an etymological significance in the name Lycidas (which the philology of the present day would not admit) and which caused him to adopt the name as bearing upon the ecclesiastical import of the poem. The name for him may have signified a *wolf-seer*, to look out for the wolf being one of the most important duties of the shepherd who has the care of the sheep and of the spiritual shepherd or pastor who watches over Christ's flock.

'The pilot of the Galilean lake,' St. Peter, 'the type and head of true episcopal power,' is introduced among the mourners of the death of King, denouncing the lewd hirelings of the priesthood of the time.

> 'How well could I have spared for thee, young swain,
> Know of such as, for their bellies' sake,
> Creep, and intrude, and climb into the fold !
> Of other care they little reckoning make
> Than how to scramble at the shearers' feast,
> And shove away the worthy bidden guest.
> Blind mouths ! that scarce themselves know how to hold
> A sheep-hook, or have learnt aught else the least
> That to the faithful herdman's art belongs !
> What recks it them? What need they? They are sped ;
> And, when they list, their lean and flashy songs
> Grate on their scrannel pipes of wretched straw ;
> The hungry sheep look up, and are not fed,
> But, swoln with wind and the rank mist they draw,
> Rot inwardly, and foul contagion spread ;
> Besides what the grim wolf with privy paw
> Daily devours apace, and nothing said.
> But that two-handed engine at the door
> Stands ready to smite once, and smite no more.'

The two last verses some commentators have explained as a prophecy of the execution of Archbishop Laud, which took place on the 10th of January, 1644, six years after the publication of 'Lycidas.' Warton thus paraphrases the lines: 'But there will soon be an end of all these evils; the axe is at hand, to take off the head of him who has been the great abettor of these corruptions of the gospel. This will be done by one stroke.'

If this is the meaning of the passage, it was certainly a very remarkable prophecy, when it was written, for the king and the archbishop were then at the height of their power, and there was little or nothing to indicate its overthrow.

The passage admits of a more probable explanation. The

two-handed engine, the epithet 'two-handed' meaning that its length and weight required it to be grasped with both hands, refers to the sword of St. Michael, the guardian and protector of the Church. In the 6th Book of the ' Paradise Lost ' (vv. 250 -253) it is said of the sword of Michael that it

> ' Smote and felled
> Squadrons at once ; with huge two-handed sway
> Brandished aloft, the horrid edge came down
> Wide-wasting. '

The poet in this passage therefore means to say that St. Michael's sword is to smite off the head of Satan, who, at the door of Christ's fold, is, ' with privy paw,' daily devouring the hungry sheep.

In a sublime invocation to the Son of God, at the conclusion of the fourth section of ' Animadversions upon the Remonstrant's Defence against Smectymnuus,' Milton says : ' As thou didst dignify our fathers' days with many revelations above all the foregoing ages, since thou tookest the flesh, so thou canst vouchsafe to us (though unworthy) as large a portion of thy spirit as thou pleasest ; for who shall prejudice thy all-governing will? Seeing the power of thy grace is not passed away with the primitive times, as fond and faithless men imagine, but thy kingdom is now at hand, and thou *standing at the door*. Come forth out of thy royal chambers, O Prince of all the kings of the earth ! put on the visible robes of thy imperial majesty, take up that unlimited sceptre which thy Almighty Father hath bequeathed thee ; for now the voice of thy bride calls thee, and all creatures sigh to be renewed.'

The view taken is strengthened by another disputed passage of the poem, a few verses farther on. The poet is addressing his drowned friend, whose body he imagines to be tossed about by the waves (vv. 154-163) :

> ' Ay me ! whilst thee the shores and sounding seas
> Wash far away, where'er thy bones are hurled;
> Whether beyond the stormy Hebrides,
> Where thou perhaps under the whelming tide
> Visitest the bottom of the monstrous world;
> Or whether thou, to our moist vows denied,
> Sleep'st by the fable of Bellerus old,
> Where the great Vision of the guarded mount
> Looks toward Namancos and Bayona's hold,
> Look homeward, Angel, now, and melt with ruth.'

By 'the fable of Bellerus old,' is meant St. Michael's Mount at the Land's End in Cornwall, anciently named Bellerium, from Bellerus, a Cornish giant, where the Vision of St. Michael was, by the old fable, represented to sit, looking toward far Namancos and the hold of Spanish Bayona.

Much of the deeper meaning of the poem centres in the three last verses of the passage quoted:

> ' Where the great Vision of the guarded mount
> Looks toward Namancos and Bayona's hold,
> Look homeward, Angel, now, and melt with ruth.'

The annotators say nothing, so far as I know, about the application of the great Vision of the guarded mount to the ecclesiastical meaning of the poem. The meaning I take to be this: in making the Archangel Michael, the guardian and defender of the Church of Christ, look toward Namancos and Bayona's hold, *i.e.* toward Spain, the great stronghold, at the time, of Papacy, and which, in the reign of Elizabeth, had threatened England with invasion and with the imposition of the Roman Catholic religion, the poet would evidently imply the Archangel's watchfulness over the Church against foreign foes. But the danger is not from *without* (this I take to be the idea shadowed forth), the danger is not from without — it lies *within* the Church. Milton, or rather 'Milton transformed in his imagination, for the time, into a poetic shepherd,' therefore says :

'Look homeward, Angel, now, and melt with ruth.'

Lycidas, who is made to represent, allegorically, the good shepherd that careth for the sheep and looketh out for the wolf, is *dead;* and the lewd hirelings who, for their bellies' sake, have crept into the fold, and to whom the hungry sheep look up and are not fed, have themselves become grim wolves, and with privy paw seize upon and devour the flock.

'Lycidas' was the last of Milton's poems produced during his residence under his father's roof at Horton, in Buckinghamshire. He set out soon after on his continental tour. Perhaps the 'fresh woods and pastures new,' in the last verse of the poem, refers to this contemplated tour. On his return to his native land, he had to bid farewell, a long farewell, to the loved haunts of the Muses, and gird himself to fight the battle of civil and religious liberty.

>Yet once more, O ye laurels, and once more,
>Ye myrtles brown, with ivy never sere,
>I come to pluck your berries harsh and crude,
>And with forced fingers rude
>Shatter your leaves before the mellowing year.   5
>Bitter constraint and sad occasion dear
>Compels me to disturb your season due ;
>For Lycidas is dead, dead ere his prime,
>Young Lycidas, and hath not left his peer.
>Who would not sing for Lycidas? He knew   10
>Himself to sing and build the lofty rhyme.
>He must not float upon his watery bier

Unwept, and welter to the parching wind,
Without the meed of some melodious tear.
    Begin, then, Sisters of the sacred well   15
That from beneath the seat of Jove doth spring;
Begin, and somewhat loudly sweep the string.
Hence with denial vain and coy excuse —
So may some gentle Muse
With lucky words favour *my* destined urn,   20
And as he passes turn,
And bid fair peace be to my sable shroud —
For we were nursed upon the self-same hill,
Fed the same flock, by fountain, shade, and rill;
Together both, ere the high lawns appeared   25
Under the opening eyelids of the Morn,
We drove a-field, and both together heard
What time the grey-fly winds her sultry horn,
Battening our flocks with the fresh dews of night,
Oft till the star that rose at evening, bright,   30
Toward heaven's descent had sloped his westering wheel.
Meanwhile the rural ditties were not mute,
Tempered to the oaten flute;
Rough Satyrs danced, and Fauns with cloven heel
From the glad sound would not be absent long;   35
And old Damœtas loved to hear our song.
    But, oh! the heavy change, now thou art gone,
Now thou art gone and never must return!
Thee, Shepherd, thee the woods, and desert caves
With wild thyme and the gadding vine o'ergrown,   40
And all their echoes, mourn.
The willows, and the hazel copses green,
Shall now no more be seen
Fanning their joyous leaves to thy soft lays.
As killing as the canker to the rose,   45

Or taint-worm to the weanling herds that graze,
Or frost to flowers, that their gay wardrobe wear,
When first the white-thorn blows;
Such, Lycidas, thy loss to shepherd's ear.
    Where were ye, Nymphs, when the remorseless deep   50
Closed o'er the head of your loved Lycidas?
For neither were ye playing on the steep
Where your old bards, the famous Druids, lie,
Nor on the shaggy top of Mona high,
Nor yet where Deva spreads her wizard stream.   55
Ay me! I fondly dream
' Had ye been there,' . . . for what could that have done?
What could the Muse herself that Orpheus bore,
The Muse herself, for her enchanting son,
Whom universal nature did lament,   60
When, by the rout that made the hideous roar,
His gory visage down the stream was sent,
Down the swift Hebrus to the Lesbian shore?
Alas! what boots it with uncessant care
To tend the homely, slighted, shepherd's trade,   65
And strictly meditate the thankless Muse?
Were it not better done, as others use,
To sport with Amaryllis in the shade,
Or with the tangles of Neæra's hair?
Fame is the spur that the clear spirit doth raise   70
(That last infirmity of noble mind)
To scorn delights and live laborious days;
But, the fair guerdon when we hope to find,
And think to burst out into sudden blaze,
Comes the blind Fury with the abhorrèd shears,   75
And slits the thin-spun life. But not the praise,'
Phœbus replied, and touched my trembling ears:
' Fame is no plant that grows on mortal soil,

Nor in the glistering foil
Set off to the world, nor in broad rumour lies, 80
But lives and spreads aloft by those pure eyes
And perfect witness of all-judging Jove;
As he pronounces lastly on each deed,
Of so much fame in heaven expect thy meed.'
O fountain Arethuse, and thou honoured flood, 85
Smooth-sliding Mincius, crowned with vocal reeds,
That strain I heard was of a higher mood.
But now my oat proceeds,
And listens to the Herald of the Sea,
That came in Neptune's plea. 90
He asked the waves, and asked the felon winds,
What hard mishap hath doomed this gentle swain?
And questioned every gust of rugged wings
That blows from off each beakèd promontory.
They knew not of his story; 95
And sage Hippotades their answer brings,
That not a blast was from his dungeon strayed:
The air was calm, and on the level brine
Sleek Panope with all her sisters played.
It was that fatal and perfidious bark, 100
Built in the eclipse, and rigged with curses dark,
That sunk so low that sacred head of thine.
    Next, Camus, reverend sire, went footing slow,
His mantle hairy, and his bonnet sedge,
Inwrought with figures dim, and on the edge 105
Like to that sanguine flower inscribed with woe.
'Ah! who has reft,' quoth he, ' my dearest pledge?'
Last came, and last did go,
The Pilot of the Galilean Lake;
Two massy keys he bore of metals twain 110
(The golden opes, the iron shuts amain).

There entertain him all the Saints above,
In solemn troops, and sweet societies,
That sing, and singing in their glory move, 180
And wipe the tears for ever from his eyes.
Now, Lycidas, the shepherds weep no more;
Henceforth thou art the genius of the shore,
In thy large recompense, and shalt be good
To all that wander in that perilous flood. 185

   Thus sang the uncouth swain to the oaks and rills,
While the still morn went out with sandals grey:
He touched the tender stops of various quills,
With eager thought warbling his Doric lay:
And now the sun had stretched out all the hills, 190
And now was dropt into the western bay.
At last he rose, and twitched his mantle blue;
To-morrow to fresh woods, and pastures new.

SAMSON AGONISTES

A DRAMATIC POEM

THE AUTHOR
JOHN MILTON

Aristot. Poet. Cap. 6.

Τραγῳδία μίμησις πράξεως σπουδαίας, etc.

Tragœdia est imitatio actionis seriæ, etc., per misericordiam et metum perficiens talium affectuum lustrationem.

SAMSON AGONISTES

'The intensest utterance of the most intense of English Poets'

IN his ' Reason of Church Government urged against Prelaty,' Milton makes the following remarkable allegorical application of the story of Samson to a king and his prelates. It is contained in ' THE CONCLUSION. *The Mischief that Prelaty does to the State* ' :

' I shall shew briefly, ere I conclude, that the prelates, as they are to the subjects a calamity, so are they the greatest underminers and betrayers of the monarch, to whom they seem to be most favourable. I cannot better liken the state and person of a king than to that mighty Nazarite Samson; who being disciplined from his birth in the precepts and the practice of temperance and sobriety, without the strong drink of injurious and excessive desires, grows up to a noble strength and perfection with those his illustrious and sunny locks, the laws, waving and curling about his godlike shoulders. And while he keeps them about him undiminished and unshorn, he may with the jawbone of an ass, that is, with the word of his meanest officer, suppress and put to confusion thousands of those that rise against his just power. But laying down his head among the strumpet flatteries of prelates, while he sleeps and thinks no harm, they wickedly shaving off all those bright and weighty tresses of his law, and just prerogatives, which were his ornament and strength, deliver him over to indirect and violent counsels, which, as those Philistines, put out the fair and far-sighted eyes of his natural discerning, and make him grind in the prison house of their sinister ends and practices upon him ; till he, knowing this prelatical razor to have bereft him of his wonted might, nourish again his puissant hair, the golden beams of law and right; and they, sternly shook, thunder with ruin upon the heads of those his evil counsellors, but not without great affliction to himself. This is the sum of their loyal service to kings; yet these are the men that still cry, The king, the king, the Lord's anointed ! We grant it; and wonder how they came to light upon anything so true; and wonder more, if kings be the Lord's anointed, how they dare thus oil over and besmear so holy an unction with the corrupt and putrid ointment of their base flatteries; which, while they smooth the skin, strike inward and envenom the lifeblood. What fidelity kings can expect from prelates, both examples past, and our present experience of their doings at this day, whereon is grounded all that hath been said, may suffice to inform us. And if they be such clippers of regal power, and shavers of the laws, how they stand affected to the lawgiving parliament, yourselves, worthy peers and commons, can best testify; the current of whose glorious and immortal actions hath been only opposed by the obscure and pernicious designs of the prelates, until their insolence broke out to such a bold affront, as hath justly immured their haughty looks within strong walls.'

'The Reason of Church Government urged against Prelaty' was published in 1641, nearly eight years before Charles I. was beheaded, and just thirty years before the publication of 'Samson Agonistes.' He little dreamed that the reigning king would, in less than eight years, be put to death, and that he should play such a rôle in the subsequent state of things, should have such experiences and such disappointments and sorrows as would make the fortunes of Samson the prototype of a great final creation embodying allegorically his own strangely similar fortunes.

In Milton's MS. jottings of subjects for a tragedy or an epic poem, in the Library of Trinity College, Cambridge, made in 1640 and some time following, and occupying seven pages of folio-sized paper, is included (No. 19 of the list of Old Testament subjects) 'Samson Pursophorus or Hybristes' [*i.e.* Samson the Firebrand-bringer or Violent, as Masson explains], 'or Samson Marrying, or Ramath-Lechi : Judges xv.'

Nothing, of course, could have been more remote from Milton's mind than that thirty years after this jotting, his swansong would be given to the world, in which Samson, blind and among the Philistines, would allegorically reflect his own condition, in the last years of his life.

The parallelisms in the fortunes of Samson and Milton have been noticed by almost every editor and every critic of the 'Samson Agonistes.' They are too obvious to escape the notice of the most careless reader who knows anything of the life of Milton. Samson is Milton in the polemic and in the post-Restoration period of his life. In all literature there is not a nobler, more exalting and pathetic egotism, than the 'Samson Agonistes' exhibits — an egotism for which every lover of the great poet must be abundantly thankful. 'How very much,' Walter Savage Landor justly remarks, 'would literature have lost, if this marvellously great and admirable man had omitted the various references to himself and his contemporaries!'

Of the numerous autobiographical passages in the 'Samson Agonistes,' which editors have noted, those most distinctly so are the following: vv. 40, 41; 67–109; 191–193; 219–226; 241–255; 268–276; 563–572; 590–598; 695–702; 760, 761; 1025–1060; 1418–1422; 1461–1471; 1687–1707.

These passages show that the allegorical significance of the 'Samson Agonistes' bears not only upon Milton's individual life and experiences, but also upon the backsliding of the English people, in their restoration of monarchy. The misgivings to which Milton gave expression in his 'Ready and easy way to establish a free commonwealth, and the excellence thereof, compared with the inconveniences and dangers of readmitting kingship in this nation,' were realized in less than three months after its publication late in February or early in March, 1660. Charles II. entered London May 29, 1660. These misgivings are expressed, or, at least, implied, in the following passage of 'The ready and easy way.' The involved construction of the language in this pamphlet shows that it must have been very hastily dictated by the blind poet :

'After our liberty and religion thus prosperously fought for, gained, and many years possessed, except in those unhappy interruptions, which God hath removed ; now that nothing remains, but in all reason the certain hopes of a speedy and immediate settlement for ever in a firm and free commonwealth, for this extolled and magnified nation, regardless both of honour won, or deliverances vouchsafed from heaven, to fall back, or rather to creep back so poorly, *as it seems the multitude would*, to their once abjured and detested thraldom of kingship, to be ourselves the slanderers of our own just and religious deeds, though done by some to covetous and ambitious ends, yet not therefore to be stained with their infamy, or they to asperse the integrity of others ; and yet these now by revolting from the conscience of deeds well done, both in church and state, to throw away and forsake, or rather to betray, a just and noble cause for the mixture of bad men who have ill-managed and abused it (which had our fathers done heretofore, and on the same pretence deserted true religion, what had long ere this become of our gospel, and all protestant reformation so much intermixed with the avarice and ambition of some reformers?), and by thus relapsing, to verify all the bitter predictions of our triumphing enemies, who will now think they wisely discerned and justly censured both us and all our actions as rash, rebellious, hypocritical, and impious ; not only argues a strange, degenerate contagion suddenly spread among us, fitted and prepared for new slavery, but will render us a scorn and derision to all our neighbours.'

OF THAT SORT OF DRAMATIC POEM WHICH IS CALLED TRAGEDY

TRAGEDY, as it was anciently composed, hath been ever held the gravest, moralest, and most profitable of all other poems; therefore said by Aristotle to be of power, by raising pity and fear, or terror, to purge the mind of those and such-like passions, — that is, to temper and reduce them to just measure with a kind of delight, stirred up by reading or seeing those passions well imitated. Nor is Nature wanting in her own effects to make good his assertion; for so, in physic, things of melancholic hue and quality are used against melancholy, sour against sour, salt to remove salt humours. Hence philosophers and other gravest writers, as Cicero, Plutarch, and others, frequently cite out of tragic poets, both to adorn and illustrate their discourse. The Apostle Paul himself thought it not unworthy to insert a verse of Euripides into the text of Holy Scripture, 1 Cor. xv. 33; and Paræus, commenting on the *Revelation*, divides the whole book, as a tragedy, into acts, distinguished each by a chorus of heavenly harpings and song between. Heretofore men in highest dignity have laboured not a little to be thought able to compose a tragedy. Of that honour Dionysius the elder was no less ambitious than before of his attaining to the tyranny. Augustus Cæsar also had begun his *Ajax*, but, unable to please his own judgment with what he had begun, left it unfinished. Seneca, the philosopher, is by some thought the author of those tragedies (at least the best of them) that go under that name. Gregory Nazianzen, a Father of the Church, thought it not unbeseeming the sanctity of his person to write a tragedy, which is entitled 'Christ Suffering.' This is mentioned to vindicate Tragedy from the small esteem, or rather infamy, which in the account of many it undergoes at this day with other common interludes; happening through the poet's error of intermixing comic stuff with tragic sadness and gravity, or introducing trivial and vulgar persons: which by all judicious hath been counted absurd, and brought in without discretion, corruptly to gratify the people. And though ancient Tragedy use no Prologue, yet using sometimes, in case of self-defence or explanation, that which Martial calls an Epistle, in behalf of this tragedy, coming forth after the ancient manner, much different from what among us passes for best, thus much beforehand may be *epistled*, — that Chorus is here introduced after the Greek manner, not ancient only, but modern, and still in use among the Italians. In the modelling therefore of this poem, with good reason, the Ancients and Italians are rather followed, as of much more authority and fame. The measure of verse used in the Chorus is of all sorts, called by the Greeks *monostrophic*, or rather *apolelymenon*, without regard had to strophe, antistrophe, or epode, — which were a kind of stanzas framed only for the music, then used with the Chorus that sung; not essential to the poem, and therefore not material; or, being divided into stanzas or pauses, they may be called *allœostropha*. Division into act and scene, referring chiefly to the stage (to which this work never was intended), is here omitted.

It suffices if the whole drama be found not produced beyond the fifth act. Of the style and uniformity, and that commonly called the plot, whether intricate or explicit, — which is nothing indeed but such economy, or disposition of the fable, as may stand best with verisimilitude and decorum, — they only will best judge who are not unacquainted with Æschylus, Sophocles, and Euripides, the three tragic poets unequalled yet by any, and the best rule to all who endeavour to write Tragedy. The circumscription of time, wherein the whole drama begins and ends, is, according to ancient rule and best example, within the space of twenty-four hours. — *M.*

THE ARGUMENT

Samson, made captive, blind, and now in the prison at Gaza, there to labour as in a common workhouse, on a festival day, in the general cessation from labour, comes forth into the open air, to a place nigh, somewhat retired, there to sit a while and bemoan his condition. Where he happens at length to be visited by certain friends and equals of his tribe, which make the Chorus, who seek to comfort him what they can; then by his old father, Manoa, who endeavours the like, and withal tells him his purpose to procure his liberty by ransom; lastly, that this feast was proclaimed by the Philistines as a day of thanksgiving for their deliverance from the hands of Samson — which yet more troubles him. Manoa then departs to prosecute his endeavour with the Philistian lords for Samson's redemption: who, in the meanwhile, is visited by other persons, and, lastly, by a public officer to require his coming to the feast before the lords and people, to play or show his strength in their presence. He at first refuses, dismissing the public officer with absolute denial to come: at length, persuaded inwardly that this was from God, he yields to go along with him, who came now the second time with great threatenings to fetch him. The Chorus yet remaining on the place, Manoa returns full of joyful hope to procure ere long his son's deliverance; in the midst of which discourse an Ebrew comes in haste, confusedly at first, and afterwards more distinctly, relating the catastrophe — what Samson had done to the Philistines, and by accident to himself; wherewith the Tragedy ends.

THE PERSONS

SAMSON.
MANOA, the Father of Samson.
DALILA, his wife.
HARAPHA, of Gath.
Public Officer.
Messenger.
Chorus of Danites.
   The SCENE, before the Prison in Gaza.

SAMSON AGONISTES

Samson. A little onward lend thy guiding hand
To these dark steps, a little further on;
For yonder bank hath choice of sun or shade.
There I am wont to sit, when any chance
Relieves me from my task of servile toil, 5
Daily in the common prison else enjoined me,
Where I, a prisoner chained, scarce freely draw
The air, imprisoned also, close and damp,
Unwholesome draught. But here I feel amends —
The breath of heaven fresh blowing, pure and sweet, 10
With day-spring born; here leave me to respire.
This day a solemn feast the people hold
To Dagon, their sea-idol, and forbid
Laborious works. Unwillingly this rest
Their superstition yields me; hence with leave 15
Retiring from the popular noise, I seek
This unfrequented place to find some ease —
Ease to the body some, none to the mind
From restless thoughts, that, like a deadly swarm
Of hornets armed, no sooner found alone 20
But rush upon me thronging, and present
Times past, what once I was, and what am now.
Oh, wherefore was my birth from Heaven foretold
Twice by an Angel, who at last, in sight
Of both my parents, all in flames ascended 25
From off the altar where an offering burned,
As in a fiery column charioting
His godlike presence, and from some great act
Or benefit revealed to Abraham's race?

Why was my breeding ordered and prescribed 30
As of a person separate to God,
Designed for great exploits, if I must die
Betrayed, captived, and both my eyes put out,
Made of my enemies the scorn and gaze,
To grind in brazen fetters under task 35
With this heaven-gifted strength? O glorious strength,
Put to the labour of a beast, debased
Lower than bond-slave! Promise was that I
Should Israel from Philistian yoke deliver!
Ask for this great deliverer now, and find him 40
Eyeless, in Gaza, at the mill, with slaves,
Himself in bonds under Philistian yoke.
Yet stay; let me not rashly call in doubt
Divine prediction. What if all foretold
Had been fulfilled but through mine own default? 45
Whom have I to complain of but myself,
Who this high gift of strength committed to me,
In what part lodged, how easily bereft me,
Under the seal of silence could not keep,
But weakly to a woman must reveal it, 50
O'ercome with importunity and tears?
O impotence of mind, in body strong!
But what is strength without a double share
Of wisdom? vast, unwieldy, burdensome,
Proudly secure, yet liable to fall 55
By weakest subtleties; not made to rule,
But to subserve where wisdom bears command.
God, when he gave me strength, to show withal
How slight the gift was, hung it in my hair.
But peace! I must not quarrel with the will 60
Of highest dispensation, which herein
Haply had ends above my reach to know.

Suffices that to me strength is my bane,
And proves the source of all my miseries —
So many, and so huge, that each apart 65
Would ask a life to wail. But chief of all,
O loss of sight, of thee I most complain!
Blind among enemies! Oh worse than chains,
Dungeon, or beggary, or decrepit age!
Light, the prime work of God, to me is extinct, 70
And all her various objects of delight
Annulled, which might in part my grief have eased.
Inferior to the vilest now become
Of man or worm, the vilest here excel me:
They creep, yet see; I, dark in light, exposed 75
To daily fraud, contempt, abuse, and wrong,
Within doors, or without, still as a fool,
In power of others, never in my own —
Scarce half I seem to live, dead more than half.
Oh dark, dark, dark, amid the blaze of noon, 80
Irrecoverably dark, total eclipse
Without all hope of day!
O first created beam, and thou great Word,
'Let there be light, and light was over all,'
Why am I thus bereaved thy prime decree? 85
The sun to me is dark
And silent as the moon,
When she deserts the night,
Hid in her vacant interlunar cave.
Since light so necessary is to life, 90
And almost life itself, if it be true
That light is in the soul,
She all in every part, why was the sight
To such a tender ball as the eye confined,
So obvious and so easy to be quenched, 95

And not, as feeling, through all parts diffused,
That she might look at will through every pore?
Then had I not been thus exiled from light,
As in the land of darkness, yet in light,
To live a life half dead, a living death,   100
And buried; but, oh yet more miserable!
Myself, my sepulchre, a moving grave;
Buried, yet not exempt,
By privilege of death and burial,
From worst of other evils, pains and wrongs;   105
But made hereby obnoxious more
To all the miseries of life,
Life in captivity
Among inhuman foes.
But who are these? for with joint pace I hear   110
The tread of many feet steering this way;
Perhaps my enemies, who come to stare
At my affliction, and perhaps to insult—
Their daily practice to afflict me more.

   Chorus. This, this is he; softly a while;   115
Let us not break in upon him.
Oh change beyond report, thought, or belief!
See how he lies at random, carelessly diffused,
With languished head unpropt,
As one past hope, abandoned,   120
And by himself given over,
In slavish habit, ill-fitted weeds
O'er-worn and soiled.
Or do my eyes misrepresent? Can this be he,
That heroic, that renowned,   125
Irresistible Samson? whom unarmed,
No strength of man, or fiercest wild beast, could withstand;
Who tore the lion, as the lion tears the kid;

Ran on embattled armies clad in iron,
And, weaponless himself, 130
Made arms ridiculous, useless the forgery
Of brazen shield and spear, the hammered cuirass,
Chalybean-tempered steel, and frock of mail
Adamantean proof;
But safest he who stood aloof, 135
When insupportably his foot advanced,
In scorn of their proud arms and warlike tools,
Spurned them to death by troops. The bold Ascalonite
Fled from his lion ramp; old warriors turned
Their plated backs under his heel, 140
Or grovelling soiled their crested helmets in the dust.
Then with what trivial weapon came to hand,
The jaw of a dead ass, his sword of bone,
A thousand foreskins fell, the flower of Palestine,
In Ramath-lechi, famous to this day. 145
Then by main force pulled up, and on his shoulders bore,
The gates of Azza, post and massy bar,
Up to the hill by Hebron, seat of giants old,
No journey of a sabbath-day, and loaded so;
Like whom the Gentiles feign to bear up Heaven. 150
Which shall I first bewail,
Thy bondage or lost sight?
Prison within prison
Inseparably dark.
Thou art become (Oh worst imprisonment!) 155
The dungeon of thyself; thy soul
(Which men enjoying sight oft without cause complain)
Imprisoned now indeed,
In real darkness of the body dwells,
Shut up from outward light 160
To incorporate with gloomy night;

For inward light, alas !
Puts forth no visual beam.
O mirror of our fickle state,
Since man on earth unparalleled, 165
The rarer thy example stands,
By how much from the top of wondrous glory,
Strongest of mortal men,
To lowest pitch of abject fortune thou art fallen.
For him I reckon not in high estate 170
Whom long descent of birth
Or the sphere of fortune raises ;
But thee, whose strength, while virtue was her mate,
Might have subdued the earth,
Universally crowned with highest praises. 175
    Samson. I hear the sound of words ; their sense the air
Dissolves unjointed ere it reach my ear.
    Chorus. He speaks, let us draw nigh. Matchless in might,
The glory late of Israel, now the grief !
We come, thy friends and neighbours not unknown, 180
From Eshtaol and Zora's fruitful vale,
To visit or bewail thee ; or, if better,
Counsel or consolation we may bring,
Salve to thy sores ; apt words have power to swage
The tumours of a troubled mind, 185
And are as balm to festered wounds.
    Samson. Your coming, friends, revives me ; for I learn
Now of my own experience, not by talk,
How counterfeit a coin they are who ' friends '
Bear in their superscription (of the most 190
I would be understood). In prosperous days
They swarm, but in adverse withdraw their head,
Not to be found, though sought. Ye see, O friends,
How many evils have enclosed me round ;

Yet that which was the worst now least afflicts me, 195
Blindness; for had I sight, confused with shame,
How could I once look up, or heave the head,
Who, like a foolish pilot, have shipwracked
My vessel trusted to me from above,
Gloriously rigged; and for a word, a tear, 200
Fool! have divulged the secret gift of God
To a deceitful woman? tell me, friends,
Am I not sung and proverbed for a fool
In every street? do they not say, 'how well
Are come upon him his deserts?' yet why? 205
Immeasurable strength they might behold
In me, of wisdom nothing more than mean.
This with the other should, at least, have paired;
These two, proportioned ill, drove me transverse.
  Chorus. Tax not divine disposal. Wisest men 210
Have erred, and by bad women been deceived;
And shall again, pretend they ne'er so wise.
Deject not, then, so overmuch thyself,
Who hast of sorrow thy full load besides.
Yet, truth to say, I oft have heard men wonder 215
Why thou shouldst wed Philistian women rather
Than of thine own tribe fairer, or as fair,
At least of thy own nation, and as noble.
  Samson. The first I saw at Timna, and she pleased
Me, not my parents, that I sought to wed 220
The daughter of an infidel. They knew not
That what I motioned was of God; I knew
From intimate impulse, and therefore urged
The marriage on, that, by occasion hence,
I might begin Israel's deliverance — 225
The work to which I was divinely called.
She proving false, the next I took to wife

(Oh that I never had ! fond wish too late !)
Was in the vale of Sorec, Dalila,
That specious monster, my accomplished snare.   230
I thought it lawful from my former act,
And the same end, still watching to oppress
Israel's oppressors. Of what now I suffer
She was not the prime cause, but I myself,
Who, vanquished with a peal of words (oh weakness !)   235
Gave up my fort of silence to a woman.
    Chorus. In seeking just occasion to provoke
The Philistine, thy country's enemy,
Thou never wast remiss, I bear thee witness :
Yet Israel still serves with all his sons.   240
    Samson. That fault I take not on me, but transfer
On Israel's governors and heads of tribes,
Who, seeing those great acts which God had done
Singly by me against their conquerors,
Acknowledged not, or not at all considered,   245
Deliverance offered. I, on the other side,
Used no ambition to commend my deeds ;
The deeds themselves, though mute, spoke loud the doer.
But they persisted deaf, and would not seem
To count them things worth notice, till at length   250
Their lords, the Philistines, with gathered powers,
Entered Judea, seeking me, who then
Safe to the rock of Etham was retired —
Not flying, but forecasting in what place
To set upon them, what advantaged best.   255
Meanwhile the men of Judah, to prevent
The harass of their land, beset me round ;
I willingly on some conditions came
Into their hands, and they as gladly yield me
To the Uncircumcised a welcome prey,   260

Bound with two cords. But cords to me were threads
Touched with the flame: on their whole host I flew
Unarmed, and with a trivial weapon felled
Their choicest youth; they only lived who fled.
Had Judah that day joined, or one whole tribe,   265
They had by this possessed the towers of Gath,
And lorded over them whom they now serve.
But what more oft in nations grown corrupt,
And by their vices brought to servitude,
Than to love bondage more than liberty —   270
Bondage with ease than strenuous liberty —
And to despise, or envy, or suspect,
Whom God hath of his special favour raised
As their deliverer? If he aught begin,
How frequent to desert him, and at last   275
To heap ingratitude on worthiest deeds!
   Chorus. Thy words to my remembrance bring
How Succoth and the fort of Penuel
Their great deliverer contemned,
The matchless Gideon, in pursuit   280
Of Madian, and her vanquished kings;
And how ingrateful Ephraim
Had dealt with Jephtha, who by argument,
Not worse than by his shield and spear,
Defended Israel from the Ammonite,   285
Had not his prowess quelled their pride
In that sore battle when so many died
Without reprieve, adjudged to death,
For want of well pronouncing *Shibboleth*.
   Samson. Of such examples add me to the roll.   290
Me easily indeed mine may neglect,
But God's proposed deliverance not so.
   Chorus. Just are the ways of God,

And justifiable to men,
Unless there be who think not God at all. 295
If any be, they walk obscure;
For of such doctrine never was there school
But the heart of the fool,
And no man therein doctor but himself.

    Yet more there be who doubt his ways not just, 300
As to his own edicts found contradicting;
Then give the reins to wandering thought,
Regardless of his glory's diminution,
Till, by their own perplexities involved,
They ravel more, still less resolved, 305
But never find self-satisfying solution.

    As if they would confine the Interminable,
And tie him to his own prescript,
Who made our laws to bind us, not himself,
And hath full right to exempt 310
Whomso it pleases him by choice
From national obstriction, without taint
Of sin, or legal debt;
For with his own laws he can best dispense.

    He would not else, who never wanted means, 315
Nor in respect of the enemy just cause,
To set his people free,
Have prompted this heroic Nazarite,
Against his vow of strictest purity,
To seek in marriage that fallacious bride, 320
Unclean, unchaste.

    Down, Reason, then; at least, vain reasonings, down;
Though Reason here aver
That moral verdict quits her of unclean:
Unchaste was subsequent, her stain not his. 325

    But see! here comes thy reverend sire,

With careful step, locks white as down,
Old Manoa: advise
Forthwith how thou ought'st to receive him.
 Samson. Ay me! another inward grief, awaked   330
With mention of that name, renews the assault.
 Manoa. Brethren and men of Dan (for such ye seem,
Though in this uncouth place), if old respect,
As I suppose, towards your once gloried friend,
My son, now captive, hither hath informed   335
Your younger feet, while mine, cast back with age,
Came lagging after, say if he be here.
 Chorus. As signal now in low dejected state,
As erst in highest, behold him where he lies.
 Manoa. Oh miserable change! is this the man?   340
That invincible Samson, far renowned,
The dread of Israel's foes, who with a strength
Equivalent to Angels', walked their streets,
None offering fight; who, single combatant,
Duelled their armies ranked in proud array,   345
Himself an army, now unequal match
To save himself against a coward armed
At one spear's length. Oh ever-failing trust
In mortal strength! and oh, what not in man
Deceivable and vain? Nay, what thing good   350
Prayed for, but often proves our woe, our bane?
I prayed for children, and thought barrenness
In wedlock a reproach; I gained a son,
And such a son as all men hailed me happy.
Who would be now a father in my stead?   355
Oh, wherefore did God grant me my request,
And as a blessing with such pomp adorned?
Why are his gifts desirable, to tempt
Our earnest prayers, then, given with solemn hand

As graces, draw a scorpion's tail behind? 360
For this did the Angel twice descend? for this
Ordained thy nurture holy, as of a plant
Select and sacred? glorious for a while,
The miracle of men; then in an hour
Ensnared, assaulted, overcome, led bound, 365
Thy foes' derision, captive, poor and blind,
Into a dungeon thrust, to work with slaves!
Alas! methinks whom God hath chosen once
To worthiest deeds, if he through frailty err,
He should not so o'erwhelm, and as a thrall 370
Subject him to so foul indignities,
Be it but for honour's sake of former deeds.

  Samson. Appoint not heavenly disposition, father.
Nothing of all these evils hath befallen me
But justly; I myself have brought them on; 375
Sole author I, sole cause. If aught seem vile,
As vile hath been my folly, who have profaned
The mystery of God, given me under pledge
Of vow, and have betrayed it to a woman,
A Canaanite, my faithless enemy. 380
This well I knew, nor was at all surprised,
But warned by oft experience. Did not she
Of Timna first betray me, and reveal
The secret wrested from me in her highth
Of nuptial love professed, carrying it straight 385
To them who had corrupted her, my spies
And rivals? In this other was there found
More faith, who, also in her prime of love,
Spousal embraces, vitiated with gold,
Though offered only, by the scent conceived 390
Her spurious first-born, Treason against me?
Thrice she assayed, with flattering prayers and sighs

And amorous reproaches, to win from me
My capital secret, in what part my strength
Lay stored, in what part summed, that she might know; 395
Thrice I deluded her, and turned to sport
Her importunity, each time perceiving
How openly and with what impudence
She purposed to betray me, and (which was worse
Than undissembled hate) with what contempt 400
She sought to make me traitor to myself.
Yet, the fourth time, when, mustering all her wiles,
With blandished parleys, feminine assaults,
Tongue-batteries, she surceased not day nor night
To storm me, over-watched, and wearied out, 405
At times when men seek most repose and rest,
I yielded, and unlocked her all my heart,
Who, with a grain of manhood well resolved,
Might easily have shook off all her snares;
But foul effeminacy held me yoked 410
Her bond-slave. Oh indignity, oh blot
To honour and religion! servile mind
Rewarded well with servile punishment!
The base degree to which I now am fallen,
These rags, this grinding, is not yet so base 415
As was my former servitude, ignoble,
Unmanly, ignominious, infamous,
True slavery; and that blindness worse than this,
That saw not how degenerately I served.
    Manoa. I cannot praise thy marriage-choices, son, 420
Rather approved them not; but thou didst plead
Divine impulsion prompting how thou might'st
Find some occasion to infest our foes.
I state not that; this I am sure — our foes
Found soon occasion thereby to make thee 425

Their captive, and their triumph; thou the sooner
Temptation found'st, or over-potent charms,
To violate the sacred trust of silence
Deposited within thee — which to have kept
Tacit, was in thy power; true; and thou bear'st   430
Enough, and more, the burden of that fault;
Bitterly hast thou paid, and still art paying,
That rigid score. A worse thing yet remains :
This day the Philistines a popular feast
Here celebrate in Gaza, and proclaim   435
Great pomp, and sacrifice, and praises loud,
To Dagon, as their god who hath delivered
Thee, Samson, bound and blind, into their hands,
Them out of thine, who slew'st them many a slain.
So Dagon shall be magnified, and God   440
Besides whom is no god, compared with idols,
Disglorified, blasphemed, and had in scorn
By the idolatrous rout amidst their wine;
Which to have come to pass by means of thee,
Samson, of all thy sufferings think the heaviest,   445
Of all reproach the most with shame that ever
Could have befallen thee and thy father's house.
　Samson. Father, I do acknowledge and confess
That I this honour, I this pomp, have brought
To Dagon, and advanced his praises high   450
Among the Heathen round; to God have brought
Dishonour, obloquy, and oped the mouths
Of idolists and atheists; have brought scandal
To Israel, diffidence of God, and doubt
In feeble hearts, propense enough before   455
To waver, or fall off and join with idols;
Which is my chief affliction, shame and sorrow,
The anguish of my soul, that suffers not

Mine eye to harbour sleep, or thoughts to rest.
This only hope relieves me, that the strife   460
With me hath end; all the contest is now
'Twixt God and Dagon.   Dagon hath presumed,
Me overthrown, to enter lists with God,
His deity comparing and preferring
Before the God of Abraham.   He, be sure,   465
Will not connive, or linger, thus provoked,
But will arise and his great name assert.
Dagon must stoop, and shall ere long receive
Such a discomfit, as shall quite despoil him
Of all these boasted trophies won on me,   470
And with confusion blank his worshippers.

   Manoa.   With cause this hope relieves thee, and these words
I as a prophecy receive; for God
(Nothing more certain) will not long defer
To vindicate the glory of his name   475
Against all competition, nor will long
Endure it doubtful whether God be Lord,
Or Dagon.   But for thee what shall be done?
Thou must not in the mean while, here forgot,
Lie in this miserable loathsome plight   480
Neglected.   I already have made way
To some Philistian lords, with whom to treat
About thy ransom: well they may by this
Have satisfied their utmost of revenge,
By pains and slaveries, worse than death, inflicted   485
On thee, who now no more canst do them harm.

   Samson.   Spare that proposal, father; spare the trouble
Of that solicitation.   Let me here,
As I deserve, pay on my punishment,
And expiate, if possible, my crime,   490
Shameful garrulity.   To have revealed

Secrets of *men*, the secrets of a friend.
How heinous had the fact been, how deserving
Contempt and scorn of all — to be excluded
All friendship, and avoided as a blab, 495
The mark of fool set on his front !
But I *God's* counsel have not kept, his holy secret
Presumptuously have published, impiously,
Weakly at least, and shamefully — a sin
That Gentiles in their parables condemn 500
To their Abyss and horrid pains confined.
 Manoa. Be penitent, and for thy fault contrite ;
But act not in thy own affliction, son.
Repent the sin ; but, if the punishment
Thou canst avoid, self-preservation bids ; 505
Or the execution leave to high disposal,
And let another hand, not thine, exact
Thy penal forfeit from thyself. Perhaps
God will relent, and quit thee all his debt ;
Who ever more approves and more accepts 510
(Best pleased with humble and filial submission)
Him who, imploring mercy, sues for life,
Than who, self-rigorous, chooses death as due ;
Which argues over-just, and self-displeased
For self-offence, more than for God offended. 515
Reject not, then, what offered means. Who knows
But God hath set before us to return thee
Home to thy country and his sacred house,
Where thou mayst bring thy offerings, to avert
His further ire, with prayers and vows renewed? 520
 Samson. His pardon I implore ; but as for life,
To what end should I seek it? when in strength
All mortals I excelled, and great in hopes,
With youthful courage, and magnanimous thoughts

Of birth from Heaven foretold and high exploits, 525
Full of divine instinct, after some proof
Of acts indeed heroic, far beyond
The sons of Anak, famous now and blazed,
Fearless of danger, like a petty god
I walked about, admired of all, and dreaded 530
On hostile ground, none daring my affront —
Then, swollen with pride, into the snare I fell
Of fair fallacious looks, venereal trains,
Softened with pleasure and voluptuous life,
At length to lay my head and hallowed pledge 535
Of all my strength in the lascivious lap
Of a deceitful concubine, who shore me
Like a tame wether, all my precious fleece,
Then turned me out ridiculous, despoiled,
Shaven, and disarmed among mine enemies. 540
 Chorus. Desire of wine and all delicious drinks,
Which many a famous warrior overturns,
Thou could'st repress; nor did the dancing ruby
Sparkling, out-poured, the flavour, or the smell,
Or taste that cheers the heart of gods and men, 545
Allure thee from the cool crystalline stream.
 Samson. Wherever fountain or fresh current flowed
Against the eastern ray, translucent, pure
With touch ethereal of Heaven's fiery rod,
I drank, from the clear milky juice allaying 550
Thirst, and refreshed; nor envied them the grape
Whose heads that turbulent liquor fills with fumes.
 Chorus. Oh madness! to think use of strongest wines
And strongest drinks our chief support of health,
When God with these forbidden made choice to rear 555
His mighty champion, strong above compare,
Whose drink was only from the liquid brook!

Samson. But what availed this temperance, not complete
Against another object more enticing?
What boots it at one gate to make defence, 560
And at another to let in the foe,
Effeminately vanquished? by which means,
Now blind, disheartened, shamed, dishonoured, quelled,
To what can I be useful? wherein serve
My nation, and the work from Heaven imposed? 565
But to sit idle on the household hearth,
A burdenous drone ; to visitants a gaze,
Or pitied object ; these redundant locks,
Robustious to no purpose, clustering down,
Vain monument of strength ; till length of years 570
And sedentary numbness craze my limbs
To a contemptible old age obscure.
Here rather let me drudge, and earn my bread,
Till vermin, or the draff of servile food,
Consume me, and oft-invocated death 575
Hasten the welcome end of all my pains.

   Manoa. Wilt thou then serve the Philistines with that gift
Which was expressly given thee to annoy them?
Better at home lie bed-rid, not only idle,
Inglorious, unemployed, with age outworn. 580
But God, who caused a fountain at thy prayer
From the dry ground to spring, thy thirst to allay
After the brunt of battle, can as easy
Cause light again within thy eyes to spring,
Wherewith to serve him better than thou hast. 585
And I persuade me so. Why else this strength
Miraculous yet remaining in those locks?
His might continues in thee not for nought,
Nor shall his wondrous gifts be frustrate thus.

   Samson. All otherwise to me my thoughts portend — 590

That these dark orbs no more shall treat with light,
Nor the other light of life continue long,
But yield to double darkness nigh at hand;
So much I feel my genial spirits droop,
My hopes all flat: Nature within me seems   595
In all her functions weary of herself;
My race of glory run, and race of shame,
And I shall shortly be with them that rest.

    Manoa. Believe not these suggestions, which proceed
From anguish of the mind, and humours black   600
That mingle with thy fancy. I, however,
Must not omit a father's timely care
To prosecute the means of thy deliverance
By ransom or how else. Mean while be calm,
And healing words from these thy friends admit.   605

    Samson. Oh, that torment should not be confined
To the body's wounds and sores,
With maladies innumerable
In heart, head, breast, and reins,
But must secret passage find   610
To the inmost mind,
There exercise all his fierce accidents,
And on her purest spirits prey,
As on entrails, joints, and limbs,
With answerable pains, but more intense,   615
Though void of corporal sense!
    My griefs not only pain me
As a lingering disease,
But, finding no redress, ferment and rage;
Nor less than wounds immedicable   620
Rankle, and fester, and gangrene,
To black mortification.
Thoughts, my tormentors, armed with deadly stings,

Mangle my apprehensive tenderest parts,
Exasperate, exulcerate, and raise 625
Dire inflammation, which no cooling herb
Or medicinal liquor can assuage,
Nor breath of vernal air from snowy Alp.
Sleep hath forsook and given me o'er
To death's benumbing opium as my only cure; 630
Thence faintings, swoonings of despair,
And sense of Heaven's desertion.
    I was his nursling once and choice delight,
His, destined from the womb,
Promised by heavenly message twice descending. 635
Under his special eye
Abstemious I grew up and thrived amain;
He led me on to mightiest deeds,
Above the nerve of mortal arm,
Against the Uncircumcised, our enemies: 640
But now hath cast me off as never known,
And to those cruel enemies,
Whom I by his appointment had provoked,
Left me all helpless, with the irreparable loss
Of sight, reserved alive to be repeated 645
The subject of their cruelty or scorn.
Nor am I in the list of them that hope;
Hopeless are all my evils, all remediless.
This one prayer yet remains, might I be heard,
No long petition, speedy death, 650
The close of all my miseries, and the balm.
    Chorus. Many are the sayings of the wise,
In ancient and in modern books enrolled,
Extolling patience as the truest fortitude,
And to the bearing well of all calamities, 655
All chances incident to man's frail life,

Consolatories writ
With studied argument, and much persuasion sought,
Lenient of grief and anxious thought.
But with the afflicted in his pangs their sound   660
Little prevails, or rather seems a tune
Harsh, and of dissonant mood from his complaint,
Unless he feel within
Some source of consolation from above,
Secret refreshings that repair his strength   665
And fainting spirits uphold.
    God of our fathers! what is Man,
That thou towards him with hand so various —
Or might I say contrarious? —
Temper'st thy providence through his short course: 670
Not evenly, as thou rul'st
The angelic orders, and inferior creatures mute,
Irrational and brute?
Nor do I name of men the common rout,
That, wand'ring loose about,   675
Grow up and perish, as the summer fly,
Heads without name, no more rememberèd;
But such as thou hast solemnly elected,
With gifts and graces eminently adorned,
To some great work, thy glory,   680
And people's safety, which in part they effect.
Yet toward these thus dignified, thou oft,
Amidst their highth of noon,
Changest thy countenance and thy hand, with no regard
Of highest favours past   685
From thee on them, or them to thee of service.
    Nor only dost degrade them, or remit
To life obscured, which were a fair dismission,
But throw'st them lower than thou didst exalt them high —

Unseemly falls in human eye, 690
Too grievous for the trespass or omission ;
Oft leav'st them to the hostile sword
Of heathen and profane, their carcasses
To dogs and fowls a prey, or else captived,
Or to the unjust tribunals, under change of times, 695
And condemnation of the ingrateful multitude.
If these they scape, perhaps in poverty
With sickness and disease thou bow'st them down,
Painful diseases and deformed,
In crude old age ; 700
Though not disordinate, yet causeless suffering
The punishment of dissolute days. In fine,
Just or unjust alike seem miserable,
For oft alike both come to evil end.
   So deal not with this once thy glorious champion, 705
The image of thy strength, and mighty minister.
What do I beg? how hast thou dealt already !
Behold him in this state calamitous, and turn
His labours, for thou canst, to peaceful end.
   But who is this? what thing of sea or land? 710
— Female of sex it seems —
That so bedecked, ornate, and gay,
Comes this way sailing,
Like a stately ship
Of Tarsus, bound for the isles 715
Of Javan or Gadire,
With all her bravery on, and tackle trim,
Sails filled, and streamers waving,
Courted by all the winds that hold them play,
An amber scent of odorous perfume 720
Her harbinger, a damsel train behind ;
Some rich Philistian matron she may seem,

And now, at nearer view, no other certain
Than Dalila thy wife. 724
   Samson. My wife? my traitress; let her not come near me.
   Chorus. Yet on she moves; now stands and eyes thee fixed,
About to have spoke; but now, with head declined,
Like a fair flower surcharged with dew, she weeps,
And words addressed seem into tears dissolved,
Wetting the borders of her silken veil. 730
But now again she makes address to speak.
   Dalila. With doubtful feet and wavering resolution
I came, still dreading thy displeasure, Samson,
Which to have merited, without excuse,
I cannot but acknowledge; yet if tears 735
May expiate (though the fact more evil drew
In the perverse event than I foresaw),
My penance hath not slackened, though my pardon
No way assured. But conjugal affection,
Prevailing over fear and timorous doubt, 740
Hath led me on, desirous to behold
Once more thy face, and know of thy estate,
If aught in my ability may serve
To lighten what thou sufferest, and appease
Thy mind with what amends is in my power, 745
Though late, yet in some part to recompense
My rash but more unfortunate misdeed.
   Samson. Out, out, hyæna! these are thy wonted arts,
And arts of every woman false like thee —
To break all faith, all vows, deceive, betray; 750
Then, as repentant, to submit, beseech,
And reconcilement move with feigned remorse,
Confess, and promise wonders in her change —
Not truly penitent, but chief to try
Her husband, how far urged his patience bears, 755

His virtue or weakness which way to assail:
Then, with more cautious and instructed skill,
Again transgresses, and again submits;
That wisest and best men, full oft beguiled,
With goodness principled not to reject 760
The penitent, but ever to forgive,
Are drawn to wear out miserable days,
Entangled with a poisonous bosom-snake,
If not by quick destruction soon cut off,
As I by thee, to ages an example. 765
   Dalila. Yet hear me, Samson; not that I endeavour
To lessen or extenuate my offence,
But that, on the other side, if it be weighed
By itself, with aggravations not surcharged,
Or else with just allowance counterpoised, 770
I may, if possible, thy pardon find
The easier towards me, or thy hatred less.
First granting, as I do, it was a weakness
In me, but incident to all our sex,
Curiosity, inquisitive, importune 775
Of secrets, then with like infirmity
To publish them — both common female faults —
Was it not weakness also to make known,
For importunity, that is for nought,
Wherein consisted all thy strength and safety? 780
To what I did thou show'd'st me first the way.
But I to enemies revealed, and should not;
Nor should'st thou have trusted that to woman's frailty:
Ere I to thee, thou to thyself wast cruel.
Let weakness, then, with weakness come to parle, 785
So near related, or the same of kind;
Thine forgive mine, that men may censure thine
The gentler, if severely thou exact not

More strength from me than in thyself was found.
And what if love, which thou interpret'st hate, 790
The jealousy of love, powerful of sway
In human hearts, nor less in mine towards thee,
Caused what I did? I saw thee mutable
Of fancy, feared lest one day thou would'st leave me
As her at Timna; sought by all means, therefore, 795
How to endear, and hold thee to me firmest:
No better way I saw than by importuning
To learn thy secrets, get into my power
Thy key of strength and safety. Thou wilt say,
'Why, then, revealed?' I was assured by those 800
Who tempted me, that nothing was designed
Against thee but safe custody and hold.
That made for me; I knew that liberty
Would draw thee forth to perilous enterprises,
While I at home sat full of cares and fears, 805
Wailing thy absence in my widowed bed;
Here I should still enjoy thee, day and night,
Mine and love's prisoner, not the Philistines',
Whole to myself, unhazarded abroad,
Fearless at home of partners in my love. 810
These reasons in love's law have passed for good,
Though fond and reasonless to some perhaps;
And love hath oft, well meaning, wrought much woe,
Yet always pity or pardon hath obtained.
Be not unlike all others, not austere 815
As thou art strong, inflexible as steel.
If thou in strength all mortals dost exceed,
In uncompassionate anger do not so.
    Samson. How cunningly the sorceress displays
Her own transgressions, to upbraid me mine! 820
That malice, not repentance, brought thee hither,

By this appears. I gave, thou say'st, the example,
I led the way; bitter reproach, but true;
I to myself was false ere thou to me.
Such pardon, therefore, as I give my folly, 825
Take to thy wicked deed; which when thou seest
Impartial, self-severe, inexorable,
Thou wilt renounce thy seeking, and much rather
Confess it feigned. Weakness is thy excuse,
And I believe it — weakness to resist 830
Philistian gold. If weakness may excuse,
What murtherer, what traitor, parricide,
Incestuous, sacrilegious, but may plead it?
All wickedness is weakness; that plea, therefore,
With God or man will gain thee no remission. 835
But love constrained thee! call it furious rage
To satisfy thy lust. Love seeks to have love;
My love how could'st thou hope, who took'st the way
To raise in me inexpiable hate,
Knowing, as needs I must, by thee betrayed? 840
In vain thou striv'st to cover shame with shame,
Or by evasions thy crime uncover'st more.
   Dalila. Since thou determin'st weakness for no plea
In man or woman, though to thy own condemning,
Hear what assaults I had, what snares besides, 845
What sieges girt me round, ere I consented;
Which might have awed the best-resolved of men,
The constantest, to have yielded without blame.
It was not gold, as to my charge thou lay'st,
That wrought with me. Thou know'st the magistrates 850
And princes of my country came in person,
Solicited, commanded, threatened, urged,
Adjured by all the bonds of civil duty
And of religion; pressed how just it was,

How honourable, how glorious, to entrap 855
A common enemy, who had destroyed
Such numbers of our nation: and the priest
Was not behind, but ever at my ear,
Preaching how meritorious with the gods
It would be to ensnare an irreligious 860
Dishonourer of Dagon. What had I
To oppose against such powerful arguments?
Only my love of thee held long debate,
And combated in silence all these reasons
With hard contest. At length, that grounded maxim, 865
So rife and celebrated in the mouths
Of wisest men, that to the public good
Private respects must yield, with grave authority
Took full possession of me, and prevailed;
Virtue, as I thought, truth, duty, so enjoining. 870
    Samson. I thought where all thy circling wiles would end—
In feigned religion, smooth hypocrisy!
But, had thy love, still odiously pretended,
Been, as it ought, sincere, it would have taught thee
Far other reasonings, brought forth other deeds. 875
I, before all the daughters of my tribe
And of my nation, chose thee from among
My enemies, loved thee, as too well thou knew'st,
Too well; unbosomed all my secrets to thee,
Not out of levity, but overpowered 880
By thy request, who could deny thee nothing;
Yet now am judged an enemy. Why, then,
Didst thou at first receive me for thy husband,
Then, as since then, thy country's foe professed?
Being once a wife, for me thou wast to leave 885
Parents and country; nor was I their subject,
Nor under their protection, but my own;

Thou mine, not theirs. If aught against my life
Thy country sought of thee, it sought unjustly,
Against the law of nature, law of nations; 890
No more thy country, but an impious crew
Of men conspiring to uphold their state
By worse than hostile deeds, violating the ends
For which our country is a name so dear;
Not therefore to be obeyed. But zeal moved thee; 895
To please thy gods thou didst it! gods unable
To acquit themselves and prosecute their foes
But by ungodly deeds, the contradiction
Of their own deity, gods cannot be;
Less therefore to be pleased, obeyed, or feared. 900
These false pretexts and varnished colours failing,
Bare in thy guilt, how foul must thou appear!
   Dalila. In argument with men a woman ever
Goes by the worse, whatever be her cause.
   Samson. For want of words, no doubt, or lack of breath!
Witness when I was worried with thy peals. 906
   Dalila. I was a fool, too rash, and quite mistaken
In what I thought would have succeeded best.
Let me obtain forgiveness of thee, Samson;
Afford me place to show what recompense 910
Towards thee I intend for what I have misdone,
Misguided. Only what remains past cure
Bear not too sensibly, nor still insist
To afflict thyself in vain. Though sight be lost,
Life yet hath many solaces, enjoyed 915
Where other senses want not their delights —
At home, in leisure and domestic ease,
Exempt from many a care and chance to which
Eye-sight exposes, daily, men abroad.
I to the lords will intercede, not doubting 920

Their favourable ear, that I may fetch thee
From forth this loathsome prison-house, to abide
With me, where my redoubled love and care,
With nursing diligence, to me glad office,
May ever tend about thee to old age, 925
With all things grateful cheered, and so supplied
That what by me thou hast lost thou least shalt miss.
    Samson. No, no; of my condition take no care;
It fits not; thou and I long since are twain;
Nor think me so unwary or accursed, 930
To bring my feet again into the snare
Where once I have been caught. I know thy trains,
Though dearly to my cost, thy gins, and toils.
Thy fair enchanted cup, and warbling charms,
No more on me have power; their force is nulled; 935
So much of adder's wisdom I have learned,
To fence my ear against thy sorceries.
If in my flower of youth and strength, when all men
Loved, honoured, feared me, thou alone could'st hate me,
Thy husband, slight me, sell me, and forgo me, 940
How would'st thou use me now, blind, and thereby
Deceivable, in most things as a child
Helpless, thence easily contemned and scorned,
And last neglected! How would'st thou insult,
When I must live uxorious to thy will 945
In perfect thraldom! how again betray me,
Bearing my words and doings to the lords
To gloss upon, and, censuring, frown or smile!
This jail I count the house of liberty
To thine, whose doors my feet shall never enter. 950
    Dalila. Let me approach at least, and touch thy hand.
    Samson. Not for thy life, lest fierce remembrance wake
My sudden rage to tear thee joint by joint.

At distance I forgive thee ; go with that ;
Bewail thy falsehood, and the pious works 955
It hath brought forth to make thee memorable
Among illustrious women, faithful wives ;
Cherish thy hastened widowhood with the gold
Of matrimonial treason : so farewell.
    Dalila. I see thou art implacable, more deaf 960
To prayers than winds and seas ; yet winds to seas
Are reconciled at length, and sea to shore :
Thy anger, unappeasable, still rages,
Eternal tempest never to be calmed.
Why do I humble thus myself, and, suing 965
For peace, reap nothing but repulse and hate?
Bid go with evil omen, and the brand
Of infamy upon my name denounced.
To mix with thy concernments I desist
Henceforth, nor too much disapprove my own. 970
Fame, if not double-faced, is double-mouthed,
And with contráry blast proclaims most deeds;
On both his wings, one black, the other white,
Bears greatest names in his wild aery flight.
My name, perhaps, among the Circumcised 975
In Dan, in Judah, and the bordering tribes,
To all posterity may stand defamed,
With malediction mentioned, and the blot
Of falsehood most unconjugal traduced.
But in my country, where I most desire, 980
In Ecron, Gaza, Asdod, and in Gath,
I shall be named among the famousest
Of women, sung at solemn festivals,
Living and dead recorded, who, to save
Her country from a fierce destroyer, chose 985
Above the faith of wedlock-bands ; my tomb

With odours visited and annual flowers;
Not less renowned than in mount Ephraim
Jael, who, with inhospitable guile,
Smote Sisera sleeping, through the temples nailed. 990
Nor shall I count it heinous to enjoy
The public marks of honour and reward
Conferred upon me for the piety
Which to my country I was judged to have shown.
At this whoever envies or repines, 995
I leave him to his lot, and like my own.
   Chorus. She's gone — a manifest serpent by her sting
Discovered in the end, till now concealed.
   Samson. So let her go. God sent her to debase me,
And aggravate my folly, who committed 1000
To such a viper his most sacred trust
Of secrecy, my safety, and my life.
   Chorus. Yet beauty, though injurious, hath strange power,
After offence returning, to regain
Love once possessed, nor can be easily 1005
Repulsed, without much inward passion felt,
And secret sting of amorous remorse.
   Samson. Love-quarrels oft in pleasing concord end,
Not wedlock-treachery endangering life.
   Chorus. It is not virtue, wisdom, valour, wit, 1010
Strength, comeliness of shape, or amplest merit,
That woman's love can win or long inherit;
But what it is, hard is to say,
Harder to hit,
Which way soever men refer it 1015
(Much like thy riddle, Samson), in one day
Or seven, though one should musing sit.
   If any of these, or all, the Timnian bride
Had not so soon preferred

Thy paranymph, worthless to thee compared, 1020
Successor in thy bed,
Nor both so loosely disallied
Their nuptials, nor this last so treacherously
Had shorn the fatal harvest of thy head.
Is it for that such outward ornament 1025
Was lavished on their sex, that inward gifts
Were left for haste unfinished, judgment scant,
Capacity not raised to apprehend
Or value what is best
In choice, but oftest to affect the wrong? 1030
Or was too much of self-love mixed,
Of constancy no root infixed,
That either they love nothing, or not long?
 Whate'er it be, to wisest men and best,
Seeming at first all heavenly under virgin veil, 1035
Soft, modest, meek, demure,
Once joined, the contrary she proves — a thorn
Intestine, far within defensive arms
A cleaving mischief, in his way to virtue
Adverse and turbulent; or by her charms 1040
Draws him awry, enslaved
With dotage, and his sense depraved
To folly and shameful deeds which ruin ends.
What pilot so expert but needs must wreck,
Embarked with such a steers-mate at the helm? 1045
 Favoured of heaven who finds
One virtuous, rarely found,
That in domestic good combines!
Happy that house! his way to peace is smooth:
But virtue which breaks through all opposition, 1050
And all temptation can remove,
Most shines and most is acceptable above.

Therefore God's universal law
Gave to the man despotic power
Over his female in due awe, 1055
Nor from that right to part an hour,
Smile she or lour:
So shall he least confusion draw
On his whole life, not swayed
By female usurpation, nor dismayed. 1060
    But had we best retire? I see a storm.
    Samson. Fair days have oft contracted wind and rain.
    Chorus. But this another kind of tempest brings.
    Samson. Be less abstruse; my riddling days are past.
    Chorus. Look now for no enchanting voice, nor fear 1065
The bait of honied words; a rougher tongue
Draws hitherward; I know him by his stride,
The giant Harapha of Gath, his look
Haughty, as is his pile high-built and proud.
Comes he in peace? what wind hath blown him hither 1070
I less conjecture than when first I saw
The sumptuous Dalila floating this way:
His habit carries peace, his brow defiance.
    Samson. Or peace or not, alike to me he comes. 1074
    Chorus. His fraught we soon shall know: he now arrives.
    Harapha. I come not, Samson, to condole thy chance,
As these perhaps, yet wish it had not been,
Though for no friendly intent. I am of Gath;
Men call me Harapha, of stock renowned
As Og, or Anak, and the Emims old 1080
That Kiriathaim held. Thou know'st me now,
If thou at all art known. Much I have heard
Of thy prodigious might and feats performed,
Incredible to me, — in this displeased,
That I was never present on the place 1085

Of those encounters, where we might have tried
Each other's force in camp or listed field;
And now am come to see of whom such noise
Hath walked about, and each limb to survey,
If thy appearance answer loud report.   1090
    Samson. The way to know were not to see, but taste.
    Harapha. Dost thou already single me? I thought
Gyves and the mill had tamed thee. Oh, that fortune
Had brought me to the field, where thou art famed
To have wrought such wonders with an ass's jaw!   1095
I should have forced thee soon with other arms,
Or left thy carcass where the ass lay thrown;
So had the glory of prowess been recovered
To Palestine, won by a Philistine
From the unforeskinned race, of whom thou bear'st   1100
The highest name for valiant acts; that honour,
Certain to have won by mortal duel from thee,
I lose, prevented by thy eyes put out.
    Samson. Boast not of what thou would'st have done, but do
What then thou would'st; thou seest it in thy hand.   1105
    Harapha. To combat with a blind man I disdain,
And thou hast need much washing to be touched.
    Samson. Such usage as your honourable lords
Afford me, assassinated and betrayed;
Who durst not with their whole united powers   1110
In fight withstand me single and unarmed,
Nor in the house with chamber-ambushes
Close-banded durst attack me, no, not sleeping,
Till they had hired a woman with their gold,
Breaking her marriage-faith, to circumvent me.   1115
Therefore, without feigned shifts, let be assigned
Some narrow place enclosed, where sight may give thee,
Or rather flight, no great advantage on me;

Then put on all thy gorgeous arms, thy helmet
And brigandine of brass, thy broad habergeon, 1120
Vant-brace and greaves and gauntlet; add thy spear,
A weaver's beam, and seven-times-folded shield:
I only with an oaken staff will meet thee,
And raise such outcries on thy clattered iron,
Which long shall not withhold me from thy head, 1125
That in a little time while breath remains thee,
Thou oft shalt wish thyself at Gath, to boast
Again in safety what thou would'st have done
To Samson, but shalt never see Gath more.
    Harapha. Thou durst not thus disparage glorious arms,
Which greatest heroes have in battle worn, 1131
Their ornament and safety, had not spells
And black enchantments, some magician's art,
Armed thee or charmed thee strong, which thou from Heaven
Feign'dst at thy birth was given thee in thy hair, 1135
Where strength can least abide, though all thy hairs
Were bristles ranged like those that ridge the back
Of chafed wild boars or ruffled porcupines.
    Samson. I know no spells, use no forbidden arts;
My trust is in the Living God, who gave me, 1140
At my nativity, this strength, diffused
No less through all my sinews, joints, and bones,
Than thine, while I preserved these locks unshorn,
The pledge of my unviolated vow.
For proof hereof, if Dagon be thy god, 1145
Go to his temple, invocate his aid
With solemnest devotion, spread before him
How highly it concerns his glory now
To frustrate and dissolve these magic spells,
Which I to be the power of Israel's God 1150
Avow, and challenge Dagon to the test,

Offering to combat thee, his champion bold,
With the utmost of his godhead seconded:
Then thou shalt see, or rather to thy sorrow
Soon feel, whose God is strongest, thine or mine. 1155
  Harapha. Presume not on thy God. Whate'er he be,
Thee he regards not, owns not, hath cut off
Quite from his people, and delivered up
Into thy enemies' hand; permitted them
To put out both thine eyes, and fettered send thee 1160
Into the common prison, there to grind
Among the slaves and asses, thy comrades,
As good for nothing else, no better service
With those thy boisterous locks; no worthy match
For valour to assail, nor by the sword 1165
Of noble warrior, so to stain his honour,
But by the barber's razor best subdued.
  Samson. All these indignities, for such they are
From thine, these evils I deserve and more,
Acknowledge them from God inflicted on me 1170
Justly, yet despair not of his final pardon,
Whose ear is ever open, and his eye
Gracious to re-admit the suppliant;
In confidence whereof I once again
Defy thee to the trial of mortal fight, 1175
By combat to decide whose god is God,
Thine, or whom I with Israel's sons adore.
  Harapha. Fair honour that thou doest thy God, in trusting
He will accept thee to defend his cause,
A murtherer, a revolter, and a robber! 1180
  Samson. Tongue-doughty giant, how dost thou prove me these?
  Harapha. Is not thy nation subject to our lords?
Their magistrates confessed it, when they took thee

As a league-breaker, and delivered bound
Into our hands: for hadst thou not committed 1185
Notorious murder on those thirty men
At Ascalon, who never did thee harm,
Then, like a robber, stripp'dst them of their robes?
The Philistines, when thou hadst broke the league,
Went up with armed powers thee only seeking, 1190
To others did no violence nor spoil.
   Samson. Among the daughters of the Philistines
I chose a wife, which argued me no foe,
And in your city held my nuptial feast;
But your ill-meaning politician lords, 1195
Under pretence of bridal friends and guests,
Appointed to await me thirty spies,
Who, threatening cruel death, constrained the bride
To wring from me, and tell to them, my secret,
That solved the riddle which I had proposed. 1200
When I perceived all set on enmity,
As on my enemies, wherever chanced,
I used hostility, and took their spoil,
To pay my underminers in their coin.
My nation was subjected to your lords! 1205
It was the force of conquest; force with force
Is well ejected when the conquered can.
But I, a private person, whom my country
As a league-breaker gave up bound, presumed
Single rebellion, and did hostile acts! 1210
I was no private, but a person raised,
With strength sufficient, and command from Heaven,
To free my country. If their servile minds
Me, their deliverer sent, would not receive,
But to their masters gave me up for nought, 1215
The unworthier they; whence to this day they serve.

I was to do my part from Heaven assigned,
And had performed it, if my known offence
Had not disabled me, not all your force.
These shifts refuted, answer thy appellant,   1220
Though by his blindness maimed for high attempts,
Who now defies thee thrice to single fight,
As a petty enterprise of small enforce.
    Harapha. With thee, a man condemned, a slave enrolled,
Due by the law to capital punishment?   1225
To fight with thee no man of arms will deign.
    Samson. Cam'st thou for this, vain boaster, to survey me,
To descant on my strength, and give thy verdict?
Come nearer; part not hence so slight informed;
But take good heed my hand survey not thee.   1230
    Harapha. O Baal-zebub! can my ears unused
Hear these dishonours, and not render death?
    Samson. No man withholds thee; nothing from thy hand
Fear I incurable; bring up thy van;
My heels are fettered, but my fist is free.   1235
    Harapha. This insolence other kind of answer fits.
    Samson. Go, baffled coward, lest I run upon thee,
Though in these chains, bulk without spirit vast,
And with one buffet lay thy structure low,
Or swing thee in the air, then dash thee down,   1240
To the hazard of thy brains and shattered sides.
    Harapha. By Astaroth, ere long thou shalt lament
These braveries in irons loaden on thee.
    Chorus. His giantship is gone somewhat crest-fallen,
Stalking with less unconscionable strides,   1245
And lower looks, but in a sultry chafe.
    Samson. I dread him not, nor all his giant brood,
Though fame divulge him father of five sons,
All of gigantic size, Goliah chief.

Chorus. He will directly to the lords, I fear, 1250
And with malicious counsel stir them up
Some way or other yet further to afflict thee.
   Samson. He must allege some cause, and offered fight
Will not dare mention, lest a question rise
Whether he durst accept the offer or not; 1255
And that he durst not plain enough appeared.
Much more affliction than already felt
They cannot well impose, nor I sustain,
If they intend advantage of my labours,
The work of many hands, which earns my keeping, 1260
With no small profit daily to my owners.
But come what will, my deadliest foe will prove
My speediest friend, by death to rid me hence;
The worst that he can give, to me the best.
Yet so it may fall out, because their end 1265
Is hate, not help to me, it may with mine
Draw their own ruin who attempt the deed.
   Chorus. Oh how comely it is, and how reviving
To the spirits of just men long oppressed,
When God into the hands of their deliverer 1270
Puts invincible might,
To quell the mighty of the earth, the oppressor,
The brute and boisterous force of violent men,
Hardy and industrious to support.
Tyrannic power, but raging to pursue 1275
The righteous, and all such as honour truth!
He all their ammunition
And feats of war defeats,
With plain heroic magnitude of mind
And celestial vigour armed; 1280
Their armories and magazines contemns,
Renders them useless, while

With wingèd expedition
Swift as the lightning glance he executes
His errand on the wicked, who, surprised,   1285
Lose their defence, distracted and amazed.
    But patience is more oft the exercise
Of saints, the trial of their fortitude,
Making them each his own deliverer,
And victor over all   1290
That tyranny or fortune can inflict.
Either of these is in thy lot,
Samson, with might endued
Above the sons of men; but sight bereaved
May chance to number thee with those   1295
Whom patience finally must crown.
    This Idol's day hath been to thee no day of rest,
Labouring thy mind
More than the working day thy hands.
And yet perhaps more trouble is behind;   1300
For I descry this way
Some other tending; in his hand
A sceptre or quaint staff he bears,
Comes on amain, speed in his look.
By his habit I discern him now   1305
A public officer, and now at hand.
His message will be short and voluble.
    Officer. Ebrews, the prisoner Samson here I seek.
    Chorus. His manacles remark him; there he sits.
    Officer. Samson, to thee our lords thus bid me say: 1310
This day to Dagon is a solemn feast,
With sacrifices, triumph, pomp, and games;
Thy strength they know surpassing human rate,
And now some public proof thereof require
To honour this great feast, and great assembly.   1315

Rise, therefore, with all speed, and come along,
Where I will see thee heartened and fresh clad,
To appear as fits before the illustrious lords.
   Samson. Thou know'st I am an Ebrew; therefore tell them
Our Law forbids at their religious rites   1320
My presence; for that cause I cannot come.
   Officer. This answer, be assured, will not content them.
   Samson. Have they not sword-players, and every sort
Of gymnic artists, wrestlers, riders, runners,
Jugglers and dancers, antics, mummers, mimics,   1325
But they must pick me out, with shackles tired,
And over-laboured at their public mill,
To make them sport with blind activity?
Do they not seek occasion of new quarrels,
On my refusal, to distress me more,   1330
Or make a game of my calamities?
Return the way thou cam'st; I will not come.
   Officer. Regard thyself; this will offend them highly.
   Samson. Myself? my conscience and internal peace.
Can they think me so broken, so debased   1335
With corporal servitude, that my mind ever
Will condescend to such absurd commands?
Although their drudge, to be their fool or jester,
And, in my midst of sorrow and heart-grief,
To show them feats, and play before their god—   1340
The worst of all indignities, yet on me
Joined with extreme contempt! I will not come.
   Officer. My message was imposed on me with speed,
Brooks no delay: is this thy resolution?
   Samson. So take it with what speed thy message needs.
   Officer. I am sorry what this stoutness will produce.   1346
   Samson. Perhaps thou shalt have cause to sorrow indeed.
   Chorus. Consider, Samson; matters now are strained

Up to the highth, whether to hold or break.
He's gone, and who knows how he may report 1350
Thy words by adding fuel to the flame?
Expect another message more imperious,
More lordly thundering than thou well wilt bear.
    Samson. Shall I abuse this consecrated gift
Of strength, again returning with my hair 1355
After my great transgression? so requite
Favour renewed, and add a greater sin
By prostituting holy things to idols,
A Nazarite, in place abominable,
Vaunting my strength in honour to their Dagon? 1360
Besides how vile, contemptible, ridiculous,
What act more execrably unclean, profane?
    Chorus. Yet with this strength thou serv'st the Philistines,
Idolatrous, uncircumcised, unclean.
    Samson. Not in their idol-worship, but by labour 1365
Honest and lawful to deserve my food
Of those who have me in their civil power.
    Chorus. Where the heart joins not, outward acts defile not.
    Samson. Where outward force constrains, the sentence holds.
But who constrains me to the temple of Dagon, 1370
Not dragging? the Philistian lords command:
Commands are no constraints. If I obey them,
I do it freely, venturing to displease
God for the fear of man, and man prefer,
Set God behind; which, in his jealousy, 1375
Shall never, unrepented, find forgiveness.
Yet that he may dispense with me, or thee,
Present in temples at idolatrous rites
For some important cause, thou need'st not doubt.
    Chorus. How thou wilt here come off surmounts my reach.
    Samson. Be of good courage; I begin to feel 1381

Some rousing motions in me, which dispose
To something extraordinary my thoughts.
I with this messenger will go along,
Nothing to do, be sure, that may dishonour   1385
Our Law, or stain my vow of Nazarite.
If there be aught of presage in the mind,
This day will be remarkable in my life
By some great act, or of my days the last.
   Chorus. In time thou hast resolved : the man returns. 1390
   Officer. Samson, this second message from our lords
To thee I am bid say : Art thou our slave,
Our captive, at the public mill our drudge,
And dar'st thou, at our sending and command,
Dispute thy coming? Come without delay ;   1395
Or we shall find such engines to assail
And hamper thee, as thou shalt come of force,
Though thou wert firmlier fastened than a rock.
   Samson. I could be well content to try their art,
Which to no few of them would prove pernicious ;   1400
Yet, knowing their advantages too many,
Because they shall not trail me through their streets
Like a wild beast, I am content to go.
—Masters' commands come with a power resistless
To such as owe them absolute subjection ;   1405
And for a life who will not change his purpose?
So mutable are all the ways of men.—
Yet this be sure, in nothing to comply
Scandalous or forbidden in our Law.
   Officer. I praise thy resolution. Doff these links : 1410
By this compliance thou wilt win the lords
To favour, and perhaps to set thee free.
   Samson. Brethren, farewell. Your company along
I will not wish, lest it perhaps offend them

To see me girt with friends; and how the sight 1415
Of me as of a common enemy,
So dreaded once, may now exasperate them,
I know not.   Lords are lordliest in their wine;
And the well-feasted priest then soonest fired
With zeal, if aught religion seem concerned; 1420
No less the people, on their holy-days,
Impetuous, insolent, unquenchable.
Happen what may, of me expect to hear
Nothing dishonourable, impure, unworthy
Our God, our Law, my nation, or myself; 1425
The last of me or no I cannot warrant.
  Chorus. Go, and the Holy One
Of Israel be thy guide
To what may serve his glory best, and spread his name
Great among the Heathen round; 1430
Send thee the Angel of thy birth, to stand
Fast by thy side, who from thy father's field
Rode up in flames after his message told
Of thy conception, and be now a shield
Of fire; that Spirit, that first rushed on thee 1435
In the camp of Dan,
Be efficacious in thee now at need!
For never was from Heaven imparted
Measure of strength so great to mortal seed,
As in thy wondrous actions hath been seen. 1440
But wherefore comes old Manoa in such haste
With youthful steps? much livelier than ere while
He seems: supposing here to find his son,
Or of him bringing to us some glad news?
  Manoa. Peace with you, brethren!   My inducement hither
Was not at present here to find my son, 1446
By order of the lords new parted hence

To come and play before them at their feast.
I heard all as I came; the city rings,
And numbers thither flock; I had no will, 1450
Lest I should see him forced to things unseemly.
But that which moved my coming now, was chiefly
To give ye part with me what hope I have
With good success to work his liberty.
    Chorus. That hope would much rejoice us to partake 1455
With thee. Say, reverend sire; we thirst to hear.
    Manoa. I have attempted, one by one, the lords,
Either at home, or through the high street passing,
With supplication prone and father's tears,
To accept of ransom for my son, their prisoner. 1460
Some much averse I found, and wondrous harsh,
Contemptuous, proud, set on revenge and spite;
That part most reverenced Dagon and his priests;
Others more moderate seeming, but their aim
Private reward, for which both God and State 1465
They easily would set to sale; a third
More generous far and civil, who confessed
They had enough revenged, having reduced
Their foe to misery beneath their fears;
The rest was magnanimity to remit, 1470
If some convenient ransom were proposed.
What noise or shout was that? it tore the sky.
    Chorus. Doubtless the people shouting to behold
Their once great dread, captive and blind before them,
Or at some proof of strength before them shown. 1475
    Manoa. His ransom, if my whole inheritance
May compass it, shall willingly be paid
And numbered down. Much rather I shall choose
To live the poorest in my tribe, than richest,
And he in that calamitous prison left. 1480

No, I am fixed not to part hence without him.
For his redemption all my patrimony,
If need be, I am ready to forgo
And quit. Not wanting him, I shall want nothing.
    Chorus. Fathers are wont to lay up for their sons;   1485
Thou for thy son art bent to lay out all;
Sons wont to nurse their parents in old age,
Thou in old age car'st how to nurse thy son,
Made older than thy age through eye-sight lost.
    Manoa. It shall be my delight to tend his eyes,   1490
And view him sitting in the house, ennobled
With all those high exploits by him achieved,
And on his shoulders waving down those locks
That of a nation armed the strength contained.
And I persuade me, God had not permitted   1495
His strength again to grow up with his hair
Garrisoned round about him like a camp
Of faithful soldiery, were not his purpose
To use him further yet in some great service —
Not to sit idle with so great a gift   1500
Useless, and thence ridiculous, about him.
And since his strength with eye-sight was not lost,
God will restore him eye-sight to his strength.
    Chorus. Thy hopes are not ill founded, nor seem vain,
Of his delivery, and thy joy thereon   1505
Conceived, agreeable to a father's love,
In both which we, as next, participate.
    Manoa. I know your friendly minds and . . . oh, what noise!
Mercy of Heaven! what hideous noise was that?
Horribly loud, unlike the former shout.   1510
    Chorus. Noise call you it, or universal groan,
As if the whole inhabitation perished!
Blood, death, and deathful deeds, are in that noise,

Ruin, destruction at the utmost point.
 Manoa. Of ruin indeed methought I heard the noise. 1515
Oh, it continues; they have slain my son!
 Chorus. Thy son is rather slaying them; that outcry
From slaughter of one foe could not ascend.
 Manoa. Some dismal accident it needs must be.
What shall we do — stay here or run and see? 1520
 Chorus. Best keep together here, lest, running thither,
We unawares run into danger's mouth.
This evil on the Philistines is fallen;
From whom could else a general cry be heard?
The sufferers then will scarce molest us here; 1525
From other hands we need not much to fear.
What if, his eye-sight (for to Israel's God
Nothing is hard) by miracle restored,
He now be dealing dole among his foes,
And over heaps of slaughtered walk his way? 1530
 Manoa. That were a joy presumptuous to be thought.
 Chorus. Yet God hath wrought things as incredible
For his people of old; what hinders now?
 Manoa. He can, I know, but doubt to think he will;
Yet hope would fain subscribe, and tempts belief. 1535
A little stay will bring some notice hither.
 Chorus. Of good or bad so great, of bad the sooner;
For evil news rides post, while good news baits.
And to our wish I see one hither speeding —
An Ebrew, as I guess, and of our tribe. 1540
 Messenger. Oh, whither shall I run, or which way fly
The sight of this so horrid spectacle,
Which erst my eyes beheld, and yet behold?
For dire imagination still pursues me.
But providence or instinct of nature seems, 1545
Or reason, though disturbed, and scarce consulted,

To have guided me aright, I know not how,
To thee first, reverend Manoa, and to these
My countrymen, whom here I knew remaining,
As at some distance from the place of horror, 1550
So in the sad event too much concerned.
  Manoa. The accident was loud, and here before thee
With rueful cry; yet what it was we hear not.
No preface needs, thou seest we long to know.
  Messenger. It would burst forth; but I recover breath, 1555
And sense distract, to know well what I utter.
  Manoa. Tell us the sum, the circumstance defer.
  Messenger. Gaza yet stands, but all her sons are fallen,
All in a moment overwhelmed and fallen.
  Manoa. Sad! but thou know'st to Israelites not saddest
The desolation of a hostile city. 1561
  Messenger. Feed on that first, there may in grief be surfeit.
  Manoa. Relate by whom.
  Messenger.   By Samson.
  Manoa.   That still lessens
The sorrow, and converts it nigh to joy.
  Messenger. Ah! Manoa, I refrain too suddenly 1565
To utter what will come at last too soon,
Lest evil tidings, with too rude irruption
Hitting thy aged ear, should pierce too deep.
  Manoa. Suspense in news is torture; speak them out. 1569
  Messenger. Take then the worst in brief: Samson is dead.
  Manoa. The worst indeed! oh, all my hope's defeated
To free him hence! but Death who sets all free
Hath paid his ransom now and full discharge.
What windy joy this day had I conceived,
Hopeful of his delivery, which now proves 1575
Abortive as the first-born bloom of spring
Nipt with the lagging rear of winter's frost!

Yet, ere I give the reins to grief, say first
How died he; death to life is crown or shame.
All by him fell, thou say'st; by whom fell he? 1580
What glorious hand gave Samson his death's wound?
   Messenger. Unwounded of his enemies he fell.
   Manoa. Wearied with slaughter, then, or how? explain.
   Messenger. By his own hands.
   Manoa.   Self-violence? what cause
Brought him so soon at variance with himself 1585
Among his foes?
   Messenger.   Inevitable cause —
At once both to destroy and be destroyed.
The edifice, where all were met to see him,
Upon their heads and on his own he pulled.
   Manoa. Oh, lastly over-strong against thyself! 1590
A dreadful way thou took'st to thy revenge.
More than enough we know; but, while things yet
Are in confusion, give us, if thou canst,
Eye-witness of what first or last was done,
Relation more particular and distinct. 1595
   Messenger. Occasions drew me early to this city,
And, as the gates I entered with sun-rise,
The morning trumpets festival proclaimed
Through each high street. Little I had dispatched,
When all abroad was rumoured that this day 1600
Samson should be brought forth, to show the people
Proof of his mighty strength in feats and games.
I sorrowed at his captive state, but minded
Not to be absent at that spectacle.
The building was a spacious theatre, 1605
Half-round, on two main pillars vaulted high,
With seats where all the lords, and each degree
Of sort, might sit in order to behold;

The other side was open, where the throng
On banks and scaffolds under sky might stand ;   1610
I among these aloof obscurely stood.
The feast and noon grew high, and sacrifice
Had filled their hearts with mirth, high cheer, and wine,
When to their sports they turned. Immediately
Was Samson as a public servant brought,   1615
In their state livery clad ; before him pipes
And timbrels ; on each side went armèd guards,
Both horse and foot ; before him and behind
Archers and slingers, cataphracts and spears.
At sight of him the people with a shout   1620
Rifted the air, clamouring their god with praise,
Who had made their dreadful enemy their thrall.
He, patient but undaunted where they led him,
Came to the place ; and what was set before him,
Which without help of eye might be assayed,   1625
To heave, pull, draw, or break, he still performed
All with incredible, stupendious force,
None daring to appear antagonist.
At length, for intermission sake, they led him
Between the pillars ; he his guide requested   1630
(For so from such as nearer stood we heard),
As over-tired, to let him lean a while
With both his arms on those two massy pillars,
That to the archèd roof gave main support.
He unsuspicious led him ; which when Samson   1635
Felt in his arms, with head a while inclined,
And eyes fast fixed, he stood, as one who prayed,
Or some great matter in his mind revolved.
At last, with head erect, thus cried aloud :
'Hitherto, Lords, what your commands imposed   1640
I have performed, as reason was, obeying,

Not without wonder or delight beheld;
Now of my own accord such other trial
I mean to show you of my strength, yet greater,
As with amaze shall strike all who behold.' 1645
This uttered, straining all his nerves, he bowed;
As with the force of winds and waters pent
When mountains tremble, those two massy pillars
With horrible convulsion to and fro
He tugged, he shook, till down they came, and drew 1650
The whole roof after them, with burst of thunder,
Upon the heads of all who sat beneath,
Lords, ladies, captains, counsellors, or priests,
Their choice nobility and flower, not only
Of this, but each Philistian city round, 1655
Met from all parts to solemnize this feast.
Samson, with these inmixed, inevitably
Pulled down the same destruction on himself;
The vulgar only scaped, who stood without.
   Chorus. Oh, dearly-bought revenge, yet glorious! 1660
Living or dying thou hast fulfilled
The work for which thou wast foretold
To Israel, and now liest victorious
Among thy slain self-killed;
Not willingly, but tangled in the fold 1665
Of dire Necessity, whose law in death conjoined
Thee with thy slaughtered foes, in number more
Than all thy life had slain before.
   Semichorus. While their hearts were jocund and sublime,
Drunk with idolatry, drunk with wine, 1670
And fat regorged of bulls and goats,
Chaunting their idol, and preferring
Before our living Dread, who dwells
In Silo, his bright sanctuary,

Among them he a spirit of phrenzy sent, 1675
Who hurt their minds,
And urged them on with mad desire
To call in haste for their destroyer.
They, only set on sport and play,
Unweetingly importuned 1680
Their own destruction to come speedy upon them.
So fond are mortal men,
Fallen into wrath divine,
As their own ruin on themselves to invite,
Insensate left, or to sense reprobate, 1685
And with blindness internal struck.
    Semichorus. But he, though blind of sight,
Despised, and thought extinguished quite,
With inward eyes illuminated,
His fiery virtue roused 1690
From under ashes into sudden flame,
And as an evening dragon came,
Assailant on the perchèd roosts
And nests in order ranged
Of tame villatic fowl, but as an eagle 1695
His cloudless thunder bolted on their heads.
So Virtue, given for lost,
Depressed and overthrown, as seemed,
Like that self-begotten bird,
In the Arabian woods embost, 1700
That no second knows nor third,
And lay erewhile a holocaust,
From out her ashy womb now teemed,
Revives, reflourishes, then vigorous most
When most unactive deemed ; 1705
And, though her body die, her fame survives,
A secular bird, ages of lives.

Manoa. Come, come ; no time for lamentation now,
Nor much more cause. Samson hath quit himself
Like Samson, and heroicly hath finished   1710
A life heroic, on his enemies
Fully revenged; hath left them years of mourning,
And lamentation to the sons of Caphtor
Through all Philistian bounds ; to Israel
Honour hath left and freedom, let but them   1715
Find courage to lay hold on this occasion ;
To himself and father's house eternal fame ;
And, which is best and happiest yet, all this
With God not parted from him, as was feared,
But favouring and assisting to the end.   1720
Nothing is here for tears, nothing to wail
Or knock the breast ; no weakness, no contempt,
Dispraise, or blame ; nothing but well and fair,
And what may quiet us in a death so noble.
Let us go find the body where it lies   1725
Soaked in his enemies' blood, and from the stream
With lavers pure, and cleansing herbs, wash off
The clotted gore. I, with what speed the while
(Gaza is not in plight to say us nay),
Will send for all my kindred, all my friends,   1730
To fetch him hence, and solemnly attend,
With silent obsequy and funeral train,
Home to his father's house. There will I build him
A monument, and plant it round with shade
Of laurel ever green, and branching palm,   1735
With all his trophies hung, and acts enrolled
In copious legend, or sweet lyric song.
Thither shall all the valiant youth resort,
And from his memory inflame their breasts
To matchless valour, and adventures high ;   1740

The virgins also shall, on feastful days,
Visit his tomb with flowers, only bewailing
His lot unfortunate in nuptial choice,
From whence captivity and loss of eyes.

Chorus. All is best, though we oft doubt,   1745
What the unsearchable dispose
Of Highest Wisdom brings about,
And ever best found in the close.
Oft He seems to hide his face,
But unexpectedly returns,   1750
And to his faithful champion hath in place
Bore witness gloriously; whence Gaza mourns,
And all that band them to resist
His uncontrollable intent.
His servants He, with new acquist   1755
Of true experience from this great event,
With peace and consolation hath dismissed,
And calm of mind, all passion spent.

NOTES

A Defence of the People of England

Page 2. *Salmasius* (Claudius), Latinized name of Claude de Saumaise, b. 1588, d. 1653; regarded in his time, throughout Europe, as the paragon of scholarship; engaged, after the execution of Charles I., to defend the royal cause against the Commonwealth, which he endeavored to do in his *Defensio Regia pro Carolo I.*, addressed to Charles II. In this work he defines a king ('if that,' says Milton, 'may be said to be defined which he makes infinite') 'to be a person in whom the supreme power of the kingdom resides, who is answerable to God alone, who may do whatsoever pleases him, who is bound by no law.'

P. 4, 5. *single person:* Milton himself, who replied to the *Eikon Basilike*, and refuted its 'maudlin sophistry' in his *Eikonoklastes; antagonist of mine:* Salmasius.

The Second Defence of the People of England

P. 7. *one eminent above the rest:* Salmasius.

P. 9, 10. *columns of Hercules:* the mountains on each side of the Straits of Gibraltar. It was fabled that they were formerly one mountain, which was rent asunder by Hercules. *Triptolemus:* the fabled inventor of the plough and the distributor of grain among men, under favor of Ceres.

P. 10. *the most noble queen of Sweden:* Christina, daughter of Gustavus Adolphus.

P. 12. *Monstrum horrendum:* a monster horrible, mis-shapen, huge, deprived of his eyesight; description of the Cyclops Polyphemus, whose one eye was put out by Ulysses. — *Virgil's Æneid*, iii. 658.

P. 14. *Tiresias:* the blind prophet of Thebes. *Apollonius Rhodius:* poet and rhetorician (B.C. 280–203), author of the *Argonautica*, a heroic poem on the Argonautic expedition to Colchis in quest of the golden fleece.

P. 14, 15. *Timoleon of Corinth:* Greek statesman and general, who expelled the tyrants from the Greek cities of Sicily, and restored the democratic form of government; died blind, 337 B.C. *Appius Claudius:* surnamed Cæcus from his blindness. Roman consul, 307 and 296; induced the senate, in his old age, to reject the terms of peace which Cineas had proposed on behalf of Pyrrhus. *Pyrrhus:* king of Epirus

(B.C. 318-272), who waged war against the Romans. *Cæcilius Metellus:* Roman consul, B.C. 251, 249; pontifex maximus for twenty-two years from 243; lost his sight in 241 while rescuing the Palladium when the temple of Vesta was on fire. *Dandolo (Enrico)*: b. 1107(?); elected Doge in 1192; d. 1205. He was ninety-six years old when, though blind, he commanded the Venetians at the taking of Constantinople, June 17, 1203.

'Oh, for one hour of blind old Dandolo!
The octogenarian chief, Byzantium's conquering foe.'
— *Byron's Childe Harold*, Canto iv. St. xii.

Ziska, or Zizka (John): military chief of the Hussites, b. 1360(?), d. 1424; his real name was Trocznow; he lost an eye in battle, and was thence called Ziska, *i.e.* one-eyed; lost his other eye from an arrow at the siege of Rubi, but his blindness did not prevent his continuing the war against ecclesiastical tyranny. *Jerome Zanchius* (Girolamo Zanchi), Italian Protestant theologian, b. 1516, d. 1590; was canon regular of the Lateran when he became a Protestant; professor of theology and philosophy, University of Strasburg, 1553-1563; professor of theology, University of Heidelberg, 1568-1576.

P. 16. *Æsculapius:* the god of medicine. *Epidaurus* (now Epidauro): chief seat of the worship of Æsculapius; *the son of Thetis:* Achilles, the hero of the Iliad. I have substituted the Earl of Derby's translation of the lines which follow from the Iliad, for that given by Robert Fellowes.

P. 18. *Prytaneum:* 'a public building in the towns of Greece, where the Prytanes (chief magistrates in the states) assembled and took their meals together, and where those who had deserved well of their country were maintained during life.'

P. 19, 20. *born in London:* 9th of December, 1608; *grammar-school:* St. Paul's, notable among the classical seminaries then in London. The head-master was a Mr. Alexander Gill, Sr., and the sub-master, or usher, Mr. Alexander Gill, Jr.; with the latter Milton afterward maintained an intimate friendship.

P. 20. *On my father's estate:* at Horton, in Buckinghamshire. *Henry Wotton:* at this time Provost of Eton. His letter to Milton is dated 13 April, 1638. In the concluding paragraph, Sir Henry writes: 'At Sienna I was tabled in the house of one Alberto Scipioni, an old Roman courtier in dangerous times, . . . at my departure toward Rome (which had been the centre of his experience) I had won confidence enough to beg his advice, how I might carry myself securely there, without offence of others, or of mine own conscience. *Signor Arrigo mio* (says he), *I pensieri stretti, & il viso sciolto:* that is, your thoughts close and your countenance loose, will go safely over the whole world. Of which Delphian oracle (for so I have found it) your judgment doth need no commentary; and therefore, Sir, I will commit you with it to the best of all securities, God's dear love, remaining your friend as much at command as any of longer date.' Milton was certainly the last man in the world to make such a prudential, or rather crafty, maxim his rule of conduct, even in such a country as Italy then was. He has stated his own rule further on in this extract. *Thomas Scudamore:* miswritten for John (*Masson*).

P. 21. *Jacopo Gaddi:* a prominent and influential literary man of Florence, member of the Florentine Academy, author of poems, historical essays, etc., in Latin and in Italian. *Carlo Dati:* his full name was Carlo Ruberto Dati; only in his 19th year when Milton visited Florence; was afterwards one of the most distinguished of the Florentine men of letters and academicians; became strongly attached to Milton, and corresponded with him after his return to England; author of 'Vite de' Pittori Antichi' (Lives of the Ancient Painters) and numerous other works.

P. 21. *Frescobaldi* (*Pietro*): a Florentine academician. *Coltellini* (*Agostino*): a Florentine advocate; founder of an academy under the name of the Apatisti (the Indifferents). 'Such were the attractions of this academy, and so energetic was Coltellini in its behalf, that within ten or twenty years after its foundation it had a fame among the Italian academies equal, in some respects, to that of the first and oldest, and counted among its members not only all the eminent Florentines, but most of the distinguished *literati* of Italy, besides cardinals, Italian princes and dukes, many foreign nobles and scholars, and at least one pope.' — *Masson*. *Bonmattei*, or *Buommattei* (*Benedetto*): an eminent member of various Florentine and other academies; author of various works, among them a commentary on parts of Dante, and a standard treatise, *Della Lingua Toscana;* by profession a priest. *Chimentelli* (*Valerio*): a priest; professor of Greek, and then of Eloquence and Politics, in Pisa; author of an archæological work, entitled *Marmor Pisanum*. *Francini* (*Antonio*): Florentine academician and poet. *Lucas Holstenius* (in the vernacular, Lukas Holste, or Holsten), secretary to Cardinal Barberini, and one of the librarians of the Vatican. *Manso:* author of a Life of Tasso, 1619. Milton, just before leaving Naples, addressed to him his Latin poem, *Mansus*.

P. 22. *so little reserve on matters of religion:* here it appears that he did not make Sir Henry Wotton's prudential maxim his rule of conduct.

P. 22, 23. *the slandering More* (Lat. *Morus*), Alexander: a Reformed minister, then resident in Holland, and at one time a friend of Salmasius. He had formerly been Professor of Greek in the University of Geneva. The real author of the *Regii Sanguinis Clamor* was the Rev. Dr. Peter Du Moulin, the younger, made, 1660, a prebendary of Canterbury. More was, indeed, the publisher of the book, the corrector of the press, and author of the dedicatory preface in the printer's name, to Charles II. Milton fully believed when he wrote the Second Defence that More was the author of the *R. S. C.*, having received convincing assurances that he was. *Diodati* (Dr. Jean, or Giovanni), uncle of Milton's friend, Carolo Diodati. He made the Italian translation of the Scriptures, known as Diodati's Bible, published in 1607. *at the time when Charles,* etc.: Milton's return to England was not, as he himself (by a slip of memory, no doubt) states, 'at the time when Charles, having broken the peace with the Scots, was renewing the second of those wars named Episcopal,' but exactly a twelvemonth previous to that time, and about eight months before the meeting of the Short Parliament. — *Keightley.*

P. 24. *two books to a friend:* 'Of Reformation in England, and the causes that hitherto have hindered it. 1641.' *two bishops:* Dr. Joseph Hall (1574–1656), Bishop of Exeter, afterward Bishop of Norwich; and Dr. James Usher (1580–1656), Archbishop of Armagh and Primate of Ireland. *Concerning Prelatical Episcopacy:* the full title is, 'Of prelatical episcopacy, and whether it may be deduced from the apostolical times, by virtue of those testimonies which are alleged to that purpose in some late treatises; one whereof goes under the name of James, Archbishop of Armagh. 1641.' *Concerning the mode of ecclesiastical government:* 'The reason of church government urged against prelaty. 1641.'

P. 24. *Animadversions:* 'Animadversions upon the remonstrant's defence against Smectymnuus. 1641.'

P. 24. *Apology:* 'An apology for Smectymnuus.' 1642. The pamphlet by Smectymnuus was published with the following title, which is sufficiently descriptive of its character: 'An Answer to a Book entituled "An Humble Remonstrance" [by Bishop Hall], in which the originall of Liturgy [and] Episcopacy is discussed and quæres propounded concerning both, the parity of Bishops and Presbyters in Scripture demonstrated, the occasion of their unparity in Antiquity discovered, the disparity of the ancient and our modern Bishops manifested, the antiquity of Ruling Elders in the Church vindicated, the Prelaticall Church bounded: Written by Smectymnuus.' 1641. The pamphlet was the joint production of five Presbyterian clergymen, Stephen Marshall, Edmund Calamy, Thomas Young, Matthew Newcomen, and William Spurstow, but written for the most part by Thomas Young, Milton's former tutor. The name Smectymnuus was made up from the several authors' initials: S. M., E. C., T. Y., M. N., U. U. (for W.) S.

P. 24. *the domestic species:* the titles of the pamphlets on marriage and divorce are: 'The Doctrine and Discipline of Divorce,' 1643, 1644; 'The Judgment of Martin Bucer concerning Divorce,' 1644; 'Tetrachordon: expositions upon the four chief places in Scripture which treat of marriage, or nullities in marriage,' 1644; 'Colasterion: a reply to a nameless answer against the Doctrine and Discipline of Divorce,' 1645.

P. 25. *Selden (John)*, 1584-1654, celebrated English lawyer, statesman, and political writer. His 'Table Talk' was long famous, 'being his sense of various matters of weight and high consequence, relating especially to religion and state.'

P. 25. *an inferior at home:* many passages in Milton's works, poetical and prose, indicate, on his part, an estimate of woman which may be attributed, in some measure, at least, to his unfortunate first marriage. His own opinions of what should be the relation of wife to husband he, no doubt, expressed in the following passages in the 'Paradise Lost,' Book iv. 635-638, x. 145-156, xi. 287-292, 629-636; and in the 'Samson Agonistes,' 1053-1060. But no one can read the several treatises on Divorce without being impressed with the loftiness of Milton's ideal of marriage, and his sense of the sacred duties appertaining thereto. The only true marriage with him was the union of *souls,* as well as of bodies, souls whom *God* hath joined together (Matt. xix. 6, Mark x. 9), not the priest nor the magistrate.

P. 25. *the principles of education:* 'Of Education. To Master Samuel Hartlib.' 1644. Hartlib was nominally a merchant in London, a foreigner by birth, the son of a Polish merchant of German extraction, settled in Elbing, in Prussia, whose wife was the daughter of a wealthy English merchant of Dantzic. He was a reformer and philanthropist, and an advocate of the views of the educational reformer, Comenius.

P. 25. '*Areopagitica:* a speech for the liberty of unlicensed printing, to the Parliament of England.' 1644.

P. 26. *what might lawfully be done against tyrants:* in his pamphlet entitled, 'The Tenure of Kings and Magistrates: proving that it is lawfu', and hath been held so through all ages, for any, who have the power, to call to account a tyrant or wicked king, and, after due conviction, to depose, and put him to death, if the ordinary magistrate have neglected, or denied to do it; and that they who of late so much blame deposing are the men that did it themselves. The author J. M. 1649.'

P. 27. *history of my country:* 'The History of Britain; that part especially now called England. From the first traditional beginning continued to the Norman Conquest.'

P. 27. *I had already finished four books:* i.e. in 1648; the work was not published till 1670. It contained the fine portrait of Milton, by William Faithorne, for which he sat in his 62d year.

P. 27. *A book . . . ascribed to the king:* ten days after the king's death, was published (9 Feb. 1649), ' Εἰκὼν Βασιλική: The True Portraicture of His Sacred Majestie in his Solitudes and Sufferings. — *Rom.* viii. *More than conquerour,* &c. — *Bona agere et mala pati Regium est.* — MDCXLVIII.' The book professed to be the king's own production, and Milton answered it as such, tho' it appears he had his suspicions as to its authorship. It was universally regarded, at the time, as the king's; but it was before long well known (though the controversy as to the authorship was long after kept up) to have been written by Dr. John Gauden, Rector of Bocking, and, after the Restoration, Bishop of Exeter, and, a short time before his death, Bishop of Worcester. Milton's reply, published 6th of Oct., 1649, is entitled ' ΕΙΚΟΝΟΚΛΆΣΤΗΣ in Answer To a Book Intitl'd Ε'ΙΚΩ'Ν ΒΑΣΙΛΙΚΗ', The Portrature of his Sacred Majesty in his Solitudes and Sufferings. The Author I. M.

Prov. xxviii. 15, 16, 17.

15. As a roaring Lyon, and a ranging Beare, so is a wicked Ruler over the poor people.

16. The Prince that wanteth understanding, is also a great oppressor; but he that hateth covetousnesse shall prolong his dayes.

17. A man that doth violence to the blood of any person, shall fly to the pit, let no man stay him.

Salust. Conjurat. Catilin.

Regium imperium, quod initio, conservandæ libertatis, atque augendæ reipub. causâ fuerat, in superbiam, dominationemque se convertit.

Regibus boni, quam mali, suspectiores sunt; semperque his aliena virtus formidolosa est.

Quidlibet impunè facere, hoc scilicet regium est.

Published by Authority.

London, Printed by Matthew Simmons, next dore to the gilded Lyon in Aldersgate street. 1649.'

P. 27. *Salmasius then appeared:* that is, with his *Defensio Regia pro Carolo I.*

To Charles Diodati

P. 28. *Chester's Dee:* the old city of Chester is situated on the Dee (Lat. *Deva.*).

P. 28. *Vergivian wave* (Lat. *Vergivium salum*): the Irish Sea.

P. 28. *it is not my care to revisit the reedy Cam,* etc.: this was the period of his rustication from Christ's College, Cambridge, due, it seems, to some difficulty which Milton had with his tutor, Mr. Chappell.

P. 28. *the tearful exile in the Pontic territory:* Ovid, who was relegated (rather than exiled) to Tomi, a town on the Euxine.

P. 28. *Maro:* the Latin poet, Publius Virgilius Maro.

P. 29. *or the unhappy boy . . . or the fierce avenger:* as Masson suggests, the allusions here may be to Shakespeare's Romeo and the Ghost in *Hamlet.*

P. 29. *the house of Pelops,* etc.: subjects of the principal Greek tragedies.

P. 29. *the arms of living Pelops:* an allusion to the ivory shoulder of Pelops, by which, when he was restored to life after having been served up at a feast of the gods, given by his father Tantalus, the shoulder consumed by Ceres was replaced.

P. 30. *thy own flower:* the anemone into which Adonis was turned by Venus, after his dying of a wound received from a wild boar during the chase.

P. 30. *alternate measures:* the alternate hexameters and pentameters of the Elegy.

To Alexander Gill, Jr. (*Familiar Letters,* No. III.)

P. 30. *Alexander Gill, Jr.:* Gill was Milton's tutor in St. Paul's School, of which his father, Alexander Gill, was head-master. Milton was sent to this school in his twelfth year (1620), and remained there till his seventeenth year (1625). He was entered very soon after at Christ's College, Cambridge, beginning residence in the Easter term of 1625.

To Thomas Young. (*Familiar Letters,* No. IV.)

P. 31. *Thomas Young:* Young had been Milton's tutor before he entered St. Paul's School, and later; he was one of the authors of the Smectymnuan pamphlet; was appointed Master of Jesus College, Cambridge, in 1644.

P. 31. *Stoa of the Iceni* (Lat. *Stoam Icenorum*): a pun for Stowmarket in Suffolk, the Iceni having been the inhabitants of the parts of Roman Britain corresponding to Suffolk, Cambridgeshire, etc.—*Masson*. Their queen was Boadicea, who led their revolt against the Romans.

P. 31. *Zeno:* Greek philosopher (about 358–260 B.C.), father of the Stoic philosophy, so called from his teaching in the *Stoa Pœcile*, in Athens, in which were the frescoes of Polygnotus (about 480–430 B.C.).

P. 31. *Serranus:* an agnomen, or fourth name, given to L. Quinctius Cincinnatus; Roman consul 460 B.C.; in 458 called from the plough to the dictatorship, whence called by Florus, *Dictator ab aratro;* the agnomen is said to have been derived from *serere*, to sow; 'Quis te, magne Cato, tacitum, aut te, Cosse, relinquat? ... vel te sulco, Serrane, serentem' (Who can leave thee unmentioned, great Cato, or thee, Cossus? ... or thee, Serranus, sowing in the furrow).—*Æneid*, vi. 844.

P. 31. *Curius:* M'. Curius Dentatus, noted for his fortitude and frugality; consul B.C. 290; a second time 275, when he defeated Pyrrhus, king of Epirus; consul a third time, 274; afterward retired to his small farm, which he cultivated himself.

To Charles Diodati, making a Stay in the Country

P. 32. *Erato:* the muse of erotic poetry.

P. 32. *the fierce dog:* Cerberus.

P. 32. *the Samian master:* Pythagoras, who was a native of Samos.

P. 32. *Tiresias:* the Theban prophet, deprived of sight by Juno; Jupiter, in compensation, bestowed upon him the power of prophecy.

P. 32. *Theban Linus:* the singer and philosopher.

P. 32. *Calchas the exile:* a famous soothsayer, who accompanied the Greeks to Troy.

P. 32. *Orpheus:* the fabulous Thracian poet and musician.

P. 32. *Circe:* See Comus, 50–53.

P. 33. *the heavenly birth of the King of Peace:* his ode *On the Morning of Christ's Nativity*, composed on and just after Christmas, 1629.

Ad Patrem

P. 35. 1. *Pieria's:* used for Pierian, from Pierus, a mountain of Thessaly sacred to the muses.

P. 36. 18. *Clio:* the Muse of History, 'inasmuch,' says Masson, 'as what he is to say about his Father is strictly true.'

P. 36. 22. *Promethean fire:* the fire which Prometheus brought down from heaven.

P. 37. 44. *Ophiuchus:* i.e. a serpent holder (ὄφις + ἔχειν); a constellation in the northern hemisphere, the outline of which is imagined to be a man holding a serpent; called also Anguitenens and Serpentarius, which have the same meaning; Ophiuchus is the translator's word; the original is *sibila serpens,* the hissing serpent.

P. 37. 45. *Orion:* a constellation with sword, belt, and club; 'Orion arm'd.' — *P. L.,* i. 305.

P. 37. 50. *Lyæus:* an epithet of Bacchus as the deliverer from care (Gk. λυαίος).

P. 37. 53. *proposed:* set forth.

P. 37. 55. *to imitation:* i.e. for imitation, to be imitated, *i.e.* the character of heroes and their deeds.

P. 38. 92. *Streams Aonian:* so called as if the resort of the muses.

P. 39. 120. *the boy:* Phaëton.

P. 40. 141-148. *Ye too, . . . my voluntary numbers:* it does not seem to me improbable that these six lines [115-120 of the original] were added to the poem just before its publication in the volume of 1645. The phrase '*juvenilia carmina*' seems to refer to that volume as containing this piece among others. Anyhow, it was a beautiful ending and prophetic. — *Masson.*

An English Letter to a Friend

P. 40. *English letter to a friend:* this letter of which there are two undated drafts in Milton's handwriting in the Library of Trinity College, Cambridge, must have been written in 1632 or 1633. In the second draft (which is given in the text), Milton is content, for the first few sentences, with simply correcting the language of the first; but in the remaining portion he throws the first draft all but entirely aside, and rewrites the same meaning more at large in a series of new sentences. Evidently he took pains with the letter. —*Masson.*

P. 41. *tale of Latmus:* i.e. of Endymion's sleeping upon Mount Latmus, and of his being visited by Selene (the moon).

P. 42. 5. *Perhaps my semblance might deceive the truth:* i.e. he appears younger than he really is. In his Second Defence, he says, 'though I am more than forty years old, there is scarcely any one to whom I do not appear ten years younger than I am.'

P. 42. 8. *timely-happy:* happy, or fortunate, in the matter of inward ripeness.

P. 42. 10. *it:* 'inward ripeness.'

P. 42. *it shall be still:* Milton very early regarded himself as dedicated to the performance of some great work for which he had to make adequate preparation, in the way of building himself up; *even:* equal, in proportion to, in conformity with.

P. 43. *Your true and unfeigned friend, etc.:* see penultimate sentence of the passage given, p. 65, from 'The Reason of Church Government urged against Prelaty.'

To Alexander Gill, Jr. (*Familiar Letters*, No. V.)

P. 43. *this ode:* Psalm cxiv.

To Charles Diodati. (*Familiar Letters*, No. VI.)

P. 44. *To Charles Diodati:* Milton's schoolfellow at St. Paul's, and his dearest friend; he died in August, 1638, while Milton was on his Continental tour; on his return he wrote the *In memoriam* poem, *Epitaphium Damonis*.

To Benedetto Bonmattei of Florence. (*Familiar Letters*, No. VIII.)

P. 46. *To Benedetto Bonmattei:* mentioned by Milton among his Florentine friends, in the autobiographical passage in the Second Defence; see note, p. 247.

Mansus

P. 47. *our native kings:* the ancient kings of Britain.

P. 47. *stirring wars even under the earth:* King Arthur, after his death, was supposed to be carried into the subterraneous land of Faerie, or of Spirits, where he still reigned as a king, and whence he was to return into Britain, to renew the Round Table, conquer all his old enemies, and reëstablish his throne. He was, therefore, *etiam movens bella sub terris*, still meditating wars under the earth. The impulse of his attachment to this subject was not entirely suppressed; it produced his History of Britain. By the expression *revocabo in carmina*, the poet means, that these ancient kings, which were once the themes of the British bards, should now again be celebrated in verse. — *Warton*. Warton renders *bella moventem* [v. 81 of the Latin] *meditating wars*, but that is not the true sense; it is waging wars, and Arthur is represented as so employed in Fairy-land in the romances. — *Keightley*.

P. 47. *Paphian myrtle:* the myrtle was sacred to Venus; Paphos was an ancient city of Cyprus, where was a temple of Venus.

Areopagitica

P. 48. *Galileo:* b. 1564, d. 1642; he was seventy-four years old when Milton visited him in 1638; whether he was actually imprisoned at the time is somewhat uncertain; he may have been, as Hales suggests, *in libera custodia, i.e.* 'only kept under a certain restraint, as that he should not move away from a specified neighborhood, or perhaps a special house.

P. 48. *never be forgotten by any revolution of time:* i.e. as Hales explains, caused to be forgotten.

P. 48. *other parts:* i.e. of the world.

P. 48. *in time of parliament:* there was no parliament assembled from 1629 to 1640.

P. 48. *without envy:* without exciting any odium against me. — *Hales.*

P. 48. *he whom an honest quæstorship:* Cicero, 75 B.C.

P. 48. *Verres:* pro-prætor in Sicily, 73–71 B.C. Cicero's Verrine orations were directed against his extortions and exactions.

To Lucas Holstenius. (*Familiar Letters*, No. IX.)

P. 49. *Lucas Holstenius:* see note, p. 21.

P. 49. *Alexander Cherubini:* Roman friend of Milton, 'known in his lifetime as a prodigy of erudition, though he died at the early age of twenty-eight.'

P. 49. *Virgil's 'penitus convalle virenti':* Virgil's 'souls enclosed within a verdant valley, and about to go to the upper light.'

P. 49. *Cardinal Francesco Barberini:* b. 1597, d. 1679; librarian of the Vatican, and founder of the Barberini Library.

Epitaphium Damonis

P. 50. In the British legends of Geoffrey of Monmouth and others, the mythical Brutus, before arriving in Britain with his Trojans, marries Imogen, daughter of the Grecian king Pandrasus; Brennus and Belinus are two legendary British princes of a much later age, sons of King Dunwallo Molmutius; Arvirach or Arviragus, son of Cunobeline, or Cymbeline, belongs to the time of the Roman conquest of Britain; the "Armorican settlers" are the Britons who removed to the French coast of Armonica to avoid the invading Saxons; Uther Pendragon, Igraine, Gorlois, Merlin, and Arthur are familiar names of the Arthurian romances. — *Masson.*

Of Reformation in England

P. 52. *their damned designs:* the restoration of Papacy and ecclesiastical despotism.

P. 53. *antichristian thraldom:* he would seem to allude to the invasions of England by the Romans, Saxons, Danes (twice), and Normans, and the War of the Roses, followed by the partial reformation under Henry VIII. — *Keightley*.

P. 53. *Thule:* some undetermined island or other land, regarded as the northernmost part of the earth; called in Latin *Ultima Thule;* often used metaphorically for an extreme limit.

P. 53. *that horrible and damned blast:* Keightley understands this as referring to the Gunpowder plot.

P. 53. *that sad intelligencing tyrant:* Philip IV., King of Spain from 1621 to 1665.

P. 53. *mines of Ophir:* used in a general sense for gold mines.

P. 53. *his naval ruins:* an allusion to the destruction of the Spanish armada, in 1588, in the reign of his grandfather, Philip II.

P. 54. *in this land:* when Milton wrote this, he must still have been meditating a poem to be based on British history.

Animadversions upon the Remonstrant's Defence, etc.

P. 56. *and thou standing at the door:* see introductory remarks on Lycidas.

The Reason of Church Government urged against Prelaty

P. 57. *Slothful, and ever to be set light by:* thou slothful one, and ever, etc.

P. 57. *infancy:* not speaking.

P. 58. *preventive:* going before, forecasting, anticipative.

P. 58. *equal:* impartial, equitable; Lat. *æqualis*.

P. 58. *the elegant and learned reader:* him only Milton addressed, not the common reader. He was no demagogue.

P. 58. *anything elaborately composed:* he had his meditated great work in mind.

P. 59. *another task:* poetical composition.

P. 59. *empyreal conceit:* lofty conceit of himself.

P. 59. *envy:* odium; Lat. *invidia*.

P. 60. *Ariosto (Lodovico)*: Italian poet; b. 1474, d. 1533; author of the *Orlando Furioso*.

P. 60. *Bembo (Pietro)*: b. 1470, d. 1547; secretary to Pope Leo X.; Cardinal, 1539; famous as a Latin scholar.

P. 60. *wits:* geniuses.

P. 61. *Tasso (Torquato)*: Italian poet; b. 1544, d. 1595; author of the *Gerusalemme Liberata* (Jerusalem Delivered).

P. 61. *a prince of Italy:* Alfonso II., Duke of Ferrara?

P. 61. *Godfrey's expedition against the Infidels:* the subject of Tasso's Jerusalem Delivered; Godfrey of Bouillon, leader of the first crusade; b. about 1058, d. 1100.

P. 61. *Belisarius:* a celebrated general, in the reign of Justinian; b. about 505 A.D., d. 565.

P. 61. *Charlemagne* (or Charles the Great): b. 742, d. 814; Emperor of the West and King of the Franks.

P. 61. *doctrinal and exemplary:* instructive and serving for example.

P. 61. *Origen:* Christian Father, of Alexandria (185–254).

P. 61. *Pareus (David)*: b. 1548, d. 1622; a Calvinist theologian, Professor of Theology, University of Heidelberg.

P. 62. *Pindarus:* Greek lyric poet, about 522–442 B.C.

P. 62. *Callimachus:* Greek poet and grammarian, about 310–235 B.C.

P. 62. *most an end:* 'almost uninterruptedly, almost always, mostly, for the most part.'—*Murray's New English Dictionary*, s.v. 'an end.' The phrase occurs again in Chap. III. Book II. of this same pamphlet: 'the patients, which most an end are brought into his [the civil magistrate's] hospital, are such as are far gone,' etc. Vol. II. p. 491, of the Bohn ed. of the P. W.

P. 63. *demean:* conduct; O. Fr. *demener*.

P. 63. *such (sports, etc.) as were authorized a while since:* i.e. in the Book of Sports. Proclamation allowing Sunday sports, issued by James I.

P. 63. *paneguries:* same as panegyrics.

P. 64. *Siren daughters:* the Muses, daughters of Memory or Mnemosyne.

P. 65. *gentle apprehension:* a refined faculty of conception or perception.

Apology for Smectymnuus

P. 66. *Solon:* Athenian statesman and lawgiver, about 638–558 B.C. 'According to Suidas it was a law of Solon that he who stood neuter in any public sedition, should be declared ἄτιμος, infamous.'

P. 66. *doubted:* hesitated; or, perhaps, in the sense of feared.

P. 66. *most nominated:* most frequently named, most prominent.

P. 66, 67. *my certain account:* the account which I shall certainly have to render.

S

P. 67. *tired out almost a whole youth:* see the extract given from 'The Reason of Church Government urged against Prelaty.'

P. 67. *this modest confuter:* Dr. Joseph Hall, Bishop of Exeter, afterward of Norwich; the reference is to his 'Modest Confutation' of Milton's 'Animadversions.'

P. 69. *Animadversions:* 'A. upon the Remonstrant's Defence against Smectymnuus.' 1641.

P. 69. *devised:* described, represented.

P. 70. *conversation:* in New Testament sense, mode or way of life, conduct, deportment (ἀναστροφή).

P. 70. *apology:* defence, vindication.

P. 71. *propense:* inclined, disposed.

P. 71. *that place:* the University.

P. 71. *to obtain with me:* prevail, succeed with me, to get the better of.

P. 71. *both she or her sister:* Cambridge or Oxford University; 'both' requires 'and'; 'or' requires 'either.'

P. 71. *that suburb sink:* the 'pretty garden-house in Aldersgate street,' as his nephew, Edward Phillips styles it, to which he removed from 'his lodgings in St. Bride's Churchyard,' in 1640, and where he was living when he wrote his 'Apology for Smectymnuus.'

P. 72. *I never greatly admired, so now much less:* in 'The Reason of Church Government urged against Prelaty' ('The Conclusion. The mischief that Prelaty does in the State'), Milton writes: 'The service of God, who is truth, her (Prelaty's) liturgy confesses to be perfect freedom; but her works and her opinions declare that the service of prelaty is perfect slavery, and by consequence perfect falsehood. Which makes me wonder much that many of the gentry, studious men as I hear, should engage themselves to write and speak publicly in her defence; but that I believe their honest and ingenuous natures coming to the universities to store themselves with good and solid learning, and there unfortunately fed with nothing else but the scragged and thorny lectures of monkish and miserable sophistry, were sent home again with such a scholastic bur in their throats, as hath stopped and hindered all true and generous philosophy from entering, cracked their voices for ever with metaphysical gargarisms, and hath made them admire a sort of formal outside men prelatically addicted, whose unchastened and unwrought minds were never yet initiated or subdued under the true lore of religion or moral virtue, which two are the best and greatest points of learning; but either slightly trained up in a kind of hypocritical and hackney course of literature to get their living by, and dazzle the ignorant, or else fondly over-studied in useless controversies, except those which they use with all the specious and delusive subtlety they are able, to defend their prelatical Sparta.'

P. 72. *wisses:* knows.

P. 72. *the bird that first rouses:* the lark; see 'L'Allegro,' 41 *et seq.*

P. 72. *old cloaks, false beards, night-walkers, and salt lotion:* the passage alluded to in the 'Animadversions,' is the following: 'We know where the shoe wrings you, you fret and are galled at the quick; and oh what a death it is to the prelates to be thus unvisarded, thus uncased, to have the periwigs plucked off, that cover your baldness, your inside nakedness thrown open to public view! The Romans had a time, once every year, when their slaves might freely speak their minds; it were hard if the free-born people of England, with whom the voice of truth for these many years, even against the proverb, hath not been heard but in corners, after all your monkish prohibitions, and expurgatorious indexes, your gags and snaffles, your proud Imprimaturs not to be obtained without the shallow surview, but *not shallow hand* of some mercenary, narrow-souled, and illiterate chaplain; when liberty of speaking, than which nothing is more sweet to man, was girded and strait-laced almost to a brokenwinded phthisic, if now, at a good time, our time of parliament, the very jubilee and resurrection of the state, if now the concealed, the aggrieved, and long-persecuted truth, could not be suffered to speak; and though she burst out with some efficacy of words, could not be excused after such an injurious strangle of silence, nor avoid the censure of libelling, it were hard, it were something pinching in a kingdom of free spirits. Some princes, and great statists, have thought it a prime piece of necessary policy, to thrust themselves under disguise into a popular throng, to stand the night long under eaves of houses, and low windows, that they might hear everywhere the utterances of private breasts, and amongst them find out the precious gem of truth, as amongst the numberless pebbles of the shore; whereby they might be the abler to discover, and avoid, that deceitful and close-couched evil of flattery, that ever attends them, and misleads them, and might skilfully know how to apply the several redresses to each malady of state, without trusting the disloyal information of parasites and sycophants; whereas now this permission of free writing, were there no good else in it, yet at some time thus licensed, is such an unripping, such an anatomy of the shyest and tenderest particular truths, as makes not only the whole nation in many points the wiser, but also presents and carries home to princes, men most remote from vulgar concourse, such a full insight of every lurking evil, or restrained good among the commons, as that they shall not need hereafter, in old cloaks and false beards, to stand to the courtesy of a night-walking cudgeller for eaves-dropping, not to accept quietly as a perfume, the overhead emptying of some salt lotion. Who could be angry, therefore, but those that are guilty, with these free-spoken and plain-hearted men, that are the eyes of their country, and the prospective glasses of their prince? But these are the nettlers, these are the blabbing books that tell, though not half your fellows' feats. You love toothless satires; let me inform you, a toothless satire is as improper as a toothed sleekstone, and as bullish.'

P. 73. *antistrophon:* reasoning turned upon an opponent.

P. 73. *mime:* a kind of buffoon play, in which real persons and events were ridiculously mimicked and represented.

P. 73. *Mundus alter et idem* (another world and the same): a satire by Bishop Hall.

P. 73. *Cephalus:* son of Mercury (Hermes), carried off by Aurora (Eos).

P. 73. *Hylas:* accompanied Hercules in the Argonautic expedition. His beauty excited the love of the Naiads, as he went to draw water from a fountain, on the coast of Mysia, and he was drawn by them into the water, and never again seen.

P. 73. *Viraginea:* the land of viragoes.

P. 73. *Aphrodisia:* the land of Aphrodite (Venus).

P. 73. *Desvergonia:* the land of shamelessness. Ital. *vergona*, shame, infamy.

P. 73. *hearsay:* the hearing of, knowing about.

P. 73. *tire:* head-dress.

P. 73. *those in next aptitude to divinity:* divinity students.

P. 73. *Trinculoes:* Trinculo is the name of a jester in Shakespeare's 'Tempest'; or, according to a note in Johnson's 'Life of Milton,' signed R, referred to by J. A. St. John, 'by the mention of this name he evidently refers to "Albemazor," acted at Cambridge in 1614.'

P. 73. *mademoiselles:* ladies' maids.

P. 73. *Atticism:* because he is here imitating a well-known passage in Demosthenes's speech against Æschines. — *Keightley.*

P. 74. *for me:* so far as I'm concerned.

P. 74. ἀπειροκαλία: ignorance of the beautiful, want of taste or sensibility (Liddell and Scott).

P. 75. *elegiac poets, whereof the schools are not scarce:* i.e. they are much read in the schools.

P. 75. *numerous:* in poetic numbers; 'in prose or numerous verse.'

P. 75. *For that:* because. — *P. L.*, v. 150.

P. 75. *severe.* serious.

P. 76. *the two famous renowners of Beatrice and Laura:* Dante and Petrarch.

P. 76. *though not in the title-page:* an allusion to his opponent's 'A *Modest* Confutation.'

P. 78. *Corinthian:* licentious, Corinth having been noted for its licentiousness.

P. 78. *the precepts of the Christian religion:* J. A. St. John quotes from Symmons's 'Life of Milton': 'It was at this early period of his life, as we may confidently conjecture, that he imbibed that spirit of devotion which actuated his bosom to his latest moment upon earth: and we need not extend our search beyond the limits of his own house for the fountain from which the living influence was derived.'

P. 78. *had been:* i.e. might have been.

P. 79. *sleekstone:* a smoothing stone; a toothed sleekstone would fail of its purpose as much as a toothless satire.

P. 79. *this champion from behind the arras:* probably an allusion to Polonius, who, in the closet scene (A. III. S. iv.), conceals himself behind the arras to overhear the interview between Hamlet and his mother.

P. 80. *Socrates:* surnamed Scholasticus; a Greek ecclesiastical historian; b. about 379, d. after 440; author of a 'History of the Church from 306 to 439 A.D.'

P. 81. *St. Martin:* there are two saints of the name; which one is alluded to is uncertain, but probably Bishop of Tours, 4th century.

P. 81. *Gregory Nazianzen:* a Greek father, surnamed the Theologian; b. about 328, d. 389 A.D.

P. 81. *Murena:* Roman consul, 63 B.C.; charged with bribery by Servius Sulpicius; defended by Cicero, in his oration *Pro Murena.* In Cicero's answer to Sulpicius, 'three months,' as given by Milton, should be 'three days': 'itaque, si mihi, homini vehementer occupato, stomachum moveritis, *triduo* me jurisconsultum esse profitebor.'

To Carlo Dati. (*Familiar Letters*, No. X.)

P. 83. *tomb of Damon:* i.e. of Carolo Diodati.

P. 83. *that poem:* 'Epitaphium Damonis.'

On his Blindness

P. 84. 1. *spent:* extinguished.

P. 84. 2. *Ere half my days:* i.e. are spent; Milton was about forty-four years old when his 'light' was fully 'spent.'

P. 85. 8. *fondly:* foolishly; *prevent:* to come before, anticipate, forestall.

P. 85. 12. *thousands:* i.e. of 'spiritual creatures.' See 'P. L.,' iv. 677.

P. 85. 14. *They also serve:* i.e. as Verity explains, those other angels too, who, etc.

To Leonard Philaras. (*Familiar Letters*, No. XII.)

P. 85. *Augier* (*René*): resident agent in Paris for the English Parliament.

To Henry Oldenburg. (*Familiar Letters*, No. XIV.)

P. 87. *Henry Oldenburg:* b. at Bremen about 1615, d. 1677; sent in 1653 by the Council of Bremen as their agent to negotiate with Cromwell some arrangement by which the neutrality of Bremen should be respected in the naval war between England and Holland ('Dict. of National Biography'); became a member and secretary of the Royal Society of London, and was afterward elected a fellow of the Society; corresponded extensively with the philosopher, Benedict Spinosa; published the 'Transactions' of the Royal Society from 1664 to 1677.

P. 87. '*Cry*' of that kind '*to Heaven*': the reference is to the *Regii Sanguinis Clamor ad Cœlum, adversus Parricidas Anglicanos* (The Cry of the Royal Blood to Heaven against the English Parricides).

P. 87. *Morus:* Alexander More, whom Milton supposed to be the author of 'The Cry of the Royal Blood to Heaven.' See note, p. 248.

To Leonard Philaras. (*Familiar Letters*, No. XV.)

P. 89. *Phineus:* see note on 'P. L.,' iii. 36, in this volume.

P. 89. *Salmydessus:* a town of Thrace, on the coast of the Black Sea.

P. 89. *Argonautica:* a heroic poem on the Argonautic expedition, by Apollonius Rhodius.

P. 89. κάρος δέ μιν ἀμφεκάλυψεν:

> 'A darkling maze now round about him drew,
> The earth from underneath seemed whirling fast,
> In languid trance he lay bereft of speech.'
>
> *Prof. Charles E. Bennett's translation.*

P. 90. *the Wise Man:* Ecclesiastes xi. 8.
P. 90. *Lynceus:* the keen-sighted Argonaut.

To Cyriac Skinner

P. 91. 1. *this three years' day:* this day three years ago. Milton became completely blind in 1652, so this sonnet must have been written in 1655. *though clear:* see passage from Second Defence, p. 13.
P. 91. 7. *bate:* from 'abate.'
P. 91. 8. *bear up and steer right onward:* the nautical sense of 'bear up,' *i.e.* to put the ship before the wind, is indicated by what follows.
P. 91. 10. *conscience:* consciousness.
P. 91. 12. *talks:* the Trin. Coll. Ms. reading; the word 'rings' was substituted by Phillips in his printed copy of 1694; 'talks' does not sound so well, in the verse, but it is more modest.
P. 91. 13. *mask:* masquerade.

On his deceased wife

P. 91. 1. *my late espoused saint:* his second wife, Catherine Woodcock, whom he married November 12, 1656; she died in February, 1658.
P. 91. 2. *Alcestis:* brought back to life by Herakles (Hercules). *her glad husband:* Admetus, King of Pheræ in Thessaly. See Browning's 'Balaustion's Adventure, including a Transcript from [the Alkestis of] Euripides.'
P. 91. 5. *as whom:* as one whom.
P. 91. 6. *Purification:* Leviticus xii.
P. 91. 10. *her face was veiled:* Alcestis was still in his mind. In Browning's 'Balaustion's Adventure,' when Hercules returns with her:

> 'Under the great guard of one arm, there leant
> A *shrouded something*, live and woman-like,
> Propped by the heart-beats 'neath the lion coat. . . .
> There is no telling how the hero twitched
> The veil off: and there stood, with such fixed eyes
> And such slow smile, Alkestis' silent self!'

To Emeric Bigot. (*Familiar Letters*, No. XXI.)

P. 92. *Emeric Bigot:* a French scholar, native of Rouen; b. 1626, d. 1689.
P. 92. *King Telephus of the Mysians:* wounded by Achilles and by him healed with the rust of his spear; and in return Telephus directed the Greeks on their way to Troy.

Autobiographic passages in the Paradise Lost

P. 96. 2. *Or of the Eternal:* or may I, unblamed, express thee as the coeternal beam of the Eternal.

P. 96. 6. *increate:* qualifies 'bright effluence.'

P. 96. 7. *Or hearest thou rather:* or approvest thou rather the appellation of pure ethereal stream; 'hearest' is a classicism: 'Matutine pater, seu Jane libentius audis' (father of the morning, or if Janus thou hearest more willingly). — *Horace*, Sat. II., vi. 20, cited by Bentley.

P. 97. 13. *wing:* flight.

P. 97. 17. *With other notes:* Orpheus made a hymn to Night, which is still extant; he also wrote of the creation out of Chaos. See 'Apoll. Rhodius,' i. 493. Orpheus was inspired by his mother Calliope only, Milton by the *heavenly Muse;* therefore he boasts that he sung with *other notes* than Orpheus, though the subjects were the same. — *Richardson*.

P. 97. 21. *hard and rare:* evidently after Virgil's Æneid, vi. 126–129.

P. 97. 25. *a drop serene:* gutta serena, *i.e.* amaurosis.

P. 97. 26. *dim suffusion:* cataract.

P. 97. 34. *So:* appears to be used optatively, as Lat. *sic*, Greek ὡς, would that I were equalled with them in renown.

P. 97. 35. *Thamyris:* a Thracian bard, mentioned by Homer, Iliad, ii. 595:

'he, over-bold,
Boasted himself preëminent in song,
Ev'n though the daughters of Olympian Jove,
The Muses, were his rivals: they in wrath,
Him of his sight at once and power of song
Amerced, and bade his hand forget the lyre.'
— *Earl of Derby's Translation*, 692–697.

P. 97. 35. *Mæonides:* a patronymic of Homer.

P. 97. 36. *Tiresias:* the famous blind soothsayer of Thebes, 'cui profundum cæcitas lumen dedit' (to whom his blindness gave deep sight), says Milton, in his *De Idea Platonica*, v. 25.

P. 97. 36. *Phineus:* a blind soothsayer, who, according to some authorities, was king of Salmydessus, in Thrace. By reason of his cruelty to his sons, who had been falsely accused, he was tormented by the Harpies, until delivered from them by the Argonauts, in return for prophetic information in regard to their voyage.

P. 97. 39. *darkling:* in the dark.

P. 97. 42. *Day:* note the emphasis imparted to this initial monosyllabic word, which receives the ictus and is followed by a pause; Milton felt that the loss of sight was fully compensated for by an inward celestial light.

P. 98. 1. *Urania:* the Heavenly Muse invoked in the opening of the poem.

P. 98. 4. *Pegaséan wing:* above the flight of 'the poet's winged steed' of classical mythology.

P. 98. 5. *the meaning, not the name:* Urania was the name of one of the Grecian Muses; he invokes not her, but what her name signifies, the Heavenly one. See vv. 38, 39.

P. 98. 8. *Before the hills appeared:* Prov. viii. 23–31.

P. 98. 10. *didst play:* the King James's version, Prov. viii. 30, reads, 'rejoicing always before him'; the Vulgate, '*ludens* coram eo omni tempore.'

P. 98. 15. *thy tempering:* the empyreal air was tempered for, adapted to, his breathing, as a mortal, by the Heavenly Muse.

P. 98. 17. *this flying steed:* i.e. this higher poetic inspiration than that represented by the classical Pegasus; *unreined:* unbridled, *infrenis.*

P. 98. 18. *Bellerophon:* thrown from Pegasus when attempting to soar upon the winged horse to heaven.

P. 99. 19. *Aleian field:* in Asia Minor, where Bellerophon, after he was thrown from Pegasus, wandered and perished; πεδίον τὸ 'Αλήϊον, Iliad, vi. 201, land of wandering (ἄλη).

P. 99. 20. *erroneous there to wander:* to wander without knowing whither; Lat. *erroneus; forlorn:* entirely lost; 'for' is intensive.

P. 99. 21. *Half yet remains unsung:* 'half of the episode, not of the whole work, . . . the episode has two principal parts, the war in heaven, and the new creation; the one was sung, but the other remained unsung, . . . *but narrower bound,* . . . this other half is not rapt so much into the invisible world as the former, it is confined in narrower compass, and bound within the visible sphere of day.' — *Newton.*

narrower: more narrowly.

P. 99. 26. *on evil days though fallen:* a pathetic emotional repetition; note the artistic change in the order of the words. Macaulay justly characterizes the thirty years which succeeded the protectorate as 'the darkest and most disgraceful in the English annals. . . . Then came those days never to be recalled without a blush — the days of servitude without loyalty, and sensuality without love, of dwarfish talents and gigantic vices, the paradise of cold hearts and narrow minds, the golden age of the coward, the bigot, and the slave. The king cringed to his rival [Louis XIV.] that he might trample on his people, sunk into a viceroy of France, and pocketed, with complacent infamy, her degrading insults and her more degrading gold. The caresses of harlots, and the jests of buffoons regulated the measures of a government which had just ability enough to deceive, and just religion enough to persecute. The principles of liberty were the scoff of every grinning courtier, and the Anathema Maranatha of every fawning dean. . . . Crime succeeded to crime, and disgrace to disgrace, till the race, accursed of God and man, was a second time driven forth, to wander on the face of the earth, and to be a by-word and a shaking of the head to the nations.'

P. 99. 33. *Bacchus and his revellers :* Charles II. and his Court, from whom Milton had reason to fear a similar fate to that of the Thracian bard, Orpheus, who was torn to pieces by the Bacchanalian women of Rhodope.

P. 99. 38. *so fail not thou :* i.e. to defend me as the Muse Calliope failed to defend her son, Orpheus.

P. 99. 1. *no more of talk :* i.e. as in the foregoing episode.

P. 99. 5. *venial :* allowable, fitting.

P. 100. 14–19. *the wrath of stern Achilles . . . Cytherea's son :* these are not the arguments (subjects) proper of the three epics, the Iliad, the Odyssey, and the Æneid; as Newton pointed out, the poet mentions certain angers or enmities, the wrath of Achilles, the rage of Turnus, Neptune's and Juno's ire; 'the anger, etc. (v. 10) of Heaven which he is about to sing is an argument more heroic, not only than the anger of men, of Achilles and Turnus, but than that even of the gods, of Neptune and Juno;' *his foe :* Hector; *Turnus :* king of the Rutuli when Æneas arrived in Italy; *Lavinia :* daughter of King Latinus, betrothed to Turnus, but afterward given in marriage to Æneas; *the Greek :* Ulysses; *Cytherea's son :* Æneas; Cytherea, a surname of Venus, from the island Cythera, famous for her worship.

P. 100. 19. *Perplexed the Greek :* a respective construction, 'perplexed the Greek' looks back to 'Neptune's ire,' 'Cytherea's son,' to Juno's ire. Bentley's note is remarkable: '*Juno's that long perplexed the Greek :* when, contrary, the *Greek* was her favourite all along.'

P. 100. 20. *answerable :* corresponding to the high argument.

P. 100. 21. *my celestial Patroness :* Urania, the Heavenly Muse.

P. 100. 23. *inspires :* Milton regarded himself as inspired by the Holy Spirit in the composition of 'Paradise Lost.'

P. 100. 25. *Since first this subject:* Milton, as has been seen, had meditated, as early as 1638, an epic poem to be based on legendary British history, with King Arthur for its hero, a subject which it appears he abandoned in the course of two or three years. While still undecided, he jotted down ninety-nine different subjects, sixty-one Scriptural, thirty-eight from British history. Among the former, 'Paradise Lost' appears first of all. These jottings occupy seven pages of the Cambridge Mss. It is evident that by 1640, Milton was quite decided as to the subject of 'Paradise Lost,' but not as to the form of his work. It was first as a tragedy that he conceived it, on the model of the Grecian drama with choruses. His nephew, Edward Phillips, informs us that several years before the poem was begun (about 1642, according to Aubrey), Satan's address to the sun (Book iv. 32-41) was shown him as designed for the beginning of the tragedy. The composition of the poem was begun, according to Phillips, about 1658, the poet being then fifty years of age. The student should read, in connection with this subject, the thirteenth chapter of Mark Pattison's 'Life of Milton.'

P. 100. 35. *Impresses:* 'devices or emblems used on shields or otherwise.' Keightley alludes to the enumeration of the devices of the nobles of England, in the tenth Canto of the 'Orlando Furioso.'

P. 100. 36. *bases:* 'the base was a skirt or kilt which hung down from the waist to the knees of the knight when on horseback.'

P. 100. 37. *marshalled feast:* ' from Minshew's " Guide into Tongues," it appears that the marshal placed the guests according to their rank, and saw that they were properly served; the sewer marched in before the meats and arranged them on the table, and was originally called *Asseour* from the French *asseoir*, to set down, or place; and the *Seneshal* was the household-steward.' — *Todd.*

P. 100. 41. *Me . . . higher argument remains :* i.e. for me.

P. 101. 44. *an age too late :* Milton might well feel, in the reign of the 'merry monarch,' that he was treating his high argument in an age too late.

P. 101. 45, 46. *my intended wing depressed:* 'wing' is used, by metonymy, for 'flight.' Keightley incorrectly puts a comma after 'wing,' 'intended wing depressed' being a case of the placing of a noun between two epithets, usual with Milton, the epithet following the noun qualifying the noun as qualified by the preceding epithet. Rev. James Robert Boyd, in his edition of the ' P. L.,' explains ' intended,' ' stretched out '; but the word is undoubtedly used in its present sense of ' purposed.'

Letter to Peter Heimbach. (*Familiar Letters*, No. XXXI.)

P. 102. *a country retreat:* 'a pretty box,' secured for him by his Quaker friend, Elwood, at Chalfont St. Giles; the house still exists, having undergone little or no change.

I hardly like to express in the text a fancy that has occurred to me in translating the letter and studying it in connection with Heimbach's, to wit, that Milton may not merely have been ironically rebuking Heimbach for his adulation and silly phraseology, but may also have been suspicious of the possibility of some trap laid for him politically. Certainly, if this letter of Milton's to a Councillor of the Elector of Brandenburg had been intercepted by the English government, it is so cleverly worded that nothing could have been made of it. But Heimbach may have been as honest as he looks. Even then, however, Milton, knowing little or nothing of Heimbach for the last nine years, had reason to be cautious. — *Masson.*

Passages in which Milton's Idea of True Liberty is Set Forth

P. 104. *Deep versed in books:* Milton would, I conceive, have thus characterized his old antagonist, Salmasius. — *Dunster.*

P. 104. *trifles for choice matters:* as choice matters.

P. 104. *worth a spunge:* deserving to be wiped out. So in his 'Areopagitica': 'sometimes five imprimaturs are seen together, dialogue-wise, in the piazza of one title-page, complimenting and ducking each to other with their shaven reverences, whether the author, who stands by in perplexity at the foot of his epistle, shall to the press or to the spunge.'

P. 111. *Uzza:* see 2 Sam. vi. 3–8.

P. 112. *Whom do we count a good man:*

'Vir bonus est quis? —
Qui consulta patrum, qui leges juraque servat;
Quo multæ magnæque secantur judice lites;
Quo res sponsore, et quo causæ teste tenentur.
Sed videt hunc omnis domus et vicinia tota
Introrsùs turpem, speciosum pelle decorâ.'
— *Epistolarum Liber,* i. 16, vv. 40–45, *Ad Quinctium.*

P. 118. *Crescentius Nomentanus:* Roman patrician, a native of Nomentum (now La Mentana), tenth century, was at the head of the Italian party against the Germans and the popes, with title of Consul; was besieged in the Castle St. Angelo, and finally capitulated on terms honorable to himself, but was basely put to death by Otho III., A.D. 998.

P. 118. *Nicholas Rentius:* Rienzi, or Rienzo (Niccolo Gabrini), or Cola di Rienzi, 'the last of the Roman Tribunes,' b. about 1313, d. 1354.

> 'Then turn we to her latest tribune's name,
> From her ten thousand tyrants turn to thee,
> Redeemer of dark centuries of shame —
> The friend of Petrarch — hope of Italy —
> Rienzi! last of Romans! while the tree
> Of Freedom's withered trunk puts forth a leaf,
> Even for thy tomb a garland let it be —
> The forum's champion, and the people's chief —
> Her new-born Numa thou — with reign, alas! too brief.'
> — *Byron's Childe Harold*, Canto iv. St. cxiv.

P. 120. *the resentment of Achilles:* the subject of the Iliad.

P. 120. *the return of Ulysses:* the subject of the Odyssey.

P. 120. *the coming of Æneas into Italy:* the subject of the Æneid.

P. 121. *As when those hinds:* he compares the reception given it [the doctrine of his Divorce pamphlets] to the treatment of the goddess Latona and her newly born twins by the Lycian rustics. These twins afterward 'held the sun and moon in fee' (*i.e.* in full possession), for they were Apollo and Diana; and yet, when the goddess, carrying them in her arms, and fleeing from the wrath of Juno, stooped in her fatigue to drink of the water of a small lake, the rustics railed at her and puddled the lake with their hands and feet; for which, on the instant, at the goddess's prayer, they were turned into frogs, to live forever in the mud of their own making (Ovid, *Met.*, vi. 335-381).'— *Masson.* Wordsworth uses the phrase, 'in fee,' in the same way in the opening verse of his sonnet on the 'Extinction of the Venetian Republic': 'Once did She hold the gorgeous east in fee.'

P. 121. *lapse:* fall.

P. 121. *twinned:* as a twin.

P. 121. *dividual:* separate.

P. 121. *undeservedly:* without right or merit; no thanks to them.

P. 121. *virtue, which is reason:* 'Virtus est recta ratio, et animi habitus, naturæ modo, rationi consentaneus.' — *Cicero.*

P. 123. 424. *his son Herod:* king of Judea when Christ was born.

P. 123. 439. *Gideon, and Jephtha;* see *Judges* vi.-viii. and xi., xii.; *the shepherd-lad:* David; see the *Books of Samuel.*

P. 123. 446. *Quintius:* Quintius Cincinnatus: *Fabricius:* the patriotic Roman who was proof against the bribes of Pyrrhus; *Curius: Curius Dentatus:* who would accept no public rewards; *Regulus:* after dissuading the Romans from making peace with the Carthaginians, returned to Carthage, knowing the consequences he would suffer.

Comus

P. 129. 4. *With Midas' ears:* i.e. with the ears of an ass; *committing:* bringing together, setting at variance (Lat. *committere*). Martial says, 'Cum Juvenale meo cur me committere tentas?' *i.e.* 'why try to match me with my Juvenal,' *i.e.* in a poetical contest with him.

P. 129. 5. *exempts:* separates, distinguishes; the compound subject 'worth and skill' is logically singular, and takes a singular verb.

P. 129. 11. *story:* 'the story of Ariadne, set by him to music,' as explained in a note in 'Choice Psalms,' 1648.

P. 129. 13. *Casella:* 'a Florentine musician and friend of Dante, who here ['Purgatorio,' ii. 91 *et seq.*] speaks to him with so much tenderness and affection as to make us regret that nothing more is known of him. — *Longfellow's note.*

milder shades: i.e. than those of the Inferno which Dante has just left.

3. *insphered:* in their several spheres.

7. *pestered:* here, as indicated by 'pinfold,' the word means 'clogged'; 'pester' is a shortened form of 'impester.' Fr. *empêtrer* (OF. *empestrer*) 'signifies properly to hobble a horse while he feeds afield. Mid. Lat. *pastorium*, a clog for horses at pasture.' — *Brachet's Etymol. Dict. of the French Language, s.v. dépêtrer.*

10. *After this mortal change:* 'mortal' I understand to be used here as a noun, the subject of 'change,' a verb in the subjunctive; there is evidently an allusion to 1 Cor. xv. 52-54, in which occur the expressions, 'we shall be changed' and 'this mortal must put on immortality.'

16. *ambrosial weeds:* immortal or heavenly garments, *i.e.* garments worn by an immortal. Gk. 'Ἀμβρόσιος, lengthened form of ἄμβροτος, immortal. See v. 83.

20. *high and nether Jove:* by metonymy for the realms of Jove and Pluto.

23. *unadorned:* i.e. but for 'the sea-girt isles.'

25. *several:* separate; *by course;* in due order.

29. *quarters:* not literally, but simply, divides, distributes.

30. *this tract that fronts the falling sun:* Wales.

31. *a noble Peer:* the Earl of Bridgewater, Lord President of Wales, before whom 'Comus' was presented at Ludlow Castle, 1634.

32. *tempered awe:* i.e. tempered with mercy; 'mercy seasons justice.'

34. *nursed in princely lore:* nurtured in high learning.

38. *horror:* ruggedness, shagginess. See v. 429. . . . 'densis hastilibus horrida myrtus.' — Virgil's *Æneid*, iii. 23. *brows:* overarching branches.

39. *forlorn and wandering:* entirely lost and, consequently, straying at random.

48. *After the Tuscan mariners transformed:* a Latinism; so, 'since created man.' — *P. L.*, i. 573. The allusion is to the story of the Etruscan or Tyrrhenian pirates, who attempted to carry off Bacchus, sell him as a slave, and were by him changed into dolphins. — *Ovid, Met.*, 660 *et seq.*

49. *listed:* pleased.

50. *On . . . fell:* happened upon.

59. *of:* from, by reason of.

60. *Celtic and Iberian fields:* France and Spain.

61. *ominous:* portentous.

65. *orient:* bright. The word was used independently of the idea of 'eastern.' In the ode 'On the Nativity,' v. 231, the *setting* sun 'pillows his chin upon an orient wave.' Fuller, in his 'Holy War,' Book ii. Chap. I., says of Godfrey of Bouillon, 'His soul was enriched with many virtues, but the most *orient* of all was his humility, which took all men's affections without resistance.'

66. *the drouth of Phœbus:* the thirst caused by the sun's heat.

67. *fond:* foolish.

88 *nor of less faith:* i.e. than of musical power; 'faith' means the fidelity of his service.

90. *Likeliest:* the best suited for impersonation by the Attendant Spirit, by reason of his office of mountain watch over the flocks. He would therefore be supposed to be near at hand if aid were needed.

92. *viewless:* invisible.

93. *The star that bids the shepherd fold:* the evening star cannot be said to hold the top of heaven, *i.e.* be in the meridian; any star, the earliest to appear, must be meant.

101. *his chamber in the east:* an allusion to Psalm xix. 5.

110. *saws:* sayings, maxims; 'grave' is used contemptuously by Comus.

116. *to the moon in wavering morrice move:* the sounds and seas beneath the moon reflect dancing lights; 'morrice,' a rapid Moorish dance, once common in England.

129. *Cotytto:* the goddess of shameless and licentious orgies. Her priests were called *Baptæ*.

> 'involved in thickest gloom,
> Cotytto's priests her secret torch illume;
> And to such orgies give the lustful night,
> That e'en Cotytto sickens at the sight.'
> — *Gifford's translation of Juvenal,* ii. 91, 92.

132. *spets:* spits.

135. *Hecate.* goddess of sorcery and magic and 'of all kinds of nocturnal ghastliness, such as spectral sights, the howlings of dogs, haunted spots, the graves of the murdered, witches at their incantations' (*Masson*). King Lear (I. i. 112) swears by ' the mysteries of Hecate and the night.'

139. *nice:* fastidious, over-scrupulous; used contemptuously by Comus.

141. *descry:* reveal.

144. *round:* a circular dance; in 'L'Allegro,' 34, we have 'the light fantastic toe.'

151. *trains:* enticements, allurements.

154. *spungy air:* which absorbs his ' dazzling spells.'

155. *blear:* dim, deceiving.

156. *false presentments:* representations which deceive the eye.

157. *quaint habits:* strange garments.

165. *virtue:* peculiar power. See v. 621; 'Il Pens.,' 113.

167. *country gear:* rural affairs.

168. *fairly:* softly.

175. *granges:* used in its original sense — barns. (Fr. *grange.*)

178. *swilled:* drunken.

180. *inform my unacquainted feet:* where else shall I learn my way than from these revellers.

203. *perfect:* perfectly distinct, sure, certain, unmistakable. There is a similar use of the word in Shakespeare : 'Thou art perfect, then, our ship hath touched upon the deserts of Bohemia ?' — *Winter's Tale,* III. iii. 1; ' I am perfect that the Pannonians and Dalmatians for their liberties are now in arms.' — *Cymb.*, III. i. 73; ' What hast thou done ? I am

perfect what ' (I know full well, I am fully aware.' *Schmidt*). — *Cymb.*, IV. ii. 118.

204. *single darkness :* pure darkness, only that and nothing more.

210. *may startle well : i.e.* may well (or indeed) startle.

212. *strong-siding :* strongly supporting.

215. *Chastity :* significantly substituted for Charity, as the companion virtue of Faith and Hope, it being the *theme*, the central idea of the poem, to which an explicit expression is given in the Elder Brother's speech, vv. 418-475, and in the speech of the Lady to Comus, 780-799.

231. *airy shell :* the dome of the sky ; 'cell' is in the margin of Milton's Ms.

248. *his :* (old neuter genitive) its, referring to 'something.'

251. *fall :* cadence.

251, 252. *smoothing . . . till it smiled :* Dr. Symmons, in his ' Life of Milton,' remarks : 'Darkness may aptly be represented by the blackness of the raven ; and the stillness of that darkness may be paralleled by an image borrowed from the object of another sense — by the softness of down ; but it is surely a transgression which stands in need of pardon when, proceeding a step further and accumulating personifications, we invest this raven-down with life and make it smile.' The metaphorical use of 'smile' or 'laugh,' applied to inanimate things that are smooth, shining, glossy, bright in colour, and the like, is, perhaps, common in all literatures. The Latin ' rideo ' and the Greek γελάω are frequently so used ; *e.g.* 'florumque coloribus almus ridet ager' (and the bounteous field laughs with the colours of its flowers).— *Ovid, Met.*, xv. 205; 'Domus ridet argento' (the house smiles with glittering silver).— *Horace, Odes*, IV. xi. 6; ' Ille terrarum mihi praeter omnes angulus ridet ' (that corner of the earth smiles for me above all others). — *Horace, Odes*, II. vi. 14.

262. *home-felt delight : i.e.* delight that keeps one at home with himself, does not carry him out of himself; in contrast with the singing of Circe and the Sirens three, which ' in sweet madness *robbed it* (the sense) *of itself.*'

267. *unless the goddess : i.e.* unless (thou be) the goddess ; 'dwell'st' should properly be 'dwells,' the antecedent of the relative 'that' being 'goddess,' third person, not 'thou' in the ellipsis.

273. *extreme shift :* last resort ; Fr. *dernier ressort.*

279. *near ushering :* attending near at hand.

285. *forestalling night :* preventing, or hindering, night came before them ; 'forestall' has here the present sense of 'prevent,' and 'prevent' its old, literal sense of come before.

T

287. *imports their loss:* does their loss signify other than your present need of them ?

290. *Hebe:* the goddess of youth ; cupbearer to the gods before Ganymedes.

293. *Swinked:* hard-worked. Spenser frequently uses the verb 'swink,' and several times in connection with 'sweat'; *severe* toil is always implied in his use of the word : 'For which men swinck and sweat incessantly.'— *F. Q.*, 2. 7, 8 ; 'And every one did swincke, and every one did sweat.— 2. 7, 36; 'For which he long in vaine did sweate and swinke,' 6. 4, 32 ; 'Of mortal men, that swincke and sweate for nought.' — *The Sheapherd's Calender, November,* 154 ; 'For they doo swinke and sweate to feed the other.' — *Mother Hubbard's Tale,* 163.

301. *plighted:* folded, involved.

313. *bosky bourn:* Masson explains 'shrubby boundary or watercourse.' Warton's explanation seems better supported by the context : 'A *bourn* . . . properly signifies here, a winding, deep, and narrow valley, with a rivulet at the bottom. In the present instance, the declivities are interspersed with trees and bushes. This sort of valley Comus knew from *side to side.* He knew *both* the *opposite sides* or ridges, and had consequently traversed the intermediate space.'

315. *attendance:* attendants.

329. *square:* adapt.

332. *wont'st:* art accustomed; *benison:* blessing.

333. *stoop:* the same idea, or *impression*, rather, in regard to the moon, is expressed in 'Il Penseroso,' 72:

'And oft, as if her head she bowed,
Stooping through a fleecy cloud.'

'And those thin clouds above, in flakes and bars,
That give away their motion to the stars.'
— *Coleridge's Dejection : an Ode.*

336. *influence:* (astrological) the effect *flowing in, or upon*, from the stars. See 'P. L.,' vii. 375, viii. 513, ix. 107, x. 662; 'L'Al.,' 122; 'Od. Nat.,' 71.

340. *rule:* long horizontal beam of light.

341. *Star of Arcady:* the constellation of the Greater Bear, by which, or by some star in which, the Greek mariner steered his course.

342. *Tyrian Cynosure:* the constellation of the Lesser Bear, or the pole star therein, by which the Phœnician (Tyrian) mariner steered.

344. *wattled cotes:* sheep-pens made of interwoven twigs.

349. *innumerous:* innumerable.

355. *leans:* subject 'she' implied in 'her,' above. See note on 'Samson Agonistes', 1671; some editors make 'head' the subject.

358. *heat:* lust.

359. *exquisite:* used literally: outsearching; 'consider not too curiously.'

366. *so to seek:* so wanting, so much at a loss.

367. *unprincipled:* ignorant of the elements, or first principles.

369. *noise:* not to be connected with 'single want of'; the meaning is, mere darkness and noise.

373. *would:* might wish.

375. *flat sea:* in 'Lycidas,' 98, 'level brine.'

376. *oft seeks to:* oft resorts to.

380. *all to-ruffled:* all ruffled up; the prefix 'to-' is an old intensive, with force of Ger. 'zer-'; generally imparts the idea of destruction: 'all to-brake,' broke all in pieces; 'all to-rent,' tore all in pieces.

382. *centre:* as in Shakespeare, centre of the earth.

386. *affects:* likes, entirely without any of its present meaning of making a show of.

390. *weeds:* garments.

391. *maple:* maple-wood.

393. *Hesperian tree:* the tree in the Hesperian gardens which bore golden apples and was guarded by the sleepless dragon Ladon, which was slain by Hercules.

395. *unenchanted:* not to be enchanted, or wrought upon by magical spells.

401. *wink on:* not take notice or advantage of.

402. *single:* solitary, alone.

404. *it recks me not:* I take no account of, care not for.

405. *events:* outcomes, consequences.

407. *unowned:* without a protector.

409. *without all doubt:* i.e. without any doubt; a Latinism.

413. *squint:* 'looking askance.' Spenser represents Suspect ('F. Q.,' 3. 12, 15) as

'ill favourèd, and grim,
Under his eiebrowes looking still askaunce.'

419. *if:* even if Heaven *did* give it.
423. *unharboured:* without harbor, or shelter.
424. *infamous:* of bad reputation.
430. *unblenched:* fearless, self-sustained.
432. *some say:* reminds, as has been often noted, of the passage in 'Hamlet': 'some say that ever 'gainst that season comes,' etc. — I. i. 158.
455. *lackey:* attend, or wait upon, as guardians.
474. *and linked itself:* and as if it were itself linked.
494. *artful:* artistic, skilful.
495. *huddling:* hurrying; Verity understands 'huddling' as the result of 'delayed.'
501. *next joy:* Thyrsis addresses the elder brother as his master's heir, and then the second brother as 'his next joy,' *i.e.* object of his joy.
503. *stealth:* the thing stolen.
509. *sadly:* seriously; *without blame: i.e.* on our part.
515, 516. *what the sage poets . . . storied:* made the theme of story:

> Tells him of trophies, statues, tombs, and stories
> His victories, his triumphs, and his glories.
> —*Shakespeare's V. and A.,* 1013, 14.

520. *navel:* centre.
526. *murmurs:* muttered spells, or incantations.
529. *mintage:* coinage.
533. *monstrous rout:* rout of monsters; so, 'monstrous world,' world of monsters.— *Lycidas,* 158.
539. *unweeting:* not knowing.
540. *by then:* by the time that.
547. *meditate:* practice; see 'Lycidas,' 66.
548. *had:* subj., should have; *close: i.e.* of his 'rural minstrelsy.'
552. *unusual stop of sudden silence:* see 145.
553. *drowsy-flighted:* this is the reading of the Cambridge Ms., which Masson adopts. Lawes's ed., 1637, and Milton's editions, 1645, 1673, read 'drowsie frighted.' Masson quite conclusively supports the reading of the Ms., which he explains, 'always drowsily flying.' Keightley retains 'drowsy frighted,' but says in his note, 'we are strongly inclined to think it [the Ms. reading] the right reading, and the present one a mistake of Lawes himself or his printer.'
558. *took:* rapt.
560. *still:* ever.

585. *period:* sentence.
586. *for me:* as for me.
603. *grisly:* horrible. 'So spake the grisly terror (Death).' — *P. L.*, ii. 704.
604. *Acheron:* a river of the lower world; here used for the lower world itself.
607. *purchase:* acquisition; the word retains here much of its original meaning, *i.e.* what has been hunted down or stolen.
610. *yet:* notwithstanding; *emprise:* here, readiness for any dangerous undertaking.
619. *a certain shepherd-lad:* a supposed compliment to Milton's dearest friend, Charles Diodati.
620. *to see to:* to look upon.
621. *virtuous:* efficacious, potent.
627. *simples:* medicinal herbs.
634. *and like esteemed:* i.e. and (un)esteemed.
635. *clouted shoon:* patched shoes.
636. *Moly:* (Gk. μώλυ) a fabulous herb, 'that Hermes [Mercury] to wise Ulysses gave,' as a protection against the spells of Circe. — *Od.*, x. 305. See Pope's note, in his translation, x. 361, Tennyson's 'Lotus Eaters,' 133.
638. *Hæmony:* supposed to be from Hæmonia, Thessaly, famous for its magic.
641. *Furies':* used objectively.
642. *little reckoning made:* see 'Lycidas,' 116.
646. *lime-twigs:* used metaphorically.
662. *root-bound:* referring to her metamorphosis into a laurel tree (δάφνη).
673. *his:* old neuter genitive, its.
675. *Nepenthes* (Gk. νηπενθές, sorrow-soothing): the drug (supposed to be opium) given by Polydamna to Helena, who put it into her husband Menelaus's wine. — *Od.*, iv. 220 *et seq.* See note to Pope's translation, v. 302.

'Quaff, oh quaff this kind nepenthe, and forget this lost Lenore.'
— *Poe's Raven*, 83.

685. *unexempt condition:* condition to which all mortal frailty is subject, namely, refreshment after toil, ease after pain.
688. *that:* referring to 'you,' 682.

695. *oughly:* the spelling in Milton's editions; 'as Milton has the common spelling, *ugly*, in all other cases where he has used the word, he must have intended a different form here, perhaps to indicate a more guttural pronunciation.' — *Masson.*

698. *visored:* masked; he appears as 'some harmless villager,' v. 166.

707. *budge:* austere, morose; *fur:* used metaphorically for order, sect, profession. Landor remarks that 'it is the first time Cynic or Stoic ever put on fur.' 'Budge' also means a kind of fur, but it certainly cannot have that meaning here; the context requires the other meaning.

708. *from the Cynic tub:* i.e. from the tub whence Diogenes, the Cynic, delivered them.

714. *curious:* careful, nice, delicate, fastidious.

719. *hutched:* hoarded, laid up, as in a hutch or chest.

724. *yet:* in addition; or, it may have the force of 'even.'

744. *it:* i.e. beauty.

750. *grain:* 'a term derived from the Latin *granum*, a seed or kernel, or grain in the sense of "grain of corn," — which word *granum* had come, in later Latin times, to be applied specifically to the *coccum*, a peculiar dye-stuff consisting of the dried, granular, or seed-like bodies of insects of the genus *Coccus*, collected in large quantities from trees in Spain and other Mediterranean countries. But that dye was distinctly red. Another name for it, and for the insect producing it, was *kermes* . . . whence our "carmine" and "crimson." "Grain," therefore, meant a dye of such red as might be produced by the use of kermes or coccum.' — From Masson's note on 'Sky-tinctured grain,' 'P. L.,' v. 285, based on George P. Marsh's dissertation on the etymology of the word, in his 'Lectures on the English Language' (1st S., 4th Am. ed., 1861, pp. 65-75). Masson's note on 'cheeks of sorry grain' is '*i.e.* of poor colour,' as if 'grain' were used in the general sense of colour merely. It is better, I think, to understand 'grain' here in its special sense of red, but used by Comus ironically, as indicated by 'sorry.' Beautiful cheeks are presumed to have a delicate reddish hue; but where the features are homely and the complexion coarse, the cheeks may be said, ironically, to be of a sorry grain, *i.e.* not red at all.

759. *pranked:* set off, adorned, decked.

760. *bolt:* sift, refine ; a metaphor from the process of separating flour from the bran. But the word may mean, as Dr. Newton explains, 'to shoot,' or, as Dr. Johnson explains, 'to blurt out, or throw out precipitantly.'

782. *sun-clad:* spiritually refulgent.

785. *the sublime notion:* see in extract from 'Apology for Smectymnuus,' in this volume.

788. *worthy:* deserving, in a bad sense.

790. *your dear wit:* the change from 'thy' to 'your' is not explainable here.

791. *her dazzling fence:* dear wit's and gay rhetoric's dazzling art of fencing. Todd quotes from Prose Works, 'Hired Masters of Tonguefence': 'dear wit' and 'gay rhetoric,' not constituting a compound idea in Milton's mind, the relative 'that,' of which they are the antecedents, takes a singular verb, and the two nouns are represented by the singular personal pronoun 'her.' In the following passage from Spenser's 'Faerie Queene,' B. II. C. ii. St. 31, two subjects take a singular verb, and are represented by a singular personal pronoun :

'But lovely concord, and most sacred peace,
Doth nourish vertue, and fast friendship breeds;
Weake she makes strong, and strong thing does increace.'

The italicized portion of the following passage from 'The Passions and Faculties of the Soul,' by Reynolds, C. xxxix, given in Trench's 'Select Glossary,' *s.v.* Wit, defines well 'dear wit': 'I take not *wit* in that common acceptation, whereby men understand *some sudden flashes of conceit whether in style or conference, which, like rotten wood in the dark, have more shine than substance, whose use and ornament are, like themselves, swift and vanishing, at once both admired and forgotten*. But I understand a settled, constant and habitual sufficiency of the understanding, whereby it is enabled in any kind of learning, theory, or practice, both to sharpness in search, subtilty in expression, and despatch in execution.'

797. *brute:* senseless ; *lend her nerves:* i.e. to this sacred vehemence.

800–806. spoken aside.

804. *speaks thunder:* threatens thunder and the chains of Erebus to some of the Titans who are disposed to be rebellious in their imprisonment in Tartarus. It seems to be meant that Erebus is a more painful region than that into which they were cast after their defeat by Jove (Zeus).

815. *snatched his wand:* see v. 653.

816. *without his rod reversed:* the process, as related in Ovid, 'Met.,' xiv. 299–305, by which the companions of Ulysses are, through his intervention, retransformed by Circe.

822. *Melibœus:* Spenser is probably referred to.

823. *soothest:* truest, most faithful.

826. *Sabrina:* the legend of Sabrina is told by Geoffrey of Monmouth, in his 'Latin History of the Britons'; by Drayton, in his 'Polyolbion,' 6th Song; by Warner, in his 'Albion's England'; by Spenser, in his 'Faerie Queene,' II. x. 14-19, and by Milton, in the first book of his 'History of Britain.'

835. *Nereus:* 'the good spirit of the Ægean Sea,' father of the nereids or sea-nymphs.

852. *old swain:* Melibœus.

867-889. *Listen, and appear to us:* *Oceanus* was the most ancient sea-god, . . . *Neptune,* with his trident, was a later being. *Tethys* was the wife of Oceanus, and mother of the river-gods. *Hoary Nereus* is the 'aged Nereus' of line 835. The *Carpathian wizard* is the subtle *Proteus,* ever shifting his shape: . . . *Triton,* son of Neptune and Aphrodite, . . . he was 'scaly,' because the lower part of him was fish. *Glaucus* was a Bœotian fisherman who had been changed into a marine god: . . . was an oracle for sailors and fishermen. *Leucothea* ('the white goddess') was originally Ino, the daughter of Cadmus, and had received her new name after she had drowned herself and been converted into a sea-deity. *Her son that rules the strands* was Melicertes, drowned and deified with her, and thenceforward known as *Palæmon,* or *Portumnus,* the god of bays and harbours. *Thetis,* one of the daughters of Nereus, and therefore a sea-deity by birth, married Peleus, and was the mother of Achilles: . . . Of the *Sirens,* or singing sea-nymphs . . . *Parthenope* and *Ligea* were two. The 'dear tomb' of the first was at Naples . . . the 'golden comb' of the second is from stories of our own mermaids. — *Masson's note, condensed.*

900. *gentle swain:* the attendant spirit is still in the person and habit of the shepherd Thyrsis.

913. *cure:* curative power.

919. *his:* old neuter genitive, its.

921. *to wait:* to attend in the bower (court) of Amphitrite (wife of Neptune).

922. *daughter of Locrine:* see vv. 827, 828. The order of the legendary 'line' is, Anchises, Æneas, Ascanius, Silvius, Brutus, Locrine.

924. *brimmed:* full to the brim or edge of the bank; *cf.* 'full-fed river.' — *Tennyson's Palace of Art.*

929. *scorch:* optative subj.

934-937. The true construction of these lines is pointed out by Mr. Calton, quoted in Todd's *variorum* ed.: 'May thy lofty head be *crowned round* with many a tower and terrace, and here and there [may] thy banks [be crowned] upon with groves of myrrh and cinnamon.'

960. *duck or nod:* i.e. of the awkward country dancers.

964. *mincing Dryades:* daintily stepping wood-nymphs.

968. *goodly:* interesting and attractive in appearance.

972. *assays:* trials.

982. *Hesperus and his daughters three:* brother of Atlas, and father of the Hesperides.

1012. *But now, etc.:* may be an independent or a subordinate sentence; if the latter, understand 'that' after 'now.' It is, perhaps, preferable to take it as an independent sentence.

1015. *bowed welkin:* arched sky; the idea is that the bend is the less noticeable at 'the green earth's end.'

1017. *corners:* horns.

1021. *higher than the sphery chime:* 'i.e. to the Empyrean, beyond the spheres which give forth their music.' — *Keightley.*

Lycidas

P. 167. *haud procul a littore Britannico:* 'the ship having struck on a rock not far from the British shore and been ruptured by the shock, he, while the other passengers were fruitlessly busy about their mortal lives, having fallen forward upon his knees, and breathing a life which was immortal, in the act of prayer going down with the vessel, rendered up his soul to God, August 10, 1637, aged 25.' — *Masson's translation.*

1-5. *Yet once more:* these verses express the poet's sense of his unripeness for the exercise of the poetic gift. See his 'English Letter to a Friend,' p. 40; laurel, myrtle, and ivy are poetical emblems.

5. *before the mellowing year:* i.e. before the mellowing year or period of his own life; 'mellowing' is intransitive, growing or becoming mellow; 'year' is not a nominative, the subject of 'does' or 'shatters,' understood, as several editors make it, but is the object of the preposition 'before.'

6. *dear:* of intimate concernment; the word was formerly applied to what is precious, or painful, to the heart; it has here, of course, the latter application.

7. *Compels me to disturb your season due:* i.e. compels me to write a poem before I have attained to the requisite 'inward ripeness.'

The compound subject, 'bitter constraint and sad occasion dear,' is logically singular, and takes a singular verb. The placing of a noun between two epithets is usual with Milton, especially when the epithet following the noun qualifies the noun as qualified by the preceding epithet; *e.g.* 'hazel copses green,' v. 42; 'flower-inwoven tresses torn.'— *Hymn on the Nativity*, 187; 'beckoning shadows dire.'— *Comus*, 207.

14. *melodious tear:* 'tear' is used, by metonymy, for an elegiac poem.

15. *sacred well:* the Pierian spring.

16. *the seat of Jove:* Mount Olympus.

17. *loudly: i.e.* as Hunter explains, in lamentation; or, perhaps, in praises.

18. *Hence with denial vain and coy excuse:* away with, etc., *i.e.* on my part; *denial:* refusal; *coy:* shrinking, hesitating, reluctant, by reason of what is expressed in the opening verses.

19-22. *So may . . . sable shroud:* these verses are parenthetical, and v. 23 must be connected with v. 18, 'Hence with denial vain,' etc. I have followed Keightley's pointing; *gentle Muse:* high-born (nobly endowed) poet; *lucky words:* words that will favorably perpetuate my memory; *bid fair peace:* pray that fair peace be, etc.

23-36. *For we were nursed:* these verses express in pastoral language the devotion to their joint studies, early and late, of Milton and King, at Christ's College, Cambridge.

25. *ere the high lawns appeared: i.e.* before daybreak.

28. *What time the grey-fly: i.e.* the sultry noontide.

30. *Oft till the star . . . had sloped his westering wheel: i.e.* they continued their studies till after midnight, while in the meantime many of their fellow-students were giving themselves to music and dancing.

33. *Tempered:* attuned, modulated.

36. *old Damœtas:* 'may be,' says Masson, 'some fellow or tutor of Christ's College, if not Dr. Bainbrigge, the master.'

37. *Now thou art gone:* emotionally repeated; *heavy:* sad.

40. *With wild thyme . . . o'ergrown:* to be connected only with 'desert caves,' not 'woods.'

44. *to:* responsively to.

45. *canker:* cankerworm.

49. *Such:* used in its etymological sense, so-like; so-like killing is thy loss; *thy:* of thee; the personal pronoun here, used objectively, and not the possessive adjective pronoun.

52. *the steep:* some one of the Welsh mountains.
53. *lie:* lie buried.
54. *Mona:* the isle of Anglesey; Mona is represented by Tacitus as the chief seat of the Druids; *shaggy:* densely wooded; 'shaggy hill.' — *P. L.*, iv. 224.

> 'They plucked the seated hills, with all their load,
> Rocks, waters, woods, and by the shaggy tops
> Uplifting, bore them in their hands.' — *P. L.*, vi. 645.

'grots and caverns shagged with horrid shades.' — *Comus*, 429.

55. *Deva:* the river Dee; called a 'wizard stream' from its associations with Druidical divinations and traditions, or Milton, in his use of the epithet, may have had more particularly in his mind the belief in regard to the river as the boundary between England and Wales, that it was itself prophetic. Drayton, in his 'Polyolbion,' 10th Song, says of the Dee:

> 'A brook, that was supposed much business to have seen,
> Which had an ancient bound twixt Wales and England been,
> And noted was by both to be an ominous flood,
> That changing of his fords, the future ill, or good,
> Of either country told; of either's war, or peace,
> The sickness, or the health, the dearth, or the increase:
> And that of all the floods of Britain, he might boast
> His stream in former times to have been honoured most,
> When as at Chester once King Edgar held his court,
> To whom eight lesser kings with homage did resort:
> That mighty Mercian lord, him in his barge bestowed,
> And was by all those kings about the river rowed.'

Aubrey, in his 'Miscellanies,' 1696, Chap. XVII., says, as quoted by Todd, 'F. Q.,' IV. xi. 39, 'when any Christian is drowned in the river Dee, there will appear over the water, where the corpse is, a light, by which means they do find the body; and it is therefore called the holy Dee.'

58. *The Muse herself:* Calliope.
59. *enchanting:* refers to the power he exercised, with the lyre given him by Apollo, over wild beasts, trees, rocks, etc.
64–69. *Alas! what boots it:* in these verses Milton, with his high ideal of the function of poetry, laments its low state, and momentarily gives way to the thought that it would be better to conform to the pre-

vailing flimsy taste than to 'strictly meditate the thankless Muse,' *i.e.* seriously devote one's self to song such as meets with no favor in these days. Amaryllis and Neæra are names of shepherdesses in Virgil's first and third Eclogues, and in other pastorals; 'meditate the thankless Muse' is after Virgil's 'Silvestrem tenui Musam meditaris avenâ.' — *Ecl.*, i. 2.

75. *Fury:* used in a general, and not in its special, mythological sense; the allusion is, of course, to Atropos, one of the Fates; called a blind fury by reason of the rashness with which she sometimes slits the thin-spun thread of life, as in the case of his friend King; 'slit' now always means to cut lengthwise; here, to cut across, sever.

76. *But not the praise:* 'slits' is understood, but it doesn't yoke well with 'praise'; the nearest substitute would be 'cuts off': but cuts not off the praise.

79. *Nor in:* *i e.* nor (lies) in, not set off in; 'set off' refers, not to 'Fame,' but to 'glistering foil,' *i.e.* the bright outside exhibited to the world.

81. *by:* as Keightley explains, by means of, under the influence of; he quotes Habakkuk i. 13: 'Thou art of purer eyes than to behold evil.'

85. *fountain Arethuse:* in the island Ortygia, near Syracuse; by metonymy for the 'Sicilian Muse' (v. 133), or the fountain-nymph, Arethusa, presiding over pastoral poetry, which originated in Sicily, and was consummated by Theocritus, a native of Syracuse. Virgil, in the opening of his fourth Eclogue, Pollio, invokes the Sicilian Muses (Sicelides Musæ, paullo majora canamus), and in his tenth Eclogue, Gallus, he invokes the fountain nymph, Arethusa, to aid him in his last pastoral song (Extremum hunc, Arethusa, mihi concede laborem); *and thou honoured flood, smooth-sliding Mincius:* Mantua, Virgil's birth town, or what he regarded as such (he was born in the neighboring village of Andes), is on an island in the river Mincius, a tributary of the Po; *honoured flood . . . crowned with vocal reeds: i.e.* by reason of its association with Virgil, and his fame as a pastoral poet. Lord Tennyson, in his ode 'To Virgil, written at the request of the Mantuans for the nineteenth centenary of Virgil's death,' speaks of him as a pastoral poet, in the fourth and fifth stanzas:

> 'Poet of the happy Tityrus
>   piping underneath his beechen bowers;
> Poet of the poet-satyr
>   whom the laughing shepherd bound with flowers;

Chanter of the Pollio, glorying
in the blissful years again to be,
Summers of the snakeless meadow,
unlaborious earth and oarless sea.'

88. *my oat proceeds:* the suspended pastoral strain is resumed.

89. *Herald of the Sea:* Triton, with 'wreathed horn.'

90. *in Neptune's plea:* Neptune's is an objective genitive: in defence, or exculpation of Neptune. This explanation of 'plea' is supported by its use in all other places in Milton's poetry:

' So spake the fiend, and with necessity,
The tyrant's plea, excused his devilish deeds.'
— *P. L.*, iv. 394.
'to make appear,
With righteous plea, their utmost vigilance.' — *P. L.*, x. 30.

' Yet of another plea bethought him soon.' — *P. R.*, iii. 149.

' Weakness is thy excuse, . . .
All wickedness is weakness; that plea therefore
With God or man will gain thee no remission.'
— *S. A.*, 834.

Keightley explains that Triton 'came, deputed by Neptune, to hold a judicial inquiry into the affair. We have the Pleas of the Crown and the Court of Common Pleas.'

96. *Hippotades:* a patronymic of Æolus, god of the winds.

98. *the level brine:* in v. 167, 'the watery floor.'

99. *Sleek Panope:* one of the sea-nymphs, daughter of Nereus; the name (in Gk. Πανόπη) seems to indicate that the nymph is a personification of a smooth sea ('level brine') which affords a *full view* all around to the horizon. The voyager on such a sea is ' ringed with the azure world.' The epithet 'sleek' is in accord with the personification.

100-102. *It was that fatal:* these verses are not part of the answer which Hippotades brings; the poet speaks in his own person.

101. *Built in the eclipse:* eclipses were believed to shed malign influences (see ' P. L.,' i. 594-599); one of the ingredients of the witches' hell-broth, in 'Macbeth,' is ' slips of yew, slivered in the moon's eclipse' ; *rigged with curses dark:* 'with,' of course, though this has been questioned, expresses accompaniment; to understand it as instrumental, makes a crazy hyperbole of the phrase.

102. *sacred head:* King was dedicated to the holy office of the ministry. He is made to represent, in the poem, a pure priesthood.

103-107. *Next Camus:* Dr. Masson's note, and the included quoted one, are the most acceptable of the numerous notes on this passage: 'Camus, the tutelary genius of the Cam, and of Cambridge University, appeared as one of the mourning figures; for had not King been one of the young hopes of the University? The garb given to Camus must doubtless be characteristic, and is perhaps most succinctly explained by a Latin note which appeared in a Greek translation of "Lycidas" by Mr. John Plumptre in 1797. "The mantle," said Mr. Plumptre in this note, "is as if made of the plant 'river-sponge,' which floats copiously in the Cam; the *bonnet* of the river-sedge, distinguished by vague marks traced somehow over the middle of the leaves, and serrated at the edge of the leaves after the fashion of the άί, άί of the hyacinth." It is said that the flags of the Cam still exhibit, when dried, these dusky streaks in the middle, and apparent scrawlings on the edge; and Milton (in whose MS. "*scrawled o'er*" was first written for "*inwrought*") is supposed to have carried away from the "*arundifer Camus*" ('Eleg.,' i. 11) this exact recollection. He identifies the edge-markings with the άί, άί (Alas! Alas!) which the Greeks fancied they saw on the leaves of the hyacinth, commemorating the sad fate of the Spartan youth from whose blood that flower had sprung.'

107. *pledge:* child; Lat. *pignus amoris.*

109. *The Pilot:* St. Peter, whom, it must be understood, Milton presents as 'the type and head of *true* episcopal power,' to which he was in no wise opposed. He wished the bishop to be a truly spiritual *overseer*, as the word signifies.

114. *Enow:* an archaic plural form of 'enough'; 'hellish foes enow.'— *P. L.*, ii. 504; 'evils enow to darken all his goodness.'— *Antony and Cleopatra*, I. iv. 11.

117. *to scramble at the shearer's feast:* to scramble for and gobble up fat benefices.

118. *the worthy bidden guest:* one who has been truly called to serve the Church.

119. *Blind mouths:* 'mouths' is used, by synecdoche, for gluttons, as the five preceding verses show. Ruskin's explanation of the phrase, in his 'Sesame and Lilies,' is very ingenious, but it is not likely that Milton meant it to have such significance. 'Those two monosyllables,' he says, 'express the precisely accurate contraries of right character in the two great offices of the Church, — those of Bishop and Pastor. A Bishop means

a person who sees. A Pastor means one who feeds. The most unbishoply character a man can have is, therefore, to be Blind. The most unpastoral is, instead of feeding, to want to be fed, — to be a Mouth. Take the two reverses together, and you have "blind mouths."'

Milton makes here his first onset upon the ecclesiastical abuses of the time. He was destined to make, not long after, fiercer onsets in his polemic prose writings.

120. *the least:* connect with 'aught else' rather than 'belongs.'

122. *What recks it them:* what does it concern them; *They are sped:* they've been successful in obtaining rich livings.

123. *list:* please; in earlier English generally used impersonally with a dative; *when they list:* i.e. when it suits them, not otherwise. They don't act from any sense of duty.

123, 124. *their lean and flashy songs grate:* their wretched sermons are wretchedly delivered with the emphasis of insincerity. Masson explains 'scrannel,' 'screeching, ear-torturing.'

126. *wind and the rank mist they draw:* i.e. the mere wind of some sermons and the poisonous doctrines of others, which their flocks inhale and drink in, and then impart the resulting spiritual disease to others.

128, 129. *the grim wolf:* generally understood to mean the Church of Rome. Bishop Newton, who first understood the passage to have reference to Archbishop Laud's 'privily introducing popery' afterward gave the alternative explanation, 'besides what the popish priests privately pervert to their religion,' which Masson conclusively supports in his 'Life of Milton,' and adopts in his note on the passage in his edition of the 'Poetical Works'; the 'privy paw' doesn't suit Archbishop Laud, who did everything above-board.

130, 131. *But that two-handed engine:* see my explanation of these verses in the Introductory Remarks.

132. *Return, Alpheus:* he invokes the return of the pastoral Muse when the dread denouncing voice of St. Peter has ceased. Alpheus, the chief river of Peloponnesus, flowing through Arcadia and Elis. The river-god loved the nymph Arethusa, of Elis, whom, in her flight from him, Diana changed into a fountain which was directed by the goddess under the sea to the island of Ortygia, near Syracuse. The river followed under sea and united with the fountain. See note on v. 85.

136. *use:* frequent.

138. *whose:* refers to 'valleys'; *the swart star:* understood by editors

to mean the dog-star Sirius. But it may mean, and I think it does, the day-star, the sun. See v. 168; 'diurnal star.' — *P. L.*, x. 1069; *swart:* used causatively; *sparely looks:* i.e. by reason of the shades.

139. *quaint enamelled eyes:* flowers of curious structure and of variegated glossy colors (?); the words are more enjoyable than distinctly intelligible; in the 'P. L.,' ix. 529, it is said of the serpent:

> 'oft he bowed
> His turret crest, and sleek enamelled neck, fawning.'

Here 'enamelled' appears to mean variegated and glossy; so in Arcades:

> 'O'er the smooth enamelled green.'

141. *purple:* an imperative, to be construed with 'throw.'

142. *rathe:* early, soon; the old positive form of 'rather,' sooner. Tennyson uses the word in his 'In Memoriam,' c. ix. 2, 'The men of rathe and riper years'; and in 'Lancelot and Elaine,' 339, 'Till rathe she rose,' etc.; *that forsaken dies:* forsaken by the sun.

153. *with false surmise:* i.e. that we have the body of Lycidas with us.

158. *monstrous world:* the world of sea-monsters.

159. *moist:* tearful.

160. *the fable of Bellerus old:* i.e. the scene of the fable.

161–163. *Where the great Vision:* see Introductory Remarks.

164. *O ye dolphins:* an allusion to the story of Arion.

166. *your sorrow:* used objectively, he who is the object of your sorrow. 'Our love, our hope, our sorrow, is not dead.' — *Shelley's Adonais.*

167. *watery floor:* what is called the level brine, v. 98; 'the shining levels of the lake.' — *Tennyson's Morte d'Arthur*, suggested, no doubt, by the classical *æquora.*

169–171. *repairs his drooping head:* Milton, in these lines, compares great things with small (*parvis componit magna*); if they are 'considered curiously,' the sun makes his toilet on rising from his ocean bed!

172. *sunk . . . mounted:* any one reading this verse for the first time would be likely to get the impression that these words are participles; this would not be the case if 'sunk' were 'sank,' originally the distinctive singular form of the preterite, 'sunk' being plural; AS. *sane, suneon.*

173. *Him that walked the waves:* a beautiful designation of the Saviour, in accord with the occasion of the poem; and so St. Peter is designated as 'the Pilot of the Galilean Lake.'

174. *along:* beside.

176. *unexpressive:* inexpressible.

184. *thy large recompense:* 'thy' is the personal, not the possessive adjective pronoun, being used objectively,— the large recompense thou hast received, in which is included thy becoming the genius of the shore; *good:* kind, propitious; 'sent by some spirit to mortals good.'— *Il Pens.*, 154.

185. *in that perilous flood:* 'in' is more poetic than 'on' or 'o'er' would be; 'that perilous flood' is spoken of as a domain in which is included the atmosphere with its winds and storms; so, to wander in the desert.

186. *uncouth:* used, it is most likely, in its original sense of 'unknown,' Milton so regarding himself, as a poet; there may be involved the idea (supported by the opening lines of the Elegy) of wanting in poetic skill and grace.

188. *tender stops:* poetic transference of epithet, 'tender' being logically applicable to the music; *various quills:* used, by metonymy, for the varied moods, strains, metres, and other features of the Elegy; *eager thought:* perhaps meant to signify as much as sharp grief; *Doric:* equivalent to pastoral, the great Greek bucolic poets having written in the Doric dialect.

190, 191. *had . . . was:* note the distinctive use of these auxiliaries, the former being used with a participle of a transitive verb, and the latter, with that of an intransitive; *all the hills:* i.e. their shadows.

192. *twitched:* Keightley explains, 'pulled, drew tightly about him on account of the chilliness of the evening.' Jerram explains, 'snatched up from where it lay beside him.'

Samson Agonistes

P. 187. *Aristotle:* Greek philosopher, B.C. 384-322; the reference is to 'The Poetics,' (Περὶ ποιητικῆς), the greater part of which is devoted to the theory of tragedy.

P. 187. *a verse of Euripides:* φθείρουσιν ἤθη χρῆσθ' ὁμιλίαι κακαί, 'evil communications corrupt good manners'; found in the fragments of both Euripides and Menander.

P. 187. *Pareus:* David Pareus, a German Calvinist theologian and biblical commentator, 1548-1622.

P. 187. *Dionysius the elder:* known as 'the tyrant of Syracuse,' B.C. 431-367; repeatedly contended for the prize of tragedy at Athens.

P. 187. *Seneca (Lucius Annæus)*: Roman Stoic philosopher, B.C. 3?-65 A.D.

P. 187. *Gregory Nazianzen:* saint; a Greek father of the Church, Bishop of Constantinople, about 328-389.

P. 188. *Martial:* M. Valerius Martialis, Latin epigrammatic poet, 43-104 A.D. or later.

P. 188. *apolelymenon:* 'a Greek word, ἀπολελυμένον, "loosed from," *i.e.* from the fetters of strophe, antistrophe, or epode; monostrophic (μονόστροφος) meaning literally "single stanzaed," *i.e.* a strophe without answering antistrophe. So allœostrophic (ἀλλοιόστροφος) signifies stanzas of irregular strophes, strophes not consisting of alternate strophe and antistrophe.' —*John Churton Collins.*

P. 188. *beyond the fifth act:* 'Neve minor, neu sit quinto productior actu Fabula.'— *Horace, Ars Poetica,* 189.

P. 191. *Agonistes:* one who contends as an athlete. 'The term is peculiarly appropriate to Samson, for he is the hero of the drama . . . and the catastrophe results from the exhibition of his strength in the public games of the Philistines.' —*J. Churton Collins.*

2. *dark:* blind.

6. *else:* otherwhile, at other times.

9. *draught:* appositive to 'air.'

11. *day-spring:* the dawn.

12. With this line Samson's soliloquy begins, the attendant having withdrawn.

13. *Dagon:* god of the Philistines; represented in the 'Paradise Lost' (i. 462, 463) as a 'sea-monster, upward man, and downward fish.' See 1 Sam. v. 1-9.

16. *popular:* of the people.

19-21. Restless thoughts, that rush thronging upon me found alone.

24. *Twice by an Angel:* see Judges xiii.

27. *charioting,* etc.: withdrawing as in a chariot his godlike presence.

28. *and from:* and (as) from.

31. *separate:* separated, set apart; 'the Holy Ghost said, Separate me Barnabas and Saul for the work whereunto I have called them.' — Acts xiii. 2.

35. *under task:* under a prescribed task.

41. *Eyeless, in Gaza,* etc.: Thomas De Quincey, in his paper entitled 'Milton *vs.* Southey and Landor,' remarks: 'Mr. Landor makes one correction by a simple improvement in the punctuation, which has a very fine effect. . . . Samson says, . . .

Ask for this great deliverer now, and find him
Eyeless in Gaza at the mill with slaves.

Thus it is usually printed, that is, without a comma in the latter line; but, says Landor, 'there ought to be commas after *eyeless*, after *Gaza*, after *mill*.' And why? because thus, 'the grief of Samson is aggravated at every member of the sentence.' He (like Milton) was 1, blind; 2, in a city of triumphant enemies; 3, working for daily bread; 4, herding with slaves — Samson literally, and Milton with those whom politically he regarded as such.'

45. *but through :* except for, had it not been for.

55. *Proudly secure :* 'secure' is subjective, free from care or fear; 'Security is mortals' chiefest enemy.'— *Macbeth*, III. v. 32.

56. *By weakest subtleties :* by those most weak but crafty creatures (women), who are not made to rule, but to serve as subordinates to the rule of wisdom, the prerogative of man. This was, unfortunately, too much Milton's own opinion of women.

58. *withal :* at the same time.

62. *above my reach :* above the reach of my capacity to know.

63. *Suffices :* it is sufficient (to know).

67. *O loss of sight :* Milton here speaks virtually *in propria persona*.

70. *Light the prime work of God.*— Gen. i. 3; 'offspring of Heaven first born.'— *P. L.*, iii. 1.

75, 76. *exposed to daily fraud :* Milton here, no doubt, drew from his own experiences as a father.

77. *still :* ever, always.

82. *all :* any; 'without all doubt.'— *Henry VIII.*, IV. i. 113; 'without all remedy.'— *Macbeth*, III. ii. 11.

87. *silent :* invisible; the epithet which pertains to one sense, that of hearing, is transferred to another, that of sight. Lat. *luna silens*.

89. *Hid in her vacant interlunar cave:* the moon is poetically represented as hid in a cave, and giving no light (vacant), between her disappearance and return, in the sky.

91, 92. *if it be true that light is in the soul :* the soul proceeding from God, and partaking of the 'Bright effluence of bright essence increate.' — *P. L.*, iii. 6.

93. *She* (the soul) *all in every part* (of the body).

95. *obvious :* literally, in the way of (Lat. *obvius*), and so, exposed; 'Not obvious, not obtrusive, but retired.'— *P. L.*, viii. 504.

106. *obnoxious:* subject, liable.

111. *steering:* directing their course; 'With radiant feet the tissued clouds down steering.' — *Ode on Nativity*, 146.

118. *at random:* anyway or anyhow; *carelessly diffused:* passively stretched upon the ground, sprawling.

'His limbs did rest
Diffused and motionless.'
— *Shelley's Alastor*.

Spenser uses two phrases of similar import; '*Pour'd out in loosnesse* on the grassy ground.' — *F. Q.*, I. vii. 7; 'carelessly displaid.' — *F. Q.*, II. v. 32. This use of 'diffused' is a Latinism.

'Publica me requies curarum somnus habebat,
*Fusa*que erant toto languida membra toro.'
— *Ovid, Ex Ponto*, III. iii. 7, 8.

122. *weeds:* garments, clothes.

128. *Who tore the lion:* see Judges xiv. 5, 6.

132. *hammered cuirass:* the cuirass was originally of leather; here of metal, formed with the hammer.

133. *Chalybean-tempered steel:* having the temper of steel wrought by the Chalybes, an ancient Asiatic people dwelling south of the Black Sea, and famous as workers in iron; hence, Lat. *chalybs*, steel, Gr. χάλυψ. Dr. Masson accents 'Chalybean' on the third syllable; it seems rather to have the accent here on the second.

134. *Adamantean proof:* having the strength of adamant.

136. *insupportably:* irresistibly.

139. *his lion ramp:* his leap or spring as of a lion. In the description of the sixth day of the creation (*P. L.*, vii. 463-466) it is said of the lion,

'now half appeared
The tawny lion, pawing to get free
His hinder parts, then springs, as broke from bonds,
And rampant shakes his brinded mane.'

144. *foreskins:* uncircumcised Philistines.

145. *Ramath-lechi:* see Judges xv. 17.

147. *Azza:* Gaza. See Judges xvi. 3. The form Azzah is used Deut. ii. 23.

148. *Hebron, seat of giants old:* for Hebron was the city of Arba,

the father of Anak, and the seat of the Anakims. — Josh. xv. 13, 14. 'And the Anakims were giants, which come of the giants.' — Num. xiii. 33. *Newton*.

149. *No journey of a sabbath-day:* Hebron was about thirty miles distant from Gaza; a sabbath-day's journey was but three-quarters of a mile.

150. *Like whom:* Atlas.

157. *complain:* directly transitive, in the sense of lament, bewail.

163. *visual beam:* ray of light, the condition of seeing.

'the air,
No where so clear, sharpen'd his visual ray.'

— *P. L.*, iii. 620.

'then [Michael] purged with euphrasy and rue
The visual nerve, for he [Adam] had much to see.'

— *P. L.*, xi. 415.

165. *Since man on earth:* a Latinism like *Post urbem conditam*, of frequent occurrence in Milton's poetry; 'Never since created man.' — *P. L.*, i. 573; 'After the Tuscan mariners transformed.' — *Comus*, 48.

169. *pitch:* usually pertains to height; here to depth.

172. *the sphere of fortune:* a constantly revolving globe.

173. *But thee:* construe with 'him,' third line above: 'For him I reckon not in high estate . . . But thee.'

181. *Eshtaol and Zora:* see Josh. xix. 41.

185. *tumours:* perturbations, agitations; so *tumor* is used in Latin: 'Cum tumor animi resedisset;' 'Erat in tumore animus.'

190. *superscription:* a continuation of the metaphor in preceding line.

191-193. *In prosperous days they swarm:* perhaps from Milton's own experience after the Restoration. — *Masson*.

207. *mean:* moderate, as compared with his physical strength.

208. *This:* i.e. wisdom.

209. *drove me transverse:* a continuation of the metaphor in 198-200. So in 'P. L.,' iii. 488:

'A violent cross wind from either coast
Blows them transverse ten thousand leagues away
Into the devious air.'

212. *pretend they ne'er so wise:* claim they to be never so wise; the idea of falseness is not in the word 'pretend' as in its present use.

219. *The first I saw at Timna:* Judges xiv.

221. *The daughter of an infidel:* Milton probably had his first wife, Mary Powell, in his mind, whose family was infidel to his own political creed.

222. *motioned:* proposed.

223. *intimate:* inward, inmost.

228. *fond:* foolish.

229. *vale of Sorec:* a valley (and stream) between Askelon and Gaza, not far from Zorah. — Judges xvi. 4.

230. *specious:* good appearing.

235, 236. *vanquished with a peal of words:* a metaphor drawn from the storming of a fortress. A similar metaphor is found in '1 Henry VI.,' III. iii. 79, 80:

'I am vanquished; these haughty words of hers
Have battered me like roaring cannon-shot.'

237. *provoke:* to call forth, to challenge. Lat. *provocare.*

241. *That fault I take not on me:* 'with an occult reference, perhaps, to the conduct of those in power in England after Cromwell's death, when Milton still argued vehemently against the restoration of the Stuarts.' — *Masson.*

247. *ambition:* used literally, going about in the service of some object, canvassing. Lat. *ambitio.*

248. *spoke loud:* proclaimed.

253. *Etham:* Judges xv. 8, 9.

257. *harass:* ravaging.

258. *on some conditions:* Judges xv. 11-13.

263. *a trivial weapon:* the jawbone of an ass. Judges xv. 15.

268-276. *But what more oft:* a plain reference to the state of England, and to Milton's own position there, after the Restoration. — *Masson.*

271. *strenuous:* ardently maintained. Newton quotes a similar sentiment from the oration of Æmilius Lepidus, the consul, to the Roman people, against Sulla: 'Annuite legibus impositis; accipite otium cum servitio;' — but for myself — 'potior visa est periculosa libertas quieto servitio.'

278. *How Succoth:* Judges viii. 4-9.

282. *how ingrateful Ephraim:* Judges xi. 15-27.

287-289. *sore battle:* the battle fought by Jephthah with Ephraim. Judges xii. 4-6.

291. *mine:* my people.

297, 298. *For of such doctrine:* 'Observe the peculiar effect of contempt given to the passage by the rapid rhythm and the sudden introduction of a rhyme in these two lines.' — *Masson.*

305. *They ravel more, still less resolved:* they become more confused, and ever less disentangled.

327. *careful step:* 'careful' is used subjectively; a step indicating that Manoa was full of care, deeply concerned. Chaucer so uses 'dredeful':

'With dredeful foot thanne stalketh Palamoun.'
— *Knight's Tale,* 1479.

333. *uncouth:* literally, unknown; strange, with the idea of the disagreeable.

334. *gloried:* a participial form derived from the noun.

335. *informed:* directed.

343. *Angels':* I have followed Keightley in making 'Angels' a genitive.

345. *Duelled:* it was an individual fight on the part of Samson.

354. *as:* that; this use of 'as' after 'so' and 'such' is not uncommon in Shakespeare and Bacon, and the later literature.

'I feel such sharp dissension in my breast,
Such fierce alarums both of hope and fear,
As I am sick with working of my thoughts.'
— 1 *Henry VI.,* V. v. 86.

364. *miracle:* wonder, admiration.

373. *Appoint:* 'Do not you arrange or direct the disposition of heavenly things.' — *Keightley.*

383. *Of Timna:* Judges xiv.

394. *my capital secret:* a play on the word 'capital' is, no doubt, designed; chief secret and the secret of his strength depending upon his hair.

433. *That rigid score:* rigorous account or reckoning.

434. *This day:* Judges xvi. 23.

453. *idolists:* idolaters.

455. *propense:* disposed.

466. *provoked:* called forth, challenged.

499, 500. *a sin that Gentiles:* supposed to be an allusion to Tantalus, who divulged the secrets of the gods.

503. *but act not:* take not a part in thy own affliction; 'thy' is objective: in afflicting thyself.

505. *self-preservation bids:* i.e. that thou do so.

509. *his debt:* debt to him.

516. *what offered means:* those offered means which.

528. *blazed:* trumpeted abroad.

531. *affront:* a front to front encounter. The word occurs as a noun but once in Shakespeare:

> 'There was a fourth man in a silly habit,
> That gave the affront with them.' — *Cymb.*, V. iii. 87.

i.e. faced or confronted the enemy (Rolfe).

533. *venereal trains:* snares of Venus, or love.

537. *me:* an ethical dative? or it may be the usual dative.

539. *Then turned me out ridiculous:* an object of ridicule, a laughing-stock.

549. *rod:* ray of light.

552. *turbulent:* used causatively.

563–572. *Now blind, disheartened:* almost literally autobiographic.

569. *robustious:* Masson explains 'full of force'; but 'vain monument of strength' in the following verse, does not seem to support this explanation.

581. *caused a fountain:* Judges xv. 18, 19.

590–598. *All otherwise:* this pathetic passage is quite literally autobiographic, if 'race of shame' be excepted; but even this might be understood, in Milton's case, to be used objectively.

599. *suggestions:* the word has a stronger meaning than at present: inward promptings.

> 'Why do I yield to that suggestion
> Whose horrid image doth unfix my hair
> And make my seated heart knock at my ribs
> Against the use of nature?' — *Macbeth*, I. iii. 34.

604. *how else:* elsewise, otherwise.

612. *all his* (torment's) *fierce accidents:* all the fierce things which *fall to*, or happen to, body or mind.

613. *her:* the mind's.

615. *answerable:* corresponding.

624. *apprehensive:* taking hold of, mentally; having the power of conception or perception.

627. *medicinal:* accented on the penult.

628. *snowy Alp:* used generically for any snowy mountain.

633. *his:* Heaven's.

635. *message:* messenger, angel.

637. *amain:* vigorously.

643. *provoked:* called forth, challenged.

645. *to be repeated:* to be again and again made the subject of their cruelty or scorn. — *Masson.*

650. *speedy death:* an appositive of 'prayer.'

658. *much persuasion:* to be construed with 'many are the sayings,' etc., and 'much persuasion (is) sought.'

662. *dissonant mood from:* mood dissonant from his complaint.

677. *Heads:* appositive to 'the common rout of men.'

683. *their highth of noon:* the meridian of their glory.

684. *Changest thy countenance:* a similar expression, but with a different meaning, to that in Job xiv. 20: 'Thou changest his (man's) countenance, and sendest him away.'

686. *or them to thee of service:* or of service (from) them to thee.

690. *Unseemly:* unbecoming in human eye; 'falls' is a noun in apposition to the preceding thought, 'thou throwest them lower than thou didst exalt them high.'

695–702. *Or to the unjust tribunals:* there has been an occult reference all through this chorus to the wreck of the Puritan cause by the Restoration; but in these lines the reference becomes distinct. Milton has the trials of Vane and the Regicides in his mind. He himself had been in danger of the law; and, though he had escaped, it was to a 'crude (premature) old age,' afflicted by painful diseases from which his temperate life might have been expected to exempt him. — *Masson.*

699. *deformed:* attended with deformity.

700. *crude:* premature.

701. *disordinate:* inordinate, irregular; yet suffering without cause.

707. *What:* the word here, perhaps, means 'why.' The following question seems to support this.

715. *Tarsus: i.e.* Tarshish, which Milton avoided from his dislike to the sound *sh.* He seems to have agreed with those who thought that Tarshish was Tarsus in Cilicia, instead of Tartessus in Spain. In the Bible, 'ships of Tarshish' signify large sea-going vessels in general; *the iles,*

etc.: *i.e.* the isles and coasts of Greece and Lesser Asia; *Javan* (pr. *Yavan*) is 'Ιάονες, "Ιωνες, the Ionians. As these were the best known of the Greeks in the south, their name was given to the whole people, just as the Greeks themselves called all the subjects of the king of Persia, Medes; *Gadire:* Γάδειρα, Gades, Cadiz. — *Keightley.*

717. *bravery:* finery, ornament; *trim:* shipshape, in good order.

719. *hold them play:* keep them in play.

720. *An amber scent:* an ambergris scent.

731. *makes address:* prepares.

732 *et seq.* 'The student will notice how thoroughly Euripidean the whole of the following scene is, not merely in the fact that two of the *dramatis personæ* are pitted dialectically against one another, but in the cast of the language and in the quality of the sentiment.' — *John Churton Collins.*

748. *hyæna:* 'a creature somewhat like a wolf, and is said to imitate a human voice so artfully as to draw people to it, and then devour them.

"'Tis thus the false hyæna makes her moan,
To draw the pitying traveller to her den;
Your sex are so, such false dissemblers all."
— *Thomas Otway's Orphan*, A. ii.

Milton applies it to a woman, but Otway to the men.' — *Newton.*

760, 761. *not to reject the penitent:* an obvious allusion to Milton's forgiveness of his first wife, after her two years' abandonment of him.

803. *That made for me:* helped my purpose (*i.e.* to keep you from leaving me as you did her at Timna).

842. *Or:* Keightley suspects that 'or' should be 'and' here, as 'or' does not connect well with what precedes.

868. *respects:* considerations; 'there's the respect that makes calamity of so long life.' — *Hamlet*, III. i. 68, 69.

906. *peals:* peals of words. See l. 235.

932, 933. *trains, gins, toils:* these words all express modes of entrapping any one or anything.

934. *thy fair enchanted cup:* an allusion to Circe and the Sirens.

948. *gloss:* comment, construe.

950. *To thine:* compared to thine.

988, 989. *in mount Ephraim Jael:* Judges iv. 5.

990. *Smote Sisera:* Judges v. 26.

1016. *thy riddle:* Judges xiv. 12-19; *in one day or seven:* connect with 'harder to hit.'

1018. *If any of these, or all:* if it be any or all of these qualities, virtue, wisdom, valor, etc., that can win or long inherit (possess) woman's love, the Timnian bride had not so soon preferred thy paranymph (bridesman). Judges xiv., xv.

1022. *Nor both:* nor both wives; *disallied:* severed.

1025. *for that:* because.

1025-1060. *Is it for that such outward ornament:* the ideas expressed in these verses, it must be admitted, were too much Milton's own, in regard to woman, as his Divorce pamphlets show.

1030. *affect:* like.

1037. *Once joined:* i.e. in marriage.

1038. *far within:* a thorn in the flesh, a cleaving mischief, deep beneath defensive armor; these may be an allusion to the poisoned shirt sent to Hercules by his wife Deianira.

1048. *combines:* i.e. with her husband.

1057. *lour:* frown, or look sullen.

1062. *contracted:* drawn together, gathered.

1068. *Harapha of Gath:* see under 1079.

1069. *pile:* the giant's body is spoken of as a pile, or large, proudly towering building.

1073. *habit:* dress.

1075. *His fraught:* the freight of commands or whatever else he is charged with. The word seems to be used contemptuously.

1076. *chance:* fate.

1079. *Men call me Harapha:* 'No such giant is mentioned by name in Scripture; but see 2 Sam. xxi. 16-22. The four Philistine giants mentioned there are said to be sons of a certain giant in Gath called "the giant"; and the Hebrew word for "the giant" there is Rapha or Harapha. Milton has appropriated the name to his fictitious giant, whom he makes out in the sequel (1248, 1249) to be the actual father of that brood of giants.' — *Masson.*

1080. *Og, or Anak:* see Deut. iii. 11, ii. 10, and Gen. xiv. 5.

1081. *Thou know'st me now:* so in 'P. L.,' iv. 830:

'Not to know me argues yourselves unknown.'

1091. *taste:* to make trial of; Fr. *tâter,* OF. *taster;*

'he now began
To taste the bow, the sharp shaft took, tugg'd hard,' etc.
— *Chapman's Homer's Od.*, xxi. 211.

1092. *single me:* challenge me to single combat. — *Keightley.*
1093. *Gyves:* handcuffs.
1105. *In thy hand:* in thy power.
1109. *assassinated:* cruelly abused or maltreated. The word is so used in Milton's 'Doctrine and Discipline of Divorce,' Book I. c. xii.
1113. *close-banded:* secretly leagued. — *Dr. Johnson.*
1116. *without feigned shifts:* without any pretended considerations for my blindness.
1118. *Or rather flight:* a cutting phrase, implying that otherwise the giant may seek safety in flight, if they were not in 'some narrow place enclosed.'
1120, 1121. *brigandine:* coat of armor for the body; *habergeon:* armor for neck and shoulders; *Vant-brace:* (*avant bras*) armor for the arms; *greaves:* leg armor; *gauntlet:* (*gant*) glove of mail.
1122. *A weaver's beam:* 1 Sam. xvii. 5-7 was in Milton's mind in lines 1119-1122. 'And he [Goliath] had an helmet of brass upon his head, and he was armed with a coat of mail; . . . And he had greaves of brass upon his legs, and a target of brass between his shoulders. And the staff of his spear was like a weaver's beam;' . . .
1132. *had not spells:* 'taken from the ritual of the combat in chivalry. When two champions entered the lists, each took an oath that he had no charm, herb, or any enchantment about him.' — *T. Warton.*
1164. *boisterous:* strong, powerful?
1169. *thine:* thy people?
1181. *Tongue-doughty:* tongue-valiant.
1186. *thirty men:* Judges xiv. 19.
1195. *politician lords:* lords of your state.
1197. *spies:* Judges xiv. 10-18. 'Milton follows Jewish tradition in supposing the thirty bridal friends there mentioned to have been spies appointed by the Philistines.' — *Masson.*
1202. *wherever chanced:* i.e. wherever by chance met with.
1219. *not all your force:* the ellipsis is, would have disabled me.
1220. *These shifts:* the charges made by Harapha of his being 'a murderer, a revolter, and a robber'; *appellant:* challenger.
1223. *enforce:* demand of strength.

1224. *With thee:* (fight) with thee?
1231. *Baal-zebub:* the god of Ekron. 2 Kings i. 16.
1238. *bulk without spirit vast:* vast bulk without spirit.
1242. *Astaroth:* the Phœnician goddess.
1243. *braveries:* bravadoes.
1266. *mine:* my end.
1274. *Hardy:* bold.
1292. *Either of these:* 'might' or 'patience.'
1309. *remark him:* plainly mark him.
1317. *heartened:* encouraged, emboldened.
1334. *Myself:* regard myself, do you say? No, my conscience and internal peace I regard. Keightley and Masson both place an (!) instead of an (?). But 'myself' requires to be uttered with an *inquiring* surprise, and should be followed by an (?).
1346. *stoutness:* firm refusal.
1369. *the sentence holds:* the sentence, 'outward acts defile not,' holds good, where outward force constrains.
1375. *which:* represents what precedes, 'If I obey ... set God behind.'
1377. *dispense with:* pardon. 'Milton here probably had in view the story of Naaman the Syrian, begging a *dispensation* of this sort from Elisha, which he seemingly grants him.' See 2 Kings v. 18, 19.— *Thyer.*
1397. *as:* used after 'such' to introduce a result, instead of 'that,' as in present English; not uncommon in Shakespeare, Bacon, and other writers of the time and later.
1399. *to try:* to test.
1408. *Yet this be sure:* looks back to 'I am content to go.'
1418–1422. *Lords are lordliest:* 'in this passage may be detected a reference to England in Milton's time.' — *Masson.*
1435. *that Spirit that first rushed on thee:* 'a young lion roared against him. And the Spirit of the Lord came mightily upon him, and he rent him as he would have rent a kid.' —*Judges* xiv. 5, 6.
1450. *I had no will:* i.e. to go thither.
1455. *That hope:* to partake that hope with thee would much rejoice us.
1461–1471. *Some much averse I found:* the different shades of feeling among the men in power in England after the Restoration may be supposed to be glanced at in this passage: obstinate and revengeful Royalism, strongest among the High Church party; and so on. — *Masson.*

1470. *The rest:* to remit the rest was magnanimity.
1471. *convenient:* fitting. Lat. *conveniens,* coming together.
1474. *Their once great dread:* former object of their great dread.
1512. *whole inhabitation:* all the inhabitants of the world, as is indicated by 'universal groan.'
1514. *ruin:* down crashing.
1529. *dole:* grief, sorrow; 'dealing dole' is not a case of the cognate accusative, as it is understood by some critics.
1538. *baits:* literally, stops for refreshment; in a general sense, tarries.
1551. *concerned in:* connected with.
1554. *needs:* is necessary.
1557. *tell us the sum:* the main fact, defer what accompanied it.
1581. *glorious:* used proleptically.
1594. *eye-witness:* ocular testimony.
1599. *high street:* main or principal street; so, highway, high seas.
1608. *sort:* rank.
1610. *banks:* benches.
1619. *cataphracts:* heavy-armed cavalry soldiers, whose horses as well as themselves were covered with a complete suit of mail armor. Gr. κατάφρακτος, covered; *spears:* spearmen.
1621. *rifted:* split.
1625. *assayed:* tried.
1626. *still:* ever.
1671. *And fat regorged:* Keightley explains, 'and the fat of bulls and goats was regorged by them who had eaten too much.' This, along with the preceding and the following verse, gives a Miltonic sublimity of the disgusting to the passage. But the prefix 're-' is, perhaps, simply intensive, and 'regorged' may mean gorged, or swallowed, voraciously. The construction is, 'And (while they, 'they' being implied in 'their,' above) fat regorged of bulls and goats, . . . Among them he (our living Dread) a spirit of phrenzy sent.'
1674. *Silo:* Shiloh. Joshua xviii. 1, Judges xxi. 19. 'He probably terms it *bright,* on account of the Shekinah which was supposed to rest on the ark.' — *Keightley.*
1688. *and thought extinguished quite:* this phrase is understood by some as a nominative absolute (the Latin ablative absolute), thought having been quite extinguished; but 'thought' is rather a past participle referring to 'he': thought to be entirely extinguished.
1692. *as an evening dragon came:* 'he' (Samson) is the subject of

'came'; he came among the Philistines as an evening dragon comes on tame farmhouse fowl, but afterward bolted his cloudless thunder on their heads, as an eagle.

1699. *that self-begotten bird:* the phœnix.

1700. *embost:* enclosed in a wood.

1702. *erewhile:* for some time before; *holocaust:* a whole burnt offering.

1703. *teemed:* brought forth.

1704. *revives:* the subject is 'Virtue,' 1697.

1707. *A secular bird:* a bird living for generations. Lat. *sæcula.*

1713. *sons of Caphtor:* the Philistines, 'originally of the island Caphtor or Crete. A colony of them settled in Palestine and there went by the name of Philistim.'— *Meadowcourt, in Todd's Var. Ed. of Milton.*

1733. *Home to his father's house:* see Judges xvi. 31.

1753. *band them:* unite themselves.

1755. *acquist:* acquisition.

www.ingramcontent.com/pod-product-compliance
Lightning Source LLC
Chambersburg PA
CBHW030744230426
43667CB00007B/840